ALSO BY MARK OPPENHEIMER

Knocking on Heaven's Door:
American Religion in the Age of Counterculture

The Bar Mitzvah Crasher:
Road-tripping Through Jewish America
(originally published as *Thirteen and a Day*)

Wisenheimer: A Childhood Subject to Debate

The Newish Jewish Encyclopedia:
From Abraham to Zabar's and Everything in Between
(with Stephanie Butnick and Liel Leibovitz)

Squirrel Hill

Squirrel Hill

The Tree of Life Synagogue Shooting
and the Soul of a Neighborhood

—⦿⦿⦿—

MARK OPPENHEIMER

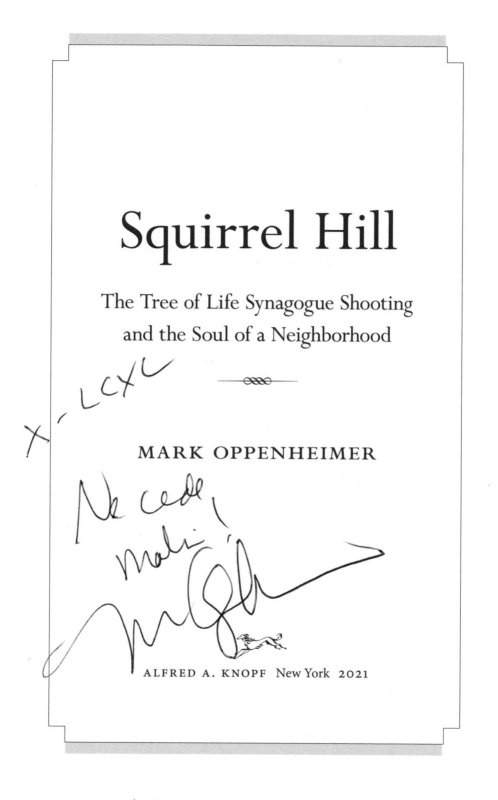

ALFRED A. KNOPF New York 2021

THIS IS A BORZOI BOOK
PUBLISHED BY ALFRED A. KNOPF

Copyright © 2021 by Mark Oppenheimer

All rights reserved. Published in the United States by Alfred A. Knopf,
a division of Penguin Random House LLC, New York, and distributed
in Canada by Penguin Random House Canada Limited, Toronto.

www.aaknopf.com

Knopf, Borzoi Books, and the colophon are registered trademarks
of Penguin Random House LLC.

Library of Congress Cataloging-in-Publication Data
Names: Oppenheimer, Mark, [date] author.
Title: Squirrel Hill : the Tree of Life Synagogue shooting
and the soul of a neighborhood / Mark Oppenheimer.
Identifiers: LCCN 2020041860 (print) | LCCN 2020041861 (ebook) |
ISBN 9780525657194 (hardcover) | ISBN 9780525657200 (ebook)
Subjects: LCSH: Tree of Life Synagogue Shooting, Pittsburgh, Pa., 2018. |
Antisemitism—Pennsylvania—Pittsburgh. |
Tree of Life–Or L'Simcha Congregation (Pittsburgh, Pa.) |
Squirrel Hill (Pittsburgh, Pa.)—Ethnic relations.
Classification: LCC HV6536.55.P58 O67 2021 (print) |
LCC HV6536.55.P58 (ebook) | DDC 364.152/340974886—dc23
LC record available at https://lccn.loc.gov/2020041860
LC ebook record available at https://lccn.loc.gov/2020041861

Jacket photograph by Brendan Smialowski / AFP / Getty Images
Jacket design by Jenny Carrow
Map by Ariana Killoran

Manufactured in the United States of America
First Edition

I am the Lord, and you shall keep my Sabbaths, and you shall venerate my sanctuary. For if you follow my laws and keep my commandments . . . I will give you peace in the land, and you shall lie down and no one shall terrify you.

—LEVITICUS 26:2—6

Contents

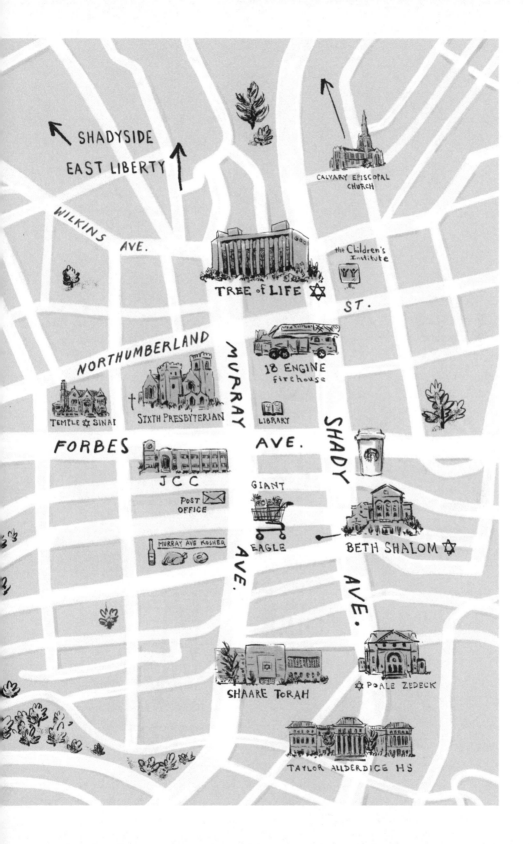

Squirrel Hill

Prologue

JUST BEFORE TEN O'CLOCK in the morning on October 27, 2018, police cars, a SWAT team, multiple fire trucks, and a fleet of ambulances converged into a serpentine caravan that sped into the Squirrel Hill neighborhood of Pittsburgh, the sirens shredding Saturday's early calm. They were responding to 911 calls about a shooter at Tree of Life, the synagogue at the corner of Shady and Wilkins avenues.

Sirens aren't unusual in Squirrel Hill; it's not a violent neighborhood, but it's densely inhabited and very alive. The houses—grand ones and smaller ones, attached dwellings and apartment buildings—are on small lots, without much margin of green at the edges; people hear their neighbors and know each other's business. There are shops, big and small, and traffic and young children and old people, and with them come grease fires and heart attacks and the small misfortunes of a thriving urban village. Plus, there is 18 Engine, the firehouse on Northumberland Street, which takes calls not just from Squirrel Hill but from other precincts in the East End of town.

But this morning there were, as local residents would recall later, "an unusual number of sirens."

Tammy Hepps lived only two blocks from Tree of Life, but she did not hear the sirens. In 2014, tired of her job as a technology executive at NBC in New York City, Hepps had moved to Pittsburgh, intending to spend a year pursuing her preferred avocation, local history. Among other things, she wanted to research the history of the synagogue her great-grandfather had founded in Homestead, the former steel town just across the Monongahela River from Pittsburgh. Hepps had grown up outside Philadelphia, but she had always been drawn to the lore of her four generations of Pittsburgh ancestors. By 2015, after spending a year in various Pittsburgh archives, she had expanded her research to include more defunct synagogues, and the bulldozed houses around them, and the family trees of long-dead Jews. So she stayed another year, then another. She joined a synagogue, made friends, and became something of a *macher,* a big shot, in her adopted neighborhood of Squirrel Hill, which had remained substantially Jewish, unlike surrounding communities that had lost their Jewish populations. Squirrel Hill had been the heart of Jewish Pittsburgh since the Great War.

That morning Hepps was planning to go to her synagogue, Beth Shalom, less than a mile up Shady Avenue from Tree of Life. Like Tree of Life, Beth Shalom was part of the Conservative movement of Judaism, but unlike Tree of Life, an elderly kind of place, Beth Shalom had a core group of young regulars. (Hepps was thirty-nine, which counts as young in a synagogue.) She always went to synagogue on the Sabbath, but like most Jews, she might roll in well after services started—a nine-thirty a.m. start time could mean a ten-thirty arrival, followed by ninety minutes of worship, then a leisurely, table-hopping lunch in the social hall.

On this particular Saturday, Hepps slept late. She was in the shower when the sirens were going by, and she didn't hear a thing. As she was toweling off, she heard her iPhone "beeping up a storm." She paused before checking her text messages. Although she had grown up with a liberal, Reform Judaism, and as a child had attended synagogue only on High Holy Days, she had become more traditional as an adult. She was not fully Sabbath-observant—she still used her laptop, turned on and off lights, and did other things prohibited under the strictest interpretation of "day of rest"—but she had been trying to use her phone less on Saturdays, to quiet the hum of technology one day a week.

As the phone kept beeping, she thought, *This is not normal.* She grabbed the phone, looked at the glowing screen. "My entire screen was people saying, 'I'm okay, I'm okay.' I was like, *Why are you telling me you're okay?*" She scrolled down and saw a text from her mother: "PLEASE CALL. SYNAGOGUE SHOOTING IN PGH?"

Hepps looked at the time stamp and saw that her mother had written ten minutes earlier. Her first thought was, *She must be terrified.* Her mom knew that she was a synagogue-goer but wouldn't have any idea which synagogue. She'd be afraid that her daughter was dead. Hepps called her mother, who instructed her to turn on the television. Numbly, she obeyed, and right away saw on TV the outside of Tree of Life. *Not my synagogue,* she thought. But she knew people there.

Having reassured her mother that she was safe, having answered the text messages already rolling in from her sister and other relatives and friends, Hepps thought to herself, *I can't just sit here alone.* Which meant she had to leave her house, and soon; she expected that barricades would go up, and her neighborhood would go into lockdown. She needed to get to her synagogue.

To get there, Hepps would normally take Shady Avenue and go past the Dunkin' Donuts—famous for having kosher certification, so that observant Jews could eat its Munchkins and drink its Coolattas—and walk up the steep hill to Beth Shalom, the massive stone structure at the highest point in Squirrel Hill. But she expected the streets would be blocked off. So she dressed, left the house, and took a detour to avoid main roads, arriving at Beth Shalom just after eleven o'clock. The detour was unnecessary; none of the streets on her way was closed. At the synagogue, there was no police cordon. The doors weren't even locked. "No one stopped me. I walked right in," said Hepps. The services were in progress—all over Squirrel Hill, with its many synagogues, services had kept going, as rabbis figured that the best response to terror was to keep praying. At noon, services ended.

After synagogue, Hepps's friend Kate Rothstein and Kate's sixteen-year-old daughter, Simone, wanted to stop by the Perlmans' house, which like Tree of Life was in the heart of Squirrel Hill. Hepps agreed to go with them. Everyone knew the Perlmans. Simone was a friend of Ada Perlman, whose father, Jonathan, was the rabbi of New Light Congregation, which met in a rented space at Tree of Life. As the world was about to learn, the Tree of Life synagogue building actually housed three congregations: its own, Tree of Life*Or L'Simcha (known to all as Tree of Life); Dor Hadash, a lay-led community that was part of the liberal Reconstructionist movement; and the small, aging New Light Congregation. New Light had sold its own building a year before and moved into the basement of Tree of Life. The gunman could have hit people from any of the three synagogues.

Which meant that Rabbi Perlman could have been shot. And what about Ada? She often went to synagogue with her dad. She, too, could be . . .

As they walked over to the Perlmans' house, they tried not to think the worst.

When they got to the house, they knocked, so as not to violate the Sabbath by ringing the doorbell. Beth Kissileff, Rabbi Perlman's wife and Ada's mother, answered the door. Ada had not gone to synagogue that morning, it turned out, so she was home, too. And her father, the rabbi, had escaped and made it home.

It was coming up on one o'clock, and around the world people knew that Jews had been murdered that morning in Squirrel Hill, but nobody knew how many, or who. As Jews from New York to Melbourne checked in with friends and relatives, they learned who was safe but still couldn't be sure who wasn't. For Orthodox and other Sabbath-observant Jews, it was tricky: they didn't use phones or other electronic technology before sundown on Saturday evening, so anything they knew about the massacre came from less religious acquaintances whom they bumped into.

The day was gray and cold, not quite fifty degrees, with light rain that kept starting and stopping. Hepps wanted to go home and get her book of Psalms.

In her research on the nearby town of Homestead, Hepps had read about laypeople stepping forward to perform the unfamiliar and sometimes uncomfortable rituals surrounding death. "They didn't have funeral homes, and they needed to figure out what to do themselves," Hepps said. In Jewish tradition, there are *shomrim,* guards, who sit with the bodies, watching over them, reciting Psalms, until the burial. In small communities like Homestead, laypeople were responsible for the tradition; they had to step up. "If they didn't do it, who was going to do it?" Today, in Squirrel Hill, it felt like her job as much as anybody's.

"There is this superstitious idea that between life and death is this serious time for a soul, and the soul doesn't find repose until the body is buried," she said. "The soul is confused, doesn't know what has happened—especially here, when death came in such a terrible way for the people in the building. I couldn't stop thinking about all the souls hovering scared over that building.

"I know this sounds crazy. I am not a Russian peasant Jew in the nineteenth century. I am a Harvard-educated engineer. But I was obsessed with this idea that what I could do for those souls was recite Psalms."

Simone and Kate walked Hepps to her house, where she picked up her small black book of Psalms. They set out for Tree of Life, two blocks away. Five minutes later, they stopped at the corner of Shady and Northumberland, yards from the 18 Engine firehouse. It was as close to the synagogue as they could get, outside the police barricades.

They huddled around Hepps as she opened her book. The table of contents was grouped by themes: the right Psalms for peace, for the Jewish people, for divine guidance, for help in troublesome times, and so forth. None of them seemed right—there was no category for *this*—the whole idea of a category for it was crazy. "What do we even call this thing? 'Psalm on the Massacre of Your Community'?" So the three women made a guess and opened the book.

"Then all these cameras appeared," Hepps said. The scene was so well composed, irresistible to photographers: three grieving women, close together around a sacred book. After a couple of minutes, Hepps got frustrated. The photographers "were right in our faces. . . . Maybe we said two or three Psalms, and then it was like, *We won't have any solitude.* They asked for our names, and we didn't think anything of it."

Within hours, photographs of Hepps and the Rothsteins were reproduced on websites around the world. They were all variations of an image showing two adult women in winter hats and glasses and one teenager in a light blue parka, huddled tight together, obviously distraught. The tall woman in the middle is Kate Rothstein, and she has one arm around the smaller woman to her right, Tammy Hepps, who is holding a small black book that matches her black hat and coat; Rothstein's left arm is around her daughter, whose gloved left hand is pressed to her mouth in grief. They are all looking down, and Hepps seems to be speaking.

(In the days to come, as the biographies of the eleven victims killed inside Tree of Life by Robert Bowers, a forty-six-year-old white nationalist from nearby Baldwin, became known, and as Squirrel Hill endured a week of funerals, there would be other images: of the victims, of Stars of

Tammy Hepps (left), outside Tree of Life with
Kate and Simone Rothstein

David in the windows of coffee shops, of armed guards, of Pittsburgh
Steelers serving as pallbearers. None of those images sticks like this one,
with its humble adjacency of hope and despair: three women praying to
offer comfort to souls whose names they have yet to learn but know with
foreboding that they soon will.)

After the photographers dispersed, the Rothsteins departed, and
Hepps encountered her friend Adam Reinherz, an Orthodox Jew who
was one of two full-time reporters for the local *Pittsburgh Jewish Chronicle*. Sabbath-observant, Reinherz was not taking phone calls, checking
social media, or watching television. But after leaving his own synagogue that morning, he had walked to the perimeter of Tree of Life, and
he knew what had happened. He insisted that Hepps join his family for
Shabbat lunch, and she agreed.

"And there," Hepps recalled, around the Reinherzes' dining room
table, with his wife and four children, "everything was weirdly okay."
For the first time since getting out of the shower that morning, she felt
a measure of calm. "I remember thinking, *This is the last time I will feel
okay. Because I don't know who was killed or what happened, but I am
about to find out, and then it will never be okay again.*"

AS TAMMY HEPPS WAS sitting down to lunch, Anne Rosenberg, sixty-two years old, a resident of Mount Laurel, New Jersey, was in Harrisburg, Pennsylvania, only three hours from Pittsburgh, with her five dachshunds, who were competing at a field trial. Her dogs were midcompetition when Rosenberg got the news about Tree of Life. Immediately, she found the organizers and told them, "I need to leave now."

In 2013, after the death of her father, Rosenberg had looked around and wondered what the rest of her life should look like. "My entire career, I was a dedicated breast cancer surgeon," she said. "I said, *I can't get lost in this job.*" She was fifty-eight years old, and she retired. "But even in retirement, I couldn't do just nothing. I had all these dogs," she said, "and the dogs were fabulous with people." Soon she and her dogs were involved with Mercury Team, a canine crisis-response team that works specifically with first responders—the dogs comfort and help police officers, ambulance workers, and firefighters who may be suffering from what they have seen. Mercury Team works locally, but Rosenberg and her dogs had also joined Crisis Response Canines, which deploys dogs nationally. She had brought her dogs to Parkland, Florida, and to Las Vegas after the shootings there. And now it seemed providential that she was close to Pittsburgh. "Growing up, I heard about all the Holocaust stuff," said Rosenberg, who is Jewish. "It was so reminiscent, how people are racially prejudiced and aggressive and angry and hostile. It was very sobering."

As it happened, the New Jersey chapter, Rosenberg's home chapter, of Crisis Response Canines had already heard from a woman named Holly, a hospital nurse in Pittsburgh, whom Rosenberg knew from dog shows. Rosenberg got relayed the message by John Hunt, a New Jersey chapter leader. "We are taking the teams out to Pittsburgh," he said. "We will meet you there." Rosenberg said she was on her way. But before she left for Squirrel Hill, there was one call that she had to make.

———

GREG ZANIS, a sixty-eight-year-old retired carpenter from Aurora, Illinois, looked at his caller ID and saw that it was his friend Anne Rosenberg. He answered, and she asked if he was going to Pittsburgh. Of course, he said. "Greg, I'll finance you," she said. He was always strapped for funds, as she knew, and for this trip she wanted to be his angel.

Not that it mattered, really. Zanis would have found a way to get to Squirrel Hill. In the olympiad of what we might call amateur crisis responders, or perhaps *extreme* amateur crisis responders—a community of comfort-dog owners, itinerant pastors, pie-bakers, and others who drop everything and hasten to the sites of mass shootings, natural disasters, and other horrific events, to be of use in their particular, and sometimes peculiar, ways—Zanis was the gold medalist. The founder, and sole member, of an organization called Crosses for Losses, Zanis had delivered over twenty-five thousand handmade memorial crosses, each about four feet tall, to the sites of murders, airplane crashes, natural disasters, and other events where people had died violently before their time. Zanis, who died in 2020, was best known for arriving at the site of mass shootings, which he had done since driving with his crosses to Columbine in 1999. Zanis built all the crosses himself. Each cross weighed about thirty pounds.

Zanis's change of life—from self-employed tradesman, building out the interiors of houses and restaurants around Chicago, to full-time Christian comfort worker—began in 1996, after he was the one to discover the lifeless body of his father-in-law, who had been shot dead. In a support group that he joined at his wife's church, he met a woman who offered him twenty dollars to make a cross in memory of her six-year-old son, who had been killed. Zanis refused payment but made a cross for her, and soon for others in the group. And then for others.

With Columbine, he went national. Zanis had a very tolerant wife, a preternatural ability to stay awake on long drives, and a new calling. Soon he was on the road most of the year. He put over half a million miles on four different trucks each. "I do everything," Zanis said. "You heard about the fires in Paradise? I put up memorials in California. I went to the tornado in Alabama, where twenty-three people were killed. I went to the Sikh temple in Wisconsin." For Jews he erected Stars of David, for Muslims crescent moons. For atheists he carved a ribbon. (Some atheists have adopted a red and black lapel-style ribbon as their sign.) He had a repertoire of "about twenty-five symbols" in his

Greg Zanis in Aurora, Illinois, 2017

garage. "I do every police officer who gets shot—like in Dallas, Baton Rouge, everywhere." Zanis brought his crosses to the sites of airplane crashes, although there are few of those in the United States today. "Like in Mississippi? A military plane crashed two years ago. Everybody died." He tried to bring a cross to the site of every homicide in Chicago, which in 2018 had 561 of them.

I spoke with Zanis on August 7, 2019, the week of mass shootings in both El Paso, Texas, and Dayton, Ohio. He was in his truck when I called, nearing his home in Chicago, having been on the road all week. "I left Saturday"—August 3, the day of the shooting in El Paso—"and then on my way down there, I heard about the other shooting, in Dayton. I drove fifteen hundred miles. It took me about thirty-six hours. I drove straight through. I set up there at four o'clock in the morning, and I stayed there for hours and hours and hours. I called the families on my radio"—he meant his mobile phone—"and asked them to come down and meet me. Then I went to Dayton. I went thirty-four hundred miles in four days. I try to limit it to one thousand miles a day.

"It was so, so hard this week. I collapsed in El Paso, when I heard about the other people dying. It just felt like a lot of responsibility here.

It seems impossible. I am more committed than anybody would under-stand. Twenty-two people died in El Paso."[*]

On Sunday morning, October 28, as news agencies were first report-ing the names of the eleven dead in Squirrel Hill, Anne Rosenberg left in her truck with her five dachshunds, driving from Harrisburg to Pittsburgh. And Greg Zanis, five hundred miles away in Aurora, Illi-nois, left in his truck, the paint wet on the wood in back. He still did not know how many Stars of David he would need, but that didn't matter. "I have my tools and my Home Depot credit card," Zanis said. "I have to build on the road."

––––––

SUNDAY AFTERNOON: the twenty-four hours leading up to it were the saddest, but also the fullest, of Tammy Hepps's life. So much to mourn, so much to do.

At about three o'clock on Saturday, Hepps finished lunch at the Rein-herzes' house. She had been checking her phone, and she made a plan so as not to be alone. "Through being on my phone, I guess, we learned that the JCC"—the nearby Jewish Community Center, at Forbes and Murray, the crossroads of Squirrel Hill—"had been set up as a gathering point." Adam Reinherz wouldn't even hold a pen or pencil on Shabbat, but he said he'd go with her to the JCC to see what was happening.

When Hepps got to the JCC, she walked down the corridor of the building, which on normal days functions as, among other things, a health club, an art gallery, a senior center, and a day care center. It did not feel like the gathering place she was looking for. "It wasn't, 'Let's sit around, hold hands, talk, have doughnuts.' I thought it was going to be a gathering of people who wanted to be with other people. People who needed someplace to be. It wasn't that." There were grief counselors, law enforcement officials, and, of course, some well-meaning gawkers, all coming and going from the largest room on the main floor, a room that seemed quieter than the rest of the building. Inside the room, look-ing from face to face of the people sitting in small groups around tables, she pieced it all together: these were the families and close friends of

––––––

[*] A twenty-third victim would die the following April of wounds suffered in the El Paso shooting.

people who had been at Tree of Life that morning. They hadn't been able to reach their loved ones. By this point in the afternoon, the odds were pretty clear: they were going to get either a miracle or the worst news of their lives.

Hepps knew she had no business being in this room. She saw Susan and Mel Melnick, the first friends she had made in Pittsburgh. "Jerry," Mel choked out. His close friend Jerry Rabinowitz was unaccounted for. Behind Susan and Mel, Jerry's wife, Miri, sat slumped in a chair. Tammy joined their group, feeling uncomfortable at having intruded on their grief.

Two tables over, she saw somebody she "sort of knew from synagogue." Judy Rosen, whose uncle, eighty-seven-year-old Melvin Wax, was still unaccounted for, told Hepps that she was a comfort to have around. "If she was telling me that I was supporting her, then I would stay." She didn't leave until shortly after six p.m., when Shabbat ended, at sundown.*

Jews don't have a clear definition of Hell, but if they did, it might be something like this, a waiting room for relatives of the just-murdered. And according to Hepps, this was a hell engineered for maximal torture. "They were so ill prepared to deal with what was going on," she said, referring to the police, the FBI, the medical examiner, the Bureau of Alcohol, Tobacco, Firearms, and Explosives—all the officials whom we trust to bring calm and order to chaos, all on-site, all seemingly impotent when faced with (to be fair) the kind of tragedy that they had no way to prepare for. It was "a hodgepodge of people who don't normally work together, who don't have clear protocols." At first, they told the families that they would release the names of the bodies in an hour, but "then an hour came and went," and there was no news. Hepps, who has never lost her fast-talking East Coast intensity, decided that she had to step up. "I remember saying, 'Can you even tell us how many bodies there are? What if we count the number of families in the room and see if they match up?'

"A couple people said, 'We are here for two people.'" It would turn out that a married couple and a pair of older, mentally disabled brothers

---

* Sunset in Pittsburgh that day was at 6:22 p.m.

were among the dead. "I was just stunned. *What do you mean you are here for two people?*" she thought. "It was beginning to unfold just how bad this was." Eventually she got a rough body count from one of the public officials, and she did a count of families in the room. And while nobody had precise information yet, and while not all the families were accounted for, and while the body count could yet be wrong, Hepps saw the truth. "It was clear," she realized, "that there was no reason for any-body in the room to have false hope."

It went on for hours. "It was horrible," she said. "People were sitting in this room all day thinking there was reason to have hope, that maybe somebody was injured in a random hospital somewhere." Desperate to learn something, family members sitting with Hepps began working the phones, calling local politicians they knew, screaming things like "You can't make us sit here any longer!" As she listened to the families plead for any information on their loved ones, Hepps had a thought: "It dawned on me that the bodies were still sitting there—that was beyond horrible."

As the sun went down, family members of some of the victims began to get the news. No official announcement had been made—that would come the next morning—but sympathetic local officials had leaked word to some of the families. People approached Hepps, told her what they knew, received hugs.

As she left the JCC, she dove back into her emails, texts, and social media, trying to catch up. The photograph of her reciting Psalms earlier that day had circled the globe. The *Daily Mail,* in England, had mis-takenly used Hepps's name under a photograph of an Ethiopian Jewish friend of the Rothsteins', hugging them at the corner by the synagogue. "My mother was like, 'You are in the *Daily Mail,* but you have turned into a Black woman,'" Hepps said.*

Hepps decided to walk to Fair Oaks Street, where her good friend Yael Silk, who was active with her in the local chapter of Bend the Arc: Jewish Action, a progressive Jewish political organization, lived. There was already some concern among local progressives that Donald Trump might come to Pittsburgh; if he did, Bend the Arc would surely organize some sort of response. When Hepps arrived at Silk's house, Silk was on

---

* Perhaps because the *Mail* quickly replaced the wrong photo with one that is indeed of Hepps, no record of the mistake exists.

a video chat that included an organizer from Bend the Arc's national headquarters in Washington, D.C. Silk motioned for Hepps to join the call. Hepps sat down in front of the computer with Silk, half paying attention while still keeping an eye on her iPhone.

Within minutes, she got a message on her phone about a victim named Daniel Stein. She had a friend *Danny* Stein, whom she knew from her Homestead research, but that had to be somebody different. She was supposed to have lunch with her Danny on Tuesday at his father's former bar in Homestead. Then she remembered that Stein was a regular at New Light, the Tree of Life tenant congregation. She tried to tell herself that she had only ever joined Danny for services there on Fridays. But then she read that he was the husband of Sharyn Stein.

"That is his wife's name," Hepps said. "And I fell apart. I walked away from this video chat, and I ran upstairs."

She called her closest friend, somebody she felt comfortable crying to. Later, when she finally got off the phone, she opened the door to the guest room where she'd found some privacy. "I looked out, and there on the floor were towels and pajamas and a toothbrush that Yael had left for me." She changed, brushed her teeth, and collapsed into bed.

———

THE NEXT MORNING, Sunday, October 28, the City of Pittsburgh held a press conference to announce the victims' names. Overnight a group of Bend the Arc activists had collaborated, using Google Docs, on a letter to President Trump, informing him that he would not be welcome in Squirrel Hill unless he renounced white nationalism. Yael suggested that Hepps help edit the letter into its final form. Hepps saw that the document was a jumble of ideas and strikethroughs and rewrites, with contributions from "like twenty different people." Eventually, she agreed that if everyone else got out of the document and let her work on the letter by herself, she would do her best.

Hepps tinkered with the letter into the afternoon, then walked home. Just after two-thirty, she had to steer around the police barricades a block from Tree of Life. When she made a turn onto Murray, a truck pulled up in front of her. On the side of it were painted three curious words: CROSSES FOR LOSSES.

As Hepps remembered it, she looked into Zanis's truck and saw a

Greg Zanis's truck as it pulled up to Tree of Life

pile of crosses in back. They were all white, and on a quick count, she decided that there were eleven of them. As soon as she grasped what she was seeing, she was incensed.

"I thought to myself, *You have got to be fucking kidding me,*" Hepps remembered. "And I looked around, and no one else was there, and I thought, *If I have to be the one to tell him he can't put crosses on the synagogue, I will be the one to tell him he can't put crosses on the synagogue.*"* Hepps had no idea who this guy was, with this kind of nerve. As she was figuring out what to say to him, trying to keep her cool, she saw, on the front seat of his truck, a pile of wooden six-pointed stars. She was relieved. "I thought, *Okay, what will happen here is he is going to put the Stars of David on the crosses, and it will be okay.*"

Zanis got out on the driver's side of the truck and approached Hepps. She looked him up and down: tired, unshaven, old. What was he doing here? Where had he come from? Then she looked down and saw his hands, and it was as if something became clear.

"I saw his hands were covered in white paint," Hepps remembered. "It's like he painted these things overnight and didn't even have time to wash his hands. He told me his intention, said to me, 'I made these

---

* She meant on the synagogue property, not literally "on the synagogue," of course.

Greg Zanis's Stars of David, affixed to his crosses

things, got in my truck, and drove nine hours.' There was white paint on his hands. He said to me, 'I have been driving the whole time. I don't even know the names of the people who died. I have to write their names on the stars.'"

And then Hepps knew what she had to do. Her mother had emailed her the full list of the dead that morning, so she had the names on her phone: Joyce Fienberg, Richard Gottfried, Rose Mallinger, Jerry Rabinowitz, Cecil Rosenthal, David Rosenthal, Bernice Simon, Sylvan Simon, Daniel Stein, Melvin Wax, Irv Younger. "I brought up this list, and he said to me, 'Can you please write the names in my notebook?' And he handed me a pen and his notebook, and I was shaking as I copied these names into his notebook—I have terrible handwriting—so he could write the names on the stars."

When Hepps had written down all eleven names, she gave Zanis's notebook back to him. Now she had a question: "I said to him, 'Why do you do this?' He said that there had been gun violence in his family, and this was his response. He said, 'Do you remember Parkland? I did that one. Do you remember Columbine? I did that one, too.'

"It had never occurred to me that it was one person who had made it his life's work to drive around the country and do this. And at that moment I realized we are just another one on the list."

A WEEKEND JOURNEY LIKE Tammy Hepps's is *very* Squirrel Hill. For one neighborhood to contain so much of Jewish life, religious and cultural, spiritual and political, liberal and traditional, all within a walkable space, in the twenty-first century, is exceptionally rare. Tammy Hepps's story is a Squirrel Hill story.

Mine is a Squirrel Hill story, too, but a different kind.

Jews have been permanently settled in Pittsburgh since the 1840s, when my great-great-great-grandfather, William Frank, and three other Jewish men founded the first Jewish burial society there. (When Jews start a graveyard, they're staying.) Frank's daughter, Julia, married my great-great-grandfather, Moses Oppenheimer, son of Isaac, another of the first Jews to put down Pittsburgh roots. They lived on Bartlett Street in Squirrel Hill. Pittsburgh Jews had settled in several neighborhoods, but by the time of the Great War, Squirrel Hill was on its way to being first among equals: not majority Jewish but with a sizable enough minority to support synagogues, Jewish bakeries, kosher butchers, a whole shopping district. My father was born, in 1945, to a prosperous family that moved, when he was four years old, to stately Aylesboro Avenue, the street where

The author's grandparents, James and Eleanor Oppenheimer,
at the Concordia Club

Tammy Hepps would later make her home. His Squirrel Hill was a little Jewish Eden.

Not that there weren't divisions. I was raised with the legends of those founding German Jewish families who went to temple together, often at the elegant Rodef Shalom Congregation; dined at the Concordia Club, which held parties and dances for their crowd; and married their children off to each other.

These fancy Jews looked down on more recent arrivals from Eastern Europe. But even such antagonisms added to the picture of a safe, lively, gemütlich urban ghetto. Upper-class Jews may have disdained their lower-class neighbors—and the disdain surely ran in the other direction—but at the end of the day, they lived side by side. North of Forbes was more upscale than south, but there were all kinds of Jewish families in both parts of the neighborhood. Everyone used the same supermarket, ate at the same delis, and attended Taylor Allderdice High School (although some lived over the line in the Peabody High district). My father's elementary school chums were not from families as fancy as his, but as a boy he couldn't have cared less. Squirrel Hill was, by midcentury, also home to a growing population of Orthodox Jews.

In Squirrel Hill, the public library, the post office, the movie theater, the ice cream shop, the shoe store, the kosher butcher, and synagogues of every denomination were all within a quarter mile of each other, give or take, so everyone walked the same sidewalks and, for the most part, nodded warmly as they passed.

The gunman who at Tree of Life perpetrated the greatest antisemitic attack in American history surely did not know that he was attacking the oldest, most stable, most internally diverse Jewish neighborhood in the United States. He did not know that, by 2018, Squirrel Hill had been a major Jewish center for a full century. It was Jewish before the Boston suburb of Newton or the Chicago suburb of Skokie, and it was still Jewish long after Philadelphia's Strawberry Mansion lost its Jews. Whereas many American cities lost their Jewish populations to white flight after World War II, the Jewish population of Pittsburgh never relocated en masse, and half of it still lives in Squirrel Hill or the immediately adjacent East End neighborhoods. Often Jews who leave return. My aunt and uncle started married life in Squirrel Hill in the 1950s, moved to the suburbs for a time, then retired to Squirrel Hill, where they live in an apartment. It's an expensive one, but they could have found one at half the price on the same street. Squirrel Hill is more economically diverse than most Jewish neighborhoods; with its mix of apartments, side-by-side duplexes, and stand-alone houses of varying sizes, you can get into the Allderdice school district for a million dollars or for less than two hundred thousand.

Jewish Squirrel Hill is not just geographically integrated, with different kinds of Jews living next door to each other, but spiritually miscegenated. The normal boundaries between Jewish denominations don't seem to apply here. It's not hard to find someone who on most weekends worships at an Orthodox synagogue but sometimes goes with a friend to a Conservative synagogue. There are "mixed" marriages, in which the Reform wife goes off to her temple while the Conservative husband goes to his. Friendships cross these lines, too. The wife of a Lubavitcher Hasidic rabbi may power-walk with a secular Jewish neighbor.

In the days after the shooting, I wondered how the people of this unusual neighborhood, my ancestral neighborhood, were doing. Given its closeness, surely the whole neighborhood felt the weight of the tragedy. I'd grown up elsewhere, but I knew that Squirrel Hill was a place of friendliness and basic midwestern decency, with a strong civic spirit that had carried it through difficult times before.* The city had also become known for its extraordinary economic and social resilience. Once a steel town, the mills had closed, one after the other, mainly in the 1970s and 1980s, as production moved overseas. But Pittsburgh had reinvented itself as a center of education, medicine, and computer technology. Carnegie Mellon University, in the western end of Squirrel Hill, was a leading center of robotics, and Google had a major outpost in the revitalized Bakery Square (its main building a rebuilt Nabisco factory).†　Pittsburgh was one of the great urban turnaround stories.

---

* There is a vigorous debate in Pittsburgh about whether it's part of "the Midwest." Many articles have been written. As to its decency, I defer to veteran Pittsburgh journalist and hometown boy John Allison, who told me, "Yes, Pittsburghers have a certain decency. But it's not the midwestern variety, which in my (limited) experience is about being nice and not talking about unpleasant things. Pittsburghers, to overgeneralize, have more of the decency of empathy—they will get nebby, they will try to do a nice thing for someone. It also stems from the Pittsburgh vibe of wanting to be seen as a nice guy—they are more actively nice. (Except for the jagoff racists.)" Now, as to the quintessential Pittsburgh epithet *jagoff* . . .

† Locals tend to talk about Carnegie Mellon University and the University of Pittsburgh as both being in Oakland, but Carnegie Mellon is in Squirrel Hill. See the Pittsburgh Neighborhoods Map archived at data.gov.

Quite understandably, much of the early reporting on the Tree of Life crime focused on the alleged killer, who apparently had spent his recent life in the ugliest depths of the racist internet. He did not interest me. And the victims were eulogized at length. I was interested in everyone else. I knew that in a neighborhood like Squirrel Hill, thousands of people would know at least one of the victims; everybody would be afraid the next time they went to synagogue (or church, or the grocery store); there would be trauma; there would be acts of extraordinary kindness. There would be discord. I was curious to know how people dealt with the aftermath of mass violence. When the cameras and the police tape were gone, what stayed behind?

Just as the shooting was an event unique in the annals of American Jewish history, the affected neighborhood was unique, too, and thus presented the perfect opportunity to look for answers to some very interesting questions. This was a neighborhood of joiners. Would it help people's recovery that the victims, many of their relatives, and those who survived the attack all belonged to houses of worship? What about faith in God, for those who had it? And what about the neighborhood's longevity—how much did it matter that Jews had been here for a century, and that many of these Jews today were third- or fourth-generation residents?

As somebody who lived in another dense, walkable neighborhood, with small lots and good sidewalks, I knew that the regularity with which I bumped into neighbors had helped me recover from my occasional troubles. I had to wonder if the Squirrel Hill topography would alleviate the isolation and depression that can follow serious misfortune.

And what would it mean for people's healing that, as *Pittsburgh Post-Gazette* editor David Shribman wrote the day after the shooting, this "anti-Semitic rampage" had occurred in "perhaps the least anti-Semitic city in the country"? That's the way my father remembered the city, too.

American Jews have had good relations with their Gentile neighbors, but not always. When I began writing, in late 2019, there were ongoing violent attacks against Orthodox Jews in Brooklyn neighborhoods where Black and Jewish residents had lived together for decades, often uneasily. On December 10, 2019, the owner of the JC Kosher Supermarket in Jersey City, New Jersey, was shot and killed, along with an employee and a customer. Eighteen days later, during Hanukkah, an intruder stabbed

five men at a rabbi's home in Monsey, New York. I was curious how the
support—and it was overwhelming support—from non-Jews helped
the Jews of Squirrel Hill.

With their dense settlement, deep roots, economic vitality, robust
Jewish life, and warm relations with their non-Jewish neighbors, the
Jews of Squirrel Hill might, I suspected, offer a model of resilience. Morbid as it is to say, if mass murder had to come, there was probably no
place in America better positioned to endure it than Squirrel Hill.

This book is about how Squirrel Hill people behaved in the aftermath of the Tree of Life shooting. Almost half the stories took place
in the first week after the shooting, a time line that reflected what the
people I interviewed shared with me. Inevitably, their memories were
heavily concentrated on the day of the shooting, beginning when they
first heard the news and going until nightfall. Then as our conversations
progressed, people would spin out memories stretching into the week
after the shooting. I would hear about anonymous acts of *hesed,* which
is often translated, beautifully, as "lovingkindness." I also heard about
professional responsibilities: rabbis who presided over multiple funerals,
for example, or the local archivist who had to collect the artifacts of people's grief, like the cards and teddy bears left at the scene. I heard about
the indispensability of the Squirrel Hill business district, strung along
Forbes and Murray avenues—how people hugged in the Giant Eagle
supermarket or planned public events in the Starbucks.

Many of the characters in these stories are Jews, but many are not. I
met a woman who was not a Jew but who decided, after the shooting, to
become one. I met a nonobservant Jew who decided that he had to look
more Jewish, so he started wearing a yarmulke.

Some lives changed in big ways, some in little ways. Some people performed the Jewish value of lovingkindness so perfectly that I still con-
template their stories shamefacedly, wondering what I have done with
my time. Such acts persisted, and not just from Jews—a Black Christian
from Minnesota came to Pittsburgh to give Jews her sweet potato pies.
In wintertime, a celebrity made a surprise visit to a boy's bar mitzvah.

When the warm weather came and the funerals seemed further in
the past, people started to feel better. There were holidays and parties,
and it became okay to have fun again.

But people struggled, too. Some non-Jews, especially African Americans, wondered why the Squirrel Hill murders got so much attention, when the murders of Black men had been so quickly forgotten. The Tree of Life synagogue remained closed, fenced off, a hulking shrine to the dead—and within the Jewish community, some wondered if Tree of Life should even reopen its badly damaged building.

There was no consensus over how to remember the dead. Many in Squirrel Hill believed that a meaningful response to their murders had to include a push for gun control and outspoken opposition to right-wing antisemitism and xenophobia—for how could we honor the dead without condemning that which had killed them? Others preferred that the deaths not occasion what they saw as partisan politicking. A year after the shooting, some of the apparent unity felt facile and dishonest. Despite all the STRONGER THAN HATE posters and merchandise, not everybody felt so strong.

Not everybody was affected, of course. Plenty of good, upstanding people stopped on the day of the shooting, shed some tears, paid attention to the news for a week or two, and then moved on. They treated Tree of Life as so many of us treat most American mass shootings. But this book is about the people who stopped what they were doing, then did something different, at least for a time. Their response to a uniquely bloody slaughter of Jews transcended religion, ethnicity, and family ties; it teaches us something about the power of proximity, how the streets we walk affect how we treat each other. This book is about people who cared about this shooting, in particular those who faced it together, because they had no choice, because they were neighbors.

I

The Attack

W HEN DID IT BEGIN, this hatred of Jews?
Some would say that all hatred began in the Garden of
Eden, when the serpent brought evil into the world, or at the
Tower of Babel, when God punished humans for their hubris by destroy-
ing their common tongue, making them strangers to one another. Others would point to the New Testament, which, as uncomfortable as it is to
admit today, does seem to lay the death of Jesus at the feet of treacherous
Jews. Or we can blame the early theologians in the centuries after Jesus,
who said things like, "The Jewish people were driven by their drunken-
ness and plumpness to the ultimate evil; they kicked about, they failed
to accept the yoke of Christ, nor did they pull the plow of his teaching. . . . Although such beasts are unfit for work, they are fit for killing.
And this is what happened to the Jews: while they were making themselves unfit for work, they grew fit for slaughter."* Over the centuries,
Christians would point to the Jews' own stubbornness as the cause of
others' antipathy toward them. There was the Jew-hating of the Quran
("Allah has cursed them on account of their unbelief"); of the medieval Europeans, with their superstition that the Jews drank the blood of
Gentile children; of the Nazis; of the Communists; of genteel Etonians;

---

* That's John Chrysostom, in "Against the Jews," from the fourth century.

of Afrocentric Black nationalists; of East Asian superstition; of rural American folk belief; of Islamic radicalism; of its left-wing apologists; of right-wing populists.

But if what we are asking is how the attack on Tree of Life *began*— not whom to blame, not who bears responsibility, since ultimately the killer does—we may start with Carolyn Ban, a Smith-, Harvard-, and Stanford-trained scholar of the European Union, who in 1997 moved to Pittsburgh to become the dean of the University of Pittsburgh's Graduate School of Public and International Affairs. Fifty-four years old and single, she had relocated a lot in her academic career, and in Pittsburgh she at last felt ready to stay put. "Within a year, I said, 'I don't think I am moving anymore,'" she recalled. "'This place feels like home.' And I went looking for a choral group." Ban had been raised in a nonobservant Jewish household, but in 1994 she had heard a concert of Jewish choral music in Albany and been "blown away." Ban was not a choral singer, but she decided, "I am going to do this, and I loved it. It connected me to Judaism." When she relocated to Pittsburgh, she found a singing group, but it didn't last. "I needed a place to sing."

She liked what she found at Dor Hadash, a small congregation in the progressive Reconstructionist movement, which emphasizes ongoing innovation and openness to change. There was no rabbi at Dor Hadash (Hebrew for "new generation"), which was part of the attraction. "I liked its informality," Ban said. "I got a kick out of the fact that everyone on the *bimah** was female. Everyone sang, they sang with heart, and they sang very well. The services are often wonderful. They are quirky, because different people lead every time. It has a reputation that is well deserved as an intellectual congregation."

Soon after Ban first attended Dor Hadash, her father died, and she needed a regular minyan, a quorum of ten adult Jews, to say the Mourner's Kaddish, the prayer for the dead. Dor Hadash gave her that. In 2005 she was diagnosed with cancer, and Dor Hadash members were there for her during a monthlong recovery at home—"I was not alone any single day." She kept up her involvement, and in 2017 she became the chairperson of the congregation's social action committee. The commit-

---

* The *bimah* is the table where the Torah scroll is unfurled to be read; it sits at the front of the congregation, or in the middle of it. The rabbi may also deliver the sermon from the *bimah*; it can be thought of as a synagogue's pulpit.

tee "had been kind of moribund," and when she called a meeting to talk about what the committee should focus on, the members present chose two issues: criminal justice reform, and immigration and refugees.

The committee began working with Jewish Family and Community Services (JFCS), a large social service organization in Squirrel Hill, to help settle refugees in the area. When committee members wanted to begin advocating for better government policies toward refugees—to move from social services into social action—JFCS recommended that Dor Hadash ally with the Hebrew Immigrant Aid Society (HIAS), a storied organization founded in 1881 to help resettle Jews fleeing persecution in Russia and Eastern Europe. Over the years, HIAS expanded its mission to helping all refugees in the United States, most of them non-Jewish. And in the summer of 2018, Ban and another committee member got an email from HIAS about the National Refugee Shabbat: on October 20, participating synagogues would use the Shabbat service to honor, welcome, or just express solidarity with refugees.

"We said, 'Great!'" Ban said. And she volunteered to lead Dor Hadash's participation in the National Refugee Shabbat. As it happened, a bat mitzvah was scheduled for October 20, so Dor Hadash held its

Carolyn Ban, hosting the first public event of Squirrel Hill Stands Against Gun Violence, at Temple Sinai, six months after the Tree of Life shooting

refugee Shabbat on October 6. The event basically involved Ban leading a discussion about refugees, but as the event's convener, she was also
responsible for publicity. "I said to the person at HIAS, 'Oh, be sure to
put us on the website of the list of congregations that are participating.'
And that's how he"—the killer—"found us."

At first, when she heard about the shooting, Ban didn't make the
connection to the synagogue's support of refugees. She found out only
in the evening, after the killings, as she sat at the Jewish Community
Center with her friend Miri Rabinowitz, whose husband, Jerry, had been
at the synagogue that morning. By then, Miri knew Jerry was dead; she
was waiting to find out what was happening with his body.

"Somebody runs over and says, 'Did you hear?' And she says that
this person—who I will not dignify by using his name—had posted that
he hated Jews, because they were supporting Muslims to help bring in
migrants who were going to kill white people. . . . And I heard later that
he said, 'Thank you HIAS for showing where your friends are.'" Ban
was right: the killer had posted on the website Gab, "You like to bring
in hostile invaders to dwell among us? We appreciate the list of friends
you have provided," and he had linked to HIAS's list of participating
congregations.

On Saturday after the shooting, authorities descending on the
alleged shooter's apartment in Baldwin, Pennsylvania

The congregation that caught Robert Bowers's eye was Dor Hadash, which since 2010 had rented space in the Tree of Life building. If he was looking for Jews to kill, it's not surprising that he went to Squirrel Hill, the heart of Jewish Pittsburgh. Perhaps he was also seeking some sort of symbolic vengeance for the death of his father, who had shot himself to death in 1979 while awaiting trial for the rape of a twenty-year-old woman. It was alleged that Bowers's father had carjacked the woman and had her drive to Squirrel Hill, where she parked her car and he assaulted her, before being caught in the act and arrested by police. Bowers was six years old when that happened, but maybe he knew that the beginning of his father's end had come in Squirrel Hill, when he was thrown in the back of the officers' K-9 van and carted off. Bowers now lived about thirty minutes away. Who knew what Squirrel Hill meant to him?

As Ban began to understand what had transpired, she "just sat there in shock." She then turned to a friend and said, about the HIAS refugee Shabbat, "Well, we don't wish we hadn't done it. That's what we were supposed to do."

———

"HIAS LIKES TO BRING invaders in that kill our people," the alleged shooter, Robert Bowers, wrote on Gab the morning of the attack. "I can't sit by and watch my people get slaughtered. Screw your optics, I'm going in." He then drove to the synagogue, bringing three Glock .357 handguns and a Colt AR-15 semiautomatic rifle, all loaded.

Depending on the route he took to get to Tree of Life, Bowers either passed right in front of Shaare Torah, a Modern Orthodox synagogue, or missed it by a city block. Either way, he apparently never knew how close he had come to the greatest concentration of Jews in Pittsburgh that weekend. At Shaare Torah, hundreds of Sabbath-observant Jews were convening for the bar mitzvah of thirteen-year-old Nate Itzkowitz. Shaare Torah always locked its doors, so there is no telling what would have happened if he had stopped there. But if he had gotten inside, he would have encountered babies, children, teens, married couples, widows, widowers. He would have been shooting Jews in a barrel.

Instead, he drove a mile farther to Tree of Life, where by the time he arrived, at about 9:50 a.m., twenty-one worshippers and one custodian were inside. By some measures, Tree of Life is the oldest continuously operating synagogue in Pittsburgh, but in recent years it had suffered a steep decline in membership, from about a thousand families a few decades ago, to half as many in 2010, to a quarter as many, between 200 and 250 families, on this October morning. But even those numbers are too rosy. The reality is that most American synagogues, at least outside Orthodoxy, are lucky to get 10 percent of their members inside the building any given week—and indeed, Tree of Life often got fewer than twenty people on Shabbat. And those whom they got were mostly the old and the very old.

Like American culture generally, houses of worship yearn for the young. For a synagogue to have young people in the pews, for a bar to have young people on the stools, for a clothing store to have young people in the checkout line—they are the desired demographic. Children are the future. At churches and synagogues, though, youth aren't reliable. With low-paying jobs, they can't always pay membership dues; with young children to look after, they can't always make it out of the house. It's empty-nesters and pensioners, with their stable incomes and free blocks of time, who come on Thursday afternoon to prepare the Saturday kiddush lunch, who have time on a Tuesday morning to visit someone dying in hospice, who can rush over to shul to be the final, tenth person to fill out the minyan. The old people do the work.

For a synagogue to survive, it needs to be multigenerational; it needs young people to replace those who stop coming when they become infirm, move to Florida, or die. By that measure, Tree of Life was struggling, and the struggle was never more apparent than on Saturday mornings.

The youngest member of Tree of Life in synagogue that morning was David Rosenthal, who was fifty-four years old. Like his older brother, Cecil, he was born with Fragile X syndrome, a genetic condition that can cause intellectual disabilities. David could not live on his own or hold down a regular job, but he had a life, with routines and friends and a sense of purpose. That life revolved around the streets of Squirrel Hill, where he had been raised and still lived, in supportive housing run by a nonprofit organization called Achieva. He knew the firefighters at the 18 Engine firehouse, he knew the mailman, he knew the proprietors of the small businesses he visited on his rounds. And he came to synagogue every week at Tree of Life. He liked to stand at the *bimah* next to Audrey Glickman, whose regular role on Shabbat was to chant the blessings and Psalms that begin the morning service. It was unclear how much he understood or what he thought he was doing, but he was *there*. How many weeks would they not have gotten to the quorum of ten without him?

Or without his older brother, Cecil? Cecil also lived in Squirrel Hill, where people knew him, talked with him, cared for him. At fifty-nine, Cecil was the second-youngest person in Tree of Life that morning, and he was among the first to get shot, moments before his brother.

"I never saw the shooter," said Audrey Glickman, one of the eleven who got out alive. As usual, on this morning, David Rosenthal was standing next to her as she chanted, and a small group of regulars followed along in their prayer books. Then there was a loud noise: "All you had to do was hear the shooter before you started running out."

Except on the High Holy Days, Tree of Life did not pray in the large sanctuary facing Shady Avenue; it had been decades since there were weekly crowds requiring a space that large. This Saturday, the worshippers were in the smaller Pervin Chapel, and at this hour there were twelve of them. Besides Rabbi Jeffrey Myers, Glickman, and the Rosenthal brothers, those in attendance included Stephen Weiss, sixty, a former executive director of the synagogue who was now a middle-school science teacher; Joe Charny, ninety, a psychiatrist and widowed father of three who had spent the last several decades as a dedicated lay leader at Tree of Life; ninety-seven-year-old Rose Mallinger, who was sitting next to her daughter, Andrea Wedner, sixty-one, a dental hygienist, who drove her mother to Tree of Life every week; Irv Younger, sixty-nine, who worked in real estate and had coached Little League baseball; Bernice and Sylvan Simon, eighty-four and eighty-six, a retired nurse and accountant, respectively, who had gotten married sixty-two years earlier in the very same small chapel in Tree of Life; and Joyce Fienberg, seventy-five, a retired researcher at the University of Pittsburgh. The custodian, Augie Siriano, was also in the building.

It sounded like a coatrack falling to the ground, several people reported. "That's why people ran out to help, and that's how they got shot," Glickman said. Within seconds, as more cracking sounds came, the people still in services realized it was gunfire. "You could hear the shots down the hallway echoing off the marble walls, and so we took off. Rabbi Myers said, 'Everyone get down!'"

At this point, Glickman and David Rosenthal turned and fled the room, leaving by a door at the front, near the ark holding the Torah. The shooter barreled toward the chapel, shooting Cecil Rosenthal, who fell to the floor, bleeding, then Irv Younger, just inside the chapel door. Once inside, the killer saw Charny, and the two men looked each other in the eye. The killer did not shoot, instead turning his gun toward other men and women in the pews. "Why he didn't shoot me, I don't know," Charny later said. Charny followed Glickman and the younger Rosenthal brother out through the door at the head of the room, and Rabbi Myers went with them.

Four people had made it to safety, at least for the moment: the rabbi, Audrey Glickman, Joe Charny, and David Rosenthal. From outside the chapel, they heard Bernice Simon screaming that her husband had been shot. Glickman looked back into the room, then realized there was

Cecil Rosenthal and New Light synagogue
president Barbara Caplan in 2017

nothing she could do. Sylvan Simon was lying on the ground, shot in the back. "He was dead, and she was screaming, and I went back with David," said Glickman. David—panicked, confused about what was going on, and scared for his brother—returned to the chapel, shouting that he wanted to call home. He was shot and killed. So were Bernice Simon, Rose Mallinger, and Joyce Fienberg. Stephen Weiss got out alive.

Charny and Glickman climbed stairs to the third floor, where they hid in a storage room, covering themselves with old bags of clothes. Myers, the rabbi, hid in the choir loft. From there he called 911 and listened as the shots continued. "I heard him execute my congregants," Myers would later say.

At about the same moment, in the basement, Barry Werber also called 911. He was a member of the other Conservative congregation housed in the building, New Light, which had an even smaller membership than Tree of Life and met in a rented room on the lower level. Only six of its members, including the rabbi, had arrived so far. When the shooting began, Werber looked out of New Light's room and saw a body on the stairs leading up to the main level, where the Tree of Life congregation met. He closed the door, then hurried—along with Rabbi Jonathan Perlman, sixty-seven-year-old congregant Carol Black, and eighty-seven-year-old Melvin Wax—toward a supply closet behind the ark. That left two members of New Light—Rich Gottfried, a sixty-five-year-old dentist who was Black's brother, and seventy-one-year-old retiree Dan Stein—in the basement kitchen, where they were preparing food for later. That's where the killer found and shot them.*

Barry Werber did not yet know his friends' fates when he called 911. Hiding in the dark, he told the dispatcher about the gunshots, then kept quiet. But Mel Wax, who was quite deaf, thought the shooting had stopped. He opened the closet door and looked out, at which point the killer shot him dead. The killer then peered into the closet, maybe even took a couple of steps in—but he didn't see Werber or Black, holding their breath in the dark. Perlman was already gone; after hurrying his congregants into the closet, he had found another exit and fled out of the building into a neighbor's yard. The killer closed the door. "I'm pressed up against the wall, Carol is kneeling on the floor to my right, and the

---

* I spoke with Carol Black once, briefly, but she did not agree to a longer interview. She and custodian Augie Siriano were the only survivors, of eleven, who did not talk with me at length.

gentleman walks in with a long gun," Werber later told the *Post-Gazette*. "I could see the jacket he was wearing and a pair of pants. . . . He didn't see us, thank God."

Meanwhile, Dan Leger, a seventy-year-old hospice nurse, and his close friend, family doctor Jerry Rabinowitz, sixty-six, had rushed toward the shooting. They had arrived at synagogue early to prepare for the twice-monthly Torah study they led for Dor Hadash. As medical professionals, both men felt that they had to try to help. "We did exactly what people who train you for crisis situations tell you not to do," Leger said the following March, when he was still recuperating from his injuries. "Instead of running away from the sound of gunfire, we thought that we could somehow be helpful. We looked at each other and said, 'That's what we have to do.'" They rushed out of their study room on the main floor, near the chapel where Tree of Life met. Both men were shot, and Rabinowitz was killed. Leger, lying on the floor, figured that he would soon bleed to death. He began to recite the Viddui, the Jewish deathbed confessional.

———

ELEVEN JEWS WERE MURDERED at Tree of Life the morning of October 27, 2018, and eleven other men and women—ten Jews and the non-Jewish custodian—were inside but survived, although two of them, Dan Leger and Andrea Wedner, were wounded.

The police received their first 911 call at 9:54 a.m., arrived at the synagogue at 9:57, and tried to enter the building at ten a.m., at which point they were met by the fleeing suspect, firing out the door. "We are pinned down by gunfire," one officer said into his radio. "He is firing out the front of the building with an automatic weapon." They returned fire, driving the shooter back inside the building. Reinforcements soon arrived, and members of a SWAT team entered the synagogue at 10:29.

As the police took control of the building, they were able to get some people out. They found Jeffrey Myers and led him to safety. Paramedics were able to remove Dan Leger, who was critically injured. Stephen Weiss got out on his own, as did Jonathan Perlman and Augie Siriano. The custodian later recalled hearing a loud *pop-pop-pop, pop-pop-pop,* and initially he had walked toward the sound. "I figured, well, maybe I'll go investigate and see what it is," he told newspaper reporters. "As I got

Pittsburgh police officers the day of the shooting

into the area where the shootings were going on, I started smelling gunpowder. Well, really, when I walked down this one aisle, heading toward the chapel, as I got out of the aisle and into the chapel, I turned and looked. There was a gentleman laying on the floor, face down, and he had blood coming out of his head." He fled through a side door and ran right into the police. "The cops were standing there, and they had the guns on me. And I says, 'Wait a minute, wait a minute.'" He fell to his knees and put his hands in the air. "And I says, 'I'm the custodian. I'm trying to get out of the building.'"

As they swept the building, looking for the shooter, police had to navigate around spent bullet casings, pools of blood and tissue, and bodies. At 10:47, the SWAT team found the shooter on the third floor, where they exchanged fire; two SWAT team members were hit, as was the shooter. At 11:03, an officer reported that they were talking with the shooter: "Spontaneous negotiations ongoing, effort to get him out, we're not going in." And by 11:08 the shooter was surrendering: "Suspect is crawling, he's injured, SWAT is telling him to continue to crawl at this time. . . . Suspect is talking about [how] all these Jews need to die." By then, the shooter had wounded four Pittsburgh police officers: Anthony Burke, Timothy Matson, Daniel Mead, and Michael Smidga (two more were wounded, but not by gunfire: one suffered a hearing injury, the other an injured knee). They all survived—as did the shooter, who was taken to Allegheny General Hospital, where he was overheard in the emergency room shouting, "I want to kill all the Jews!" He was treated by a team that included at least three Jewish doctors and nurses. "We're here to take care of sick people," hospital president Jeffrey K. Cohen, himself a member of Tree of Life, told television reporters.

————

THE DAY AFTER the shooting, the media pieced together the time line of what had happened, identified the dead, and told the ever-tantalizing near-miss stories. For example: Judah Samet, eighty, of Squirrel Hill, a survivor of the Bergen-Belsen concentration camp, had been late for synagogue that morning and had pulled into the Tree of Life parking lot as his friends were being murdered inside. As he was getting out of his car, somebody approached him and suggested that he back out carefully, which he did, but not before he saw the shooter, at the synagogue door, spraying rounds at the police outside. "I was talking to my housekeeper here; she comes once a week," he told *The Washington Post,* and so he "was four minutes late . . . getting to shul," which had likely saved his life. Samet, a garrulous little fire hydrant of a man, was a Trump supporter, and he would achieve renown as the president's guest for the State of the

Union address in January. That night was his eighty-first birthday, and the entire Congress sang "Happy Birthday" to him on television.

The media got some things wrong. Early reports indicated that all the victims were members of Tree of Life. It was an understandable mistake—reporters, under tremendous pressure to disseminate the news, had no reason to know that one synagogue building housed three congregations. A second error, widely repeated, was that the attack occurred during a bris, a baby boy's circumcision. It's impossible to say for sure where this error originated, but state senator Jay Costa sent a tweet at 11:51 that morning that read, "In a room at Tree of Life today was a bris— one of Judaism's most important rituals, a tradition that welcomes an 8-day-old baby into the faith's ancient covenant with G-d. The sanctity of this ceremony—and its importance in celebrating new life—makes today even more devastating."* A spokeswoman for Costa later said that the senator had been "on-site" at the synagogue just after the shooting, and may have heard about the supposed bris from someone there. Pennsylvania's attorney general, Josh Shapiro, saw Costa's tweet and ran with it. "When gunfire erupted, a bris, a circumcision ceremony had been in progress," according to the *New York Post.* That story went live on the web at 11:14 a.m., but if Shapiro's office is correct that he got his information from Costa's tweet, then his quotation must have been added in a later update: "Pennsylvania's Attorney General Josh Shapiro said the shooting happened during the portion of the rite when the child is given a Hebrew name. The 'shooter claimed innocent lives—and injured first responders—at a baby-naming,' Shapiro said." Soon the cable network MSNBC repeated the error, tweeting at 12:16 p.m., "President Trump on Pittsburgh synagogue attack: 'This was an anti-Semitic act' during a baby-naming ceremony." In the embedded video accompanying the tweet, Trump expresses dismay at the attack but says nothing about a baby-naming ceremony (which could, in Judaism, be part of a boy's circumcision ceremony or a special event for a newborn daughter). It seems that MSNBC had added that detail without any attribution.

Handed a plotline with great drama—and coming straight from an attorney general named Shapiro!—other media outlets did not hesi-

---

* By writing "G-d," Costa was honoring the tradition of some Jews not to write out the full name of the deity, to show respect.

tate to repeat the circumcision detail. That afternoon, at 3:12 p.m., PBS posted a story on its *NewsHour* website that mentioned a bris. *The New York Times* joined the chorus: "Though a bris, a ceremony to mark a child's birth, was among the ceremonies taking place Saturday, no children were among the casualties, law enforcement officials said." The Jewish parenting website *Kveller* had the bris detail. At seven the next morning, *The Washington Post* ran an opinion essay by Danya Ruttenberg, a rabbi and author popular on Twitter. "Some were there to celebrate a brit milah—to welcome a new baby boy into the community," she wrote (using the Hebrew *brit,* rather than the Yiddish *bris,* for "covenant," as in the covenant of circumcision). "Perhaps some of them went primarily to be with friends, or to pour out their hearts in prayer. Maybe some were there for a combination of reasons. But they were all together in a sacred space, in holy time, when a gunman opened fire."

Other publications embellished further. At 12:50 p.m., *The Advocate,* a national gay and lesbian publication, posted an article that read, "The mass shooting at a Pittsburgh synagogue reportedly happened during a ceremony for the children of a gay couple." Later in the article, the reporter quoted a Facebook post from the Delta Foundation of Pittsburgh, a local LGBTQ group: "'We were just informed that this morning's tragedy was happening during a Briss for a set of twins adopted by a gay couple,' the organization posted Saturday on Facebook, in a post that has since been edited to exclude this information, pending the final confirmation. 'Our hearts and prayers go out to all that were involved including the members of the Synagogue, law-enforcement and first responders.'"

The detail about the gay couple was still circulating several days later, on November 1, when the *Philadelphia Gay News* quoted a Philadelphia rabbi asserting that "the shooter targeted the Tree of Life synagogue, located in the diverse and LGBTQ-friendly neighborhood of Squirrel Hill, 'because of the openness and values that it held.'" The writers continued: "A bris, a ritual circumcision and baby-naming ceremony, was being held for the son of a gay male couple at the synagogue that morning. No children were physically harmed in the attack, which was the worst single attack on Jews in U.S. history." In this account, the twins had become just one boy, and the ideology behind the attack was now anti-queer animus.

Within Pittsburgh's Jewish community, the false report that the shooter had disrupted a bris at Tree of Life was an occasion for some gallows humor, along the lines of "Tree of Life should be so lucky to have a baby in the building." As it happened, there was a baby-naming ceremony in Pittsburgh that morning—for a girl, the second daughter of a gay male couple—but it took place at Rodef Shalom, the large Reform temple just north of Squirrel Hill.

Both of these errors, soon corrected in the national narrative of the Tree of Life shooting, paradoxically reflected a sense of optimism. As horrifying as this story was, American Jews would have been cheered to know that there was a large, thriving congregation in the heart of Squirrel Hill, where that morning the parents of a newborn son were celebrating his circumcision, his entry into the covenant. But the reality was that the shooter arrived at a mostly empty building, with no babies or teens or recently married couples anywhere to be found. By choosing Tree of Life, the killer guaranteed that his body count would be lower than it would have been at practically any other house of worship, at any other time Saturday morning, in Squirrel Hill.

On the other hand, who *is* in synagogue at ten to ten on a normal Saturday morning, when it's not a holiday, when there's no wedding or bat mitzvah or bris? It's a mix of the most committed Jews and the Jews with no place else to go, the widowed or disabled or simply lonely, who wake up early and can't wait to see other people. Jews have a word for people like this: *amcha*, "your people." It means the common folk, the ordinary ones, the humble masses. It's people like Cecil and David Rosenthal, who always came early to have tea with Augie Siriano. "This was a weekly ritual," the *Post-Gazette* later reported, "the longtime building janitor taking tea with two longtime congregants, men he considered brothers, in a place they all loved."

That's who came early. That's who got shot.

2

⸺ ∞ ⸺

Those Inside

THE JEWS INSIDE Tree of Life that morning were a varied group. Some had never spoken to one another, and some knew each other only in passing. They were under one roof because the landlord synagogue needed money; one of the tenant congregations had just sold a building it could ill afford to keep; and the other tenant, a rolling-stone congregation that refused to own property, had been settled there for the past few years. They were different kinds of communities, and to the extent the members mixed, it was because they were all Squirrel Hill Jews. They had that much in common, and now something else in common, too.

────

IN THE SUMMER OF 1970, when Jeffrey Myers was fifteen years old, Samuel Seidelman, his beloved cantor and choir director at the Suburban Jewish Center, a Conservative synagogue in Linden, New Jersey, suffered a stroke. The stroke was not fatal, but it paralyzed the cantor's vocal cords. With the fall holidays approaching, the cantor's numerous roles would have to be filled by others. Somebody suggested that the choir be put in the hands of a certain talented boy tenor. It was an unorthodox suggestion, but as people looked at their limited options, it began to make sense.

As Myers remembered it, "The elders of the choir met, and they reviewed their choices, and they felt the person best qualified to go into every part and do the best was me. I was a musician, I played clarinet. . . . I knew all the music, all the parts." Myers ended up leading the synagogue choir through the rest of high school and during his college years at nearby Rutgers. Then he enrolled at Jewish Theological Seminary (JTS), in New York City, first for a degree in Jewish education, then for training as a cantor, too. He was ordained a cantor in 1984 and could now look for work as the music leader of a Conservative synagogue.

For a man of his gifts, this seemed like a perfect career choice. Myers was born into a suburban Conservative Judaism then at its zenith. His father, Donald, modeled what it was to be a proud Jew and a patriotic American. A prosecutor and later a municipal judge, he gave speeches on behalf of Israel Bonds; joined B'nai Brith, the Jewish fraternal order, eventually becoming an international vice president; served as president of his synagogue, the one where his son would direct the choir; and was included in an edition of *Who's Who in World Jewry*. Donald Myers was a leader in a suburban Conservative Jewish culture that perfectly suited the professional aspirations of men like him, who wanted out of the urban ghetto—he had grown up in New York City, been educated in its public schools—but wanted to stay emphatically, even clannishly, Jewish. Men like him worked in the cities, lived in the suburbs. Some might have wanted to integrate Gentile suburbs, but many were happy to stick with their own kind: chewing the fat with Jewish neighbors as they took breaks from mowing their quarter-acre lawns. Many were even content with Jewish country clubs, while others chafed at the restrictions that stubbornly persisted. Donald Myers was the municipal judge in a community where, according to his son, a local swim club did not welcome Jews. Jews were half in, half out.

These suburban Jews were no longer Orthodox, not by any stretch; their observance of kosher laws, for example, often turned on compromises, unspoken or maybe chuckled about. For many families—although not for the Myerses—shrimp was permissible in Chinese food, on the theory that under the sauce you couldn't tell what you were eating. (But no leftovers could be brought home to sully the kosher kitchen!) Yet they eschewed the Reform movement's mostly English Sabbath services, often accompanied by organ music or, as the 1960s turned into the '70s, guitars. The synagogue choir that young Jeffrey sang in, then led, was the product of a typical Conservative-movement compromise; a "choir" was very churchy, more typical of the Reform movement, but the music sung by the Suburban Jewish Center choir was probably all Hebrew, a hat tip to more Orthodox tradition.

When Myers entered cantorial school, he had no way of knowing that Conservatism was about to begin its great contraction. In the decades to come, it would lose adherents to the left, to the right, and to nothing at all. To its left, Reform Judaism was reconnecting with tradition, bringing more Hebrew back into its services, embracing Zionism, and thus becoming a more acceptable option for Jews who wanted a more ample dose of Judaism on Friday nights or Saturdays. To its right, Orthodoxy, once seen to be a dying, old-world atavism, was enjoying a rebirth in the United States. Of course, all streams of Judaism—all streams of American religion—were losing adherents to the newly acceptable secularism, the choice to pray nowhere at all. And because Judaism is an ethnic affiliation—or a tribe, or a nation—as well as a religion, many American Jews realized that they could stop paying synagogue dues while continuing to identify, proudly, as Jews.

Between 1971 and 2013, Conservative Judaism went from being the denominational home of 41 percent of American Jews to representing only 18 percent. Along the way, the career of Jeffrey Myers would suffer the same fortunes as the movement.

After graduating from seminary, Myers taught seventh-grade Hebrew in Matawan, New Jersey, then became cantor of a small congregation in Rock Island, Illinois. He returned east in 1991 for a bigger job, at Temple Beth-El in Massapequa, Long Island, a job he held until 2010, when he looked at "the continued shrinkage on the south shore of Long Island and saw no future" for him and his family there. After leaving Beth-El, Myers found work at Beth Judah, in Ventnor, New Jersey, a position that lasted until 2017, when Beth Judah merged with a Reform temple to create a new congregation.

The cantor, the musical leader of a synagogue, the one who sings the prayers and chants from the Torah scroll, is often beloved but expendable. If a congregation is shrinking and losing money, the rabbi stays and the cantor may go. While still in Massapequa, Myers had decided to get ordained as a rabbi. "I saw there were challenges ahead for those of us who wanted to serve as professional cantors," he would later tell the *Pittsburgh Jewish Chronicle*. "There is a downturn in synagogues, and with that, fewer cantors are needed in the United States. I felt this [ordination] would be something critically important to have, to be able to one day provide a way to continue to take care of my family as best as I could." So in about 2000—he could not remember the exact year—he enrolled in Mesifta Adath Wolkowisk, an online seminary, based in Queens, that was unaffiliated with any Jewish denomination.

Mesifta Adath Wolkowisk was largely unknown in the Jewish world, and to the extent that it was known, it was because of a negative article in the Jewish press about "quick-route" seminaries that would ordain rabbis in as little as two years, compared to the five years of intensive study required by the Conservative movement's Jewish Theological Seminary, among others. "Rabbi Eli Kavon's colleagues don't consider him a rabbi," began a 2012 article in the *Forward* about rabbis with fast-track, online ordination. The article went on to say that Kavon, who like Myers had ordination from Mesifta Adath Wolkowisk, had been hired to replace a rabbi with proper Conservative credentials. "Rabbis with questionable qualifications are nothing new in South Florida, where some local rabbis have been ordaining rabbinical candidates on their own for years. The recent hiring of the two nontraditional rabbis to Conservative pulpits, however, may point to a growing acceptance of their less-recognized credentials in this financially beleaguered Jewish community." Understandably, establishment Conservative and Reform rabbis were not pleased. "'It's a plague down here,' said Rabbi Gerry Weiss, the JTS graduate who lost his job at Beth Ami to Kavon. Others argue, however, that the shift answers an economic need, and one that isn't going away."

To enroll at a small, online school was risky. Myers said that when he inquired about rabbinic ordination at JTS, where he had received his cantorial training, he had "found their expectations untenable at the time." (Was this because he had a family and a full-time job? Because of the cost of tuition? He would not answer directly, saying only that I should "not make any assumptions" about his finances. "That is irrelevant.") Mesifta Adath Wolkowisk would do.

It turned out to be a perfectly acceptable choice. As the *Forward* noted, by the time Myers looked toward Pittsburgh, financially strapped congregations were becoming receptive to rabbis with less traditional ordination. Tree of Life was shrinking faster than almost any synagogue in the world. In 1995 it had a membership roll of about 850 families, but by the time it was searching for a new rabbi in 2017, it had fewer than 250. It had also been through a great deal of recent, very public turmoil, having bought out the contract of Rabbi Chuck Diamond, a colorful local figure in whom many congregants had lost faith. The synagogue needed somebody seasoned, steady, and cheap. And after interviewing three candidates in the spring of 2017, they knew they had found their man in Myers. He was a rabbi (if one with unusual training) who was also a cantor. He was articulate but not bombastic, soft-spoken but cheery, quietly forceful but also agreeable. He was, above all, reassuring. He had light eyes and a trim, white beard; he was not handsome, but he was pleasing to look at, which may have been even better. He dressed tastefully and chose his words carefully. If he was perhaps a little too reserved, even a little prim, that was preferable to the unbridled, uninhibited gregariousness of his predecessor.

"Rabbi Myers was by far the clear choice," Michael Eisenberg, the synagogue president, told the *Jewish Chronicle*. "He had a very professional approach to the pulpit, he had a very nice voice, and he interacted with the people on both a ritual and a secular level. He's down-to-earth, but he takes his job very seriously."

Rabbi Jeffrey Myers speaking at the Sunday evening memorial
service at Soldiers & Sailors Memorial Hall and Museum

Myers started his job on August 1, 2017, and began using an unusual double honorific: he would be known as Rabbi Hazzan Jeffrey Myers (*hazzan* is Hebrew for "cantor"). Their two children having grown, Rabbi Hazzan Myers and his wife, Janice, moved to Pittsburgh, where she got a job teaching special education at Community Day School, a Jewish school in Squirrel Hill. Synagogues can be sleepy places over the summer, and it was not until the fall of 2017 that Myers began to get to know his congregants. Rosh Hashanah came on the evening of September 20, Yom Kippur a week later, and in that week, the members of Tree of Life got their first glimpse of their rabbi. Attendance being what it was, most of them wouldn't see him again for a year, until the following High Holy Days—and after that, the next time they would see him would be right after the shooting: on the local news, in the *Post-Gazette*, or on network morning shows.[*]

"I could only save some," he told CBS on Sunday evening, in an interview that ran the next morning. "The people in the back of the sanctuary I could not save. . . . I carry that regret with me, and I will the rest of my life, that I could have done more." His eyes looked wet, but he was composed. He was somber but showed a bit of reassuring levity. "How are you coping with that trauma?" the reporter asked him. "Badly," he replied, with a hint of a lopsided grin. It was just right. He was good at this. He did not ask for the spotlight, but he knew how to handle it. He was still largely unknown in Pittsburgh, still a newcomer to his own flock, but he was now the most famous rabbi in America.

———

JONATHAN PERLMAN GREW UP in Shadyside, adjacent to Squirrel Hill, in a Reform Jewish family. His father died when he was eleven, and he was raised by his mother. Perlman was an excellent student at Peabody High School, where he was in the class of 1981. He was admitted to Yale, but before college, he had some unfinished business to attend to. Although he had grown up in a proudly Jewish household, he felt that his Jewish education, received mostly at his Reform temple's Hebrew school in the run-up to his bar mitzvah, was inadequate. He wanted to know

---

[*] When I shared with Myers my observation that most of his congregants would not see him between High Holy Day seasons, he wrote to me, "I find the reference that most of my congregants would not see me for another year to be insulting to both my congregants and my efforts."

more Hebrew and to see Israel. So he took a year off and enrolled in a yearlong program in Israel run by Young Judaea, a youth Zionist organization. During that year, he began to think that maybe he would become a rabbi . . . or teacher . . . or something. A Jewish something.

At Yale, Perlman tried on all kinds of futures, seeing how they felt. For a time, he wanted to be a writer. Then he thought maybe he wanted to be a doctor. One summer he went home to Pittsburgh and worked for AAA, the car-and-driver group. His sophomore year he got deep into the works of Henry David Thoreau, and that summer, eager to get back to nature, he borrowed his grandfather's car, drove up Route 17, and presented himself for employment at various Jewish resorts in the Catskills. He said no to the Concord, where he would have had to live in a decrepit dormitory known to employees as "the slave quarters," and said yes to the legendary Grossinger's, where he worked the dining room and the cocktail lounge, pouring wine and catching comedy acts for free. He saw the Black comedian Nipsey Russell tell jokes in Yiddish, and he saw Miss America, Vanessa Williams, do her song-and-dance show just weeks before she had to resign her crown, after *Penthouse* published nude photographs of her. It was a formative summer for Perlman: he painted houses during the day, read books at a local college library, hitchhiked to work, deejayed at nearby hotels, and worked backstage for Phyllis Diller. He lived a few towns over from Grossinger's, in Loch Sheldrake, with a roommate who "drank a lot—mostly Night Train," the sweet flavored wine. His coworkers were mostly Jewish guys, about his age, many of them Deadheads. Perlman didn't know the Grateful Dead so well, but he was a good singer, very musical, and he liked to talk bands. "It was one of my favorite summers," he said. "A lot of characters in it."

He never worked the Catskills again. He was thinking that maybe he would make aliyah, move to Israel, and with that in mind he went to Israel again the summer before his senior year, enrolling in a summer program at Tel Aviv University. It was another fun summer—his girlfriend came to visit in the middle, and they traveled around the country together. A relative cautioned him against settling in Israel, pointing to the severe hyperinflation wracking the country at that time. But when he returned to Yale for his senior year, he was more serious than ever about Judaism, Israel, all of it. He had been having long conversations with Yale's charismatic young rabbi, Jim Ponet (who, decades later, would achieve a moment of fame as the rabbi who performed Chelsea Clinton's interfaith wedding), and Judaism began to seem like a possible career plan. He wasn't committed to being a rabbi, not if that meant the traditional kind, who gave sermons to a congregation every Saturday, taught bar mitzvah boys, and so on. But he figured that five years of seminary education would give him the space and time to figure out just what he needed from Judaism, and what Judaism could do with him.

Perlman was accepted at Jewish Theological Seminary, which just a couple years earlier had graduated Jeffrey Myers from its cantorial program. (The two men would not meet until decades later, when Myers moved to Pittsburgh.) During his five years at JTS, Perlman met Beth Kissileff, a Columbia undergraduate who would become his wife. In an essay she wrote in 2017 for the online magazine *Tablet,* she recalled the day they met thirty years earlier: "One Saturday afternoon in April, I went for a walk in Riverside Park with a friend, and we bumped into a guy playing Frisbee. He was in the Jewish Theological Seminary's Hebrew production of *Yankim Arurim—Damn Yankees*—with my friend. He was skinny and handsome, with a head full of thick, beautiful hair and gorgeous blue eyes. We talked, and, though he was friendly, he didn't seem all that interested in me—which I found out later was because he liked my friend, who did not reciprocate his feelings in the slightest. I tried again, remembering where he said he studied in the JTS library; I went looking for him one day at lunchtime, pretending my careful plan was a coincidence." They had lunch, and she followed up with a telephone call asking if he would help her prepare a speech she'd been asked to give about the Jewish ritual of Havdalah, the candlelighting that ends Shabbat. He agreed, then came to hear her give the talk. He found her beforehand, nervously walking from her dormitory. "He put his arm around me," she wrote. "Instantly, I felt comfortable." They dated that spring and summer, and then she left for study in Israel. "That year we were apart, he and I used to make tapes, actual cassette tapes (I am dating myself here), and mail them to each other. I would walk around Jerusalem in 1987 and '88 with my now impossibly clunky-seeming Walkman and my future husband's voice in my ears, telling me about his classes, things he was thinking about, and what was going on in his life."

A year after she got back from Israel, they got engaged. "He loved

Billy Joel and the Beatles," she wrote, "and comedy recordings of all per-
suasions, a legacy from his Grandpa Dave, who loved to tell jokes. He
was a slight hypochondriac, and we joked about the bulging medicine
kit he needed to bring even to travel for short periods. We loved to discuss current events and intellectual matters, Jewish texts and modern
novels. He knew way more about Shakespeare than I—a future comp
lit Ph.D.—did, and his religion major in college gave him a great deal of
knowledge about the minutiae of almost any major religion that the rest
of us have no clue about."

The professional journey of an American rabbi is unpredict-
able. There's no straight highway, more like a winding, poorly maintained rural route. As synagogue membership declines, the supply of
rabbis often outstrips the demand. A small number of large, wealthy
synagogues—usually in urban areas with large Jewish populations—
have multiple rabbis on staff. But far more jobs are with small, struggling congregations; these jobs are part-time, poorly paid, or both. And a
rabbi whose first job is at one of these failing synagogues may have trouble moving up to a more successful place for his or her next job; after all,
if the synagogue that hires you—at the age of twenty-seven, with almost
no experience—is full of elderly members, in an area that is losing population, with almost no young Jewish families, how do you demonstrate
your gifts? When that synagogue folds, or merges with the other one in
town, how do you sell yourself to the next potential employer?

So in every graduating class at JTS, somebody gets a job at the shiny
place in New York or Los Angeles, and someone else gets a job at the
shabby old-timers' shul whose best days are thirty years in the past. And
someone else gets hired at a Jewish community center running "adult
education"—the senior citizens' book club, the Torah class for a few souls
every Sunday morning, the Jewish singles' night at the art museum. And
somebody lands a part-time gig at a nursing home, and hopes to pick
up adjunct work at a Jewish elementary school. It's a tough racket, the
rabbinate, hardly any better than the cantorial world Jeffrey Myers had
been released into a few years before.

After being ordained in 1992, Perlman took a job at Beth El Synagogue, a small congregation in East Windsor, New Jersey. After two
years, his contract was not renewed, but he was hired on at a bigger synagogue, in Raleigh, North Carolina, where in addition to his rabbinic

work he supervised the kosher certification at the local Whole Foods bakery. In 1999 he left to become the director of education at the Jewish Community Center in Springfield, Massachusetts, a job that included everything from supervising preschool education to leading Israel trips for adults; for many of those years, he was also the part-time rabbi in Athol, Massachusetts, an hour's drive to the northeast. In February 2007 he and his family, which by now included three daughters, moved to Minnesota, where he worked at the large JCC in St. Louis Park, a suburb of Minneapolis. It was not a good fit, and he left the following year. He soon found work as the rabbi of Temple Sholom in Eau Claire, Wisconsin, a hundred miles away; he was part-time and commuted to Eau Claire one weekend a month, while beginning a training program in Minneapolis to be a hospital chaplain.

Put simply, at this point in his career, twenty-five years after college, Perlman was still seeking, trying to find his place in the Jewish world. He had never made much money, never lasted very long within one community. But he had not become a rabbi to get his name above a doorway; he had never put money or prestige first. He had looked for jobs only in regions where his wife might find teaching work, and they were always looking for better schools, and a more robust Jewish com-

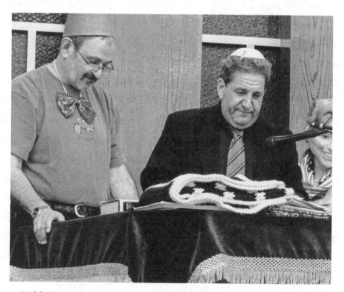

Rabbi Jonathan Perlman (right) and Rich Gottfried reading
from the book of Esther for the holiday of Purim

munity, for their daughters. But still, Perlman might have hoped to be at a more stable place.

And so it was back home to Pittsburgh. In the spring of 2010, Perlman was hired by New Light, a small congregation he had known a bit as a child. And what he had known of it was that it was for old people. "It has never, ever attracted young families," he recalled. "And I know that because when I was sixteen, seventeen years old, I used to come here with my friend whose aunt was a member. And you'd always walk in on a Friday night, and it would always be the same older people. The only young people would be the rabbi and his family."

But still, this was where he was offered a job, and so he went. The Squirrel Hill to which he moved his wife and children was not the one he had such fond memories of growing up near. It still felt Jewish, but not the way it once did. The bakeries and delis were all but gone, and some synagogues had closed. Pittsburgh, which when he was a child was reeling from the loss of the steel industry, had rebounded, but the biotech and computer firms that powered the new economy had done nothing to reconstruct the landscape of his memory. He was haunted by the Pittsburgh of his youth. His new life often felt "like being in a time machine, and taking it to something that was no longer recognizable."

His job at New Light was not full-time, and he combined it with chaplaincy work; one gig, with a hospice agency, lasted five years, into 2016, and he picked up another hospice job in the summer of 2018, but that one, too, soon ended. Meanwhile, his synagogue's membership was declining, in both senses: shrinking numbers, aging members. In June 2017, New Light put its building up for sale and announced it would move into Tree of Life, taking over the former Sisterhood Room as its sanctuary. Dor Hadash was already renting space from Tree of Life, whose president, Michael Eisenberg, talked up the new tenant. "With New Light there, it will be bustling even more," he told the *Jewish Chronicle*. On November 12, 2017, a procession of about seventy-five people carried New Light's six Torah scrolls through Squirrel Hill to their new home in a basement room at Tree of Life. The synagogue was at the beginning of a three-year lease, one that they prayed would see the rejuvenation of its small community.

New Light had been in its new home not quite a year when the shooting took place. The sale of its old building had given the congregation

Rich Gottfried carrying one of New Light's Torah scrolls to the
congregation's new home in the Tree of Life building, November 2017

some cash to keep going, but it was tough pulling together a minyan on Saturdays. On the morning of October 27, 2018, Rabbi Perlman was a little late to show, so at 9:45, Barry Werber tapped his watch, signaling that it was time for the service to start. Cecil Rosenthal, who had been hanging out in the New Light room, got up and left, heading upstairs to join the Tree of Life service, and Melvin Wax went up to the *bimah* to start morning prayers. Within five minutes, Perlman arrived, bringing the total New Light community in the building to six: four in their small sanctuary, two in the kitchen. When the shooting began, Werber looked out of the room, saw a body on the stairs, and turned back inside; Perlman motioned for him, Carol Black, and Mel Wax to follow him. "The rabbi immediately dragged us into the storeroom," Werber said, which "was perfectly dark."

At some point in this confusion, as the shooter opened the door to the storeroom, shooting Mel Wax dead but not seeing Barry Werber or Carol Black in the darkness, Perlman found another door, one that he had not known existed, which led him up some stairs and out of the building. When he emerged into the light outside the building, safe from the shooter, no one was behind him. "I was in the backyard of the neighboring home," Perlman recalled, "and told an officer about the door and where Carol and Barry were hidden. He told me to get the hell out of here." He walked away from the synagogue toward his house, three-quarters of a mile away. He arrived home at about ten-fifteen and told his wife that somebody had just tried to kill him.

"What?" Beth shouted, awakening their fourteen-year-old daughter, Ada, in her downstairs bedroom. Minutes later she went into Ada's room and sat down on her bed. "Abba is okay," she told her, using the Hebrew for "Dad," "but there was a shooting at Tree of Life."

"I sprinted up the stairs faster than I've ever run before," Ada recounted in an essay she wrote a month later, "and to my relief, there was my dad. I hugged him and squeezed him tight. 'I love you. I am so glad you are here.'" Her father had his phone out, something he never did on Shabbat. "He was scrolling through his contacts to see if he could get in touch with any of his congregants or their spouses who were at the shul that day. One picked up, the wife of a man who had been in synagogue. "'Rabbi, Rabbi!' she shouted. 'I do not know where he is! Rabbi, I do not know what to do!'"

The calls continued, as he got news that two of the congregants had been able to get out as well: "One of them said he saw someone from our congregation being shot." As Ada listened to her father make his calls, she gathered that Mel Wax had been shot, and that Dan Stein and Rich Gottfried were not accounted for. Sitting with her father, she began to cry. "I started crying, fearing for my shul, for my future, for my religion, for my city. Will the gunman go to the other shuls? What if he is not acting alone? Will people be afraid to come to shul? Will my dad lose his job because no one will want to come anymore? What about Dan and Rich? Are they alive?"

———

DANIEL LEGER WAS BORN in 1948 and grew up in Homewood, a working-class neighborhood north and east of Squirrel Hill. The neighborhood was nearly all white, but it was religiously mixed, with Catholics, like the Legers, amicably sharing the blocks with Protestants and Jews. After Black families began to move in, the white families began to leave. Leger was a bookish, reflective boy, and as a teenager he attended a Catholic high school seminary that prepared boys for the priesthood.

He planned to be a priest, at least until he was in his late teens, when he realized that celibacy was not for him. And he was being pulled in other directions by the counterculture, the Vietnam War, the whole era. He began to lose his Catholic faith, but he lost none of his spirituality. He began to "question basic things . . . separating out religion and exploring what was bigger," looking to ascend other sides of the mountain of truth. "It expanded my world," all this seeking, and when it came time to serve in the army, he was able to honestly say that his religion, however he might describe it, prevented him from picking up a gun.

Conscientious objectors were usually not allowed to do alternative service in their hometowns—the government did not want draft-dodging to be too appealing—but Leger was, surprisingly, allowed to stay in Pittsburgh. It was 1969, and he was detailed to the Home for Crippled Children, a pediatric rehabilitation facility in Squirrel Hill, just across from Tree of Life synagogue. Working as "a nurse's aide, basically," he helped treat children with developmental disabilities, spina bifida, and polio, among other challenges. "I just loved the place," Leger said. After two years of the required alternative military service, Leger kept working at the facility—it is now called the Children's Institute—and enrolled in nursing school. He would stay at the institute for thirty years, before leaving to work as a nurse and chaplain at other facilities.

Leger formed close friendships with other conscientious objectors in the Pittsburgh area, whom he remembers as a creative, inspiring bunch. One became an actor and mime, while another, Yitzhak Husbands-Hankin, is now a noted cantor, rabbi, and progressive activist in Eugene, Oregon. Husbands-Hankin gave Leger some of his first sustained exposure to Judaism, but Leger was also learning a little about Judaism from his first wife, to whom he was married from 1969 to 1992 and with whom he raised two sons. She was not particularly religious, but the family performed some Jewish rituals together, like lighting Hanukkah candles, and a spiritually attuned dad like Leger got curious about the theology behind the actions. "At Hanukkah I would say, 'So what does that mean that you just sang?'" Whenever a family member couldn't answer one of his questions, he would think to himself, *Hmm, I guess I should find out.*

Leger had begun to notice, too, that in addition to his wife, many of the people he most enjoyed being around—"so many people that I connected with, and made friendships with"—were Jews. In the mid-1970s he attended a bat mitzvah at Dor Hadash and was enchanted by the spirit he encountered. "This was just amazing to me, to see a group of people who were so socially engaged. I mean, that was the reason that you practiced religion: to get in touch with those values and to live them out through social action. Not study just for the sake of study." And the questioning, anti-authoritarian ethos of the congregation spoke to him. Seeing that kind of Judaism in action, getting to know a community that seemed like one he could call home, helped make his own Judaism feel inevitable.

The decision to convert, then, was a slow, organic process. There was no one moment of decision. At some point "in the 1970s" he had a formal conversion, supervised by the rabbi at the University of Pittsburgh, but he'd felt Jewish long before that. "He spent forty-five years learning and studying and practicing and being totally immersed in it," Dan's second wife, Ellen, whom he married in 1998, said of his relationship to Judaism. Over the years, Leger had become a passionate Jew: studying Hebrew and Jewish texts, donating thousands of hours to Dor Hadash, even blowing the shofar, the ram's horn that heralds the new year, on Rosh Hashanah—a duty that he shared with his close friend Jerry Rabinowitz.

Dan Leger

Dor Hadash, which was founded in 1963 in Squirrel Hill, never owned a building. Its members decided from the start that they did not want to be saddled with real estate or debt. They would rent, borrow, squat, meet where they could. It wasn't just a financial decision but also a spiritual one. Often its members were fleeing the brick-and-mortar institutions of their childhoods, a Judaism of large, sturdy buildings wherein one could find soulless worship led by uninspired, and sometimes hypocritical, clergy. They wanted Dor Hadash to be about the people, not the space. In 2010, after meeting for many years at Community Day School, the non-Orthodox Jewish day school in Squirrel Hill, the congregation began renting space at Tree of Life. In recent years it had met there twice a month: one Friday for evening services, and one Saturday morning for brief services followed by Torah study. It was on such a Saturday, the fatal one, that Leger and Rabinowitz arrived around nine-thirty.

By the time the medics got inside Tree of Life, Rabinowitz was mortally wounded. Leger had been shot and was bleeding profusely. They got him on a stretcher and out to an ambulance, which took him to the former Presbyterian Hospital, now a branch of the University of Pittsburgh Medical Center. That evening the *Post-Gazette* posted an article on its website with updates about those injured in the attack: "Of the 17 people shot Saturday at the Tree of Life Congregation in Pittsburgh's Squirrel Hill neighborhood, four police officers and two others survived." One of the survivors was "Daniel Leger, 70, of Squirrel Hill, a nurse and UPMC chaplain. . . . He was in critical condition late Saturday afternoon after undergoing surgery at UPMC Presbyterian in Oakland, his brother Paul Leger said. 'He may be going into a second surgery. He has a number of surgeries ahead of him,' Paul said. 'But they did expect that [he] would be surviving.'" The article quoted Randall Bush, the pastor of nearby East Liberty Presbyterian Church, who had presided with Leger at an interfaith wedding the previous spring: "'He was extremely sensitive when we were shaping the wedding experience to balance out the Christian and Jewish traditions,' Rev. Bush said."

Dor Hadash may have never had a rabbi, but it boasted congregants, like Leger, who performed the roles that we associate with the clergy. Leger had always defined his life by service, and he had found in the Dor Hadash community a perfect vehicle through which to serve, often with Jerry. They were, for example, among the most active members of the

New Community Chevra Kadisha. A *chevra kadisha*—one can translate this as "holy society"—performs *tahara,* the ritual preparation of a body for burial according to ancient Jewish rites. (Most American Jews today are content to rely on funeral homes.) The members wash and clean the body, then dress it in a muslin or linen shroud, while saying prayers and reciting Psalms. Men do this for men, women for women. The holy society is supposed to do its work quietly and anonymously. Because Jews bury their dead as quickly as possible, ideally within twenty-four hours, members of the holy society are always on call. They may be awakened in the middle of the night, multiple times a month. Yet in most Jewish communities, nobody knows who they are.

"It just seemed like a logical extension of the work that I had been doing as a hospice nurse," Leger said, recovering at home several months after he was shot. "It was not so unusual for me to have had a patient in hospice, been present at their *tahara,* and then do their funeral and bury them."

Whenever Leger wondered how he would die, he had assumed, had trusted, that his friends in the holy society would clean and dress his body. When he lay bleeding on the floor of Tree of Life, he believed that the end was near. As the medics carried him into the ambulance, he lost consciousness. Then, at the hospital, he saw what he took to be the shadows of four people. He thought he was dead, and he wasn't afraid. What he thought was *My God, it's the* chevra kadisha. *And they're taking care of me.*

3

The Gentiles

THE MORNING OF the shooting, forty-year-old graphic designer Tim Hindes and Robert Bowers, the alleged shooter, both left their homes south of Pittsburgh and drove north, across the Monongahela River, into town. The shooter went all the way to Squirrel Hill, while Hindes went to Greenfield, the neighborhood just south of Squirrel Hill, to help a friend move. He was about a mile from Tree of Life.

When Hindes was driving home, he began getting text alerts about the shooting. As it happened, he had been thinking about antisemitism lately: a close Jewish friend had just that week been the target of some antisemitic remarks, and Hindes had been wondering what he, as a non-Jew, could do to help. "I had struggled with knowing the right thing to do, to say, and ended up not saying anything," he said.

Hindes thus felt especially determined to take action now. He got home, turned on the television news, and fired up his desktop Mac. "I just started doodling," he said. Within ten minutes, he had decided on two design elements that would form the heart of whatever his final design would be: a Star of David, the iconic Jewish symbol, and a hypocycloid.

Geometrically speaking, a hypocycloid is a curve traced by a point on the circumference of one circle, inside another circle, rolling internally on the circumference of the larger circle. But Pittsburgh-wise, and football-wise, the hypocycloid is the universally known symbol of the Pittsburgh Steelers, the city's beloved NFL team. Their logo, found on their helmets, contains four elements, arranged in a diamond: the left point is the word STEELERS, while the top, right, and bottom points are, respectively, yellow, red, and blue hypocycloids. Old-time Pittsburghers know that the Steelers logo, adopted in 1962, is based on a design by U.S. Steel, later adopted by the entire steel industry, meant to represent domestic steel in its battle—which it lost—with foreign imports. The three hypocycloids (to be precise, they are astroids, or hypocycloids with four cusps—diamond-like hypocycloids) thus carry the banner of local pride as remembered in two lost glories: they simultaneously recall the Steelers—the dominant NFL team of the 1970s, with four Super Bowl victories between 1975 and 1980—and the steel industry for which the team was named.

The six-pointed Star of David, known in Hebrew as the Magen David, or Shield of David, was not originally Jewish. It is found nowhere in the Hebrew Bible or in the Talmud. It was used decoratively by many peoples for hundreds of years. During the Renaissance, it began to proliferate as a design element in Jewish books and on Jewish flags and buildings. But only after 1897, when it was used as a symbol for the First Zionist Congress, did world Jewry come to embrace the Star of David, and only after it appeared on the flag of Israel, in 1948, did the world come to know it as Jewish.

Hindes fiddled around with his two basic images, playing with color, size, and placement, putting a Star of David up top. He liked where this was going. But the word STEELERS had to go. "In thinking through the words, I actually thought of Boston and BOSTON STRONG and of ORLANDO STRONG. You see those 'strong' things whenever a tragedy happens. It seemed too common and monotonous. Pittsburgh is different. It's not like any other city. It needed a different message." He decided on the legend STRONGER THAN HATE to replace STEELERS as the left-side element of his design.

Hindes had no big plans for his design. It was just a way to feel like he was doing *something*. He posted the image to his private Facebook page. A couple of friends liked the image and asked if he would make the post public, so that they could share it. He said sure, why not, and changed the post's status. He got up from his computer, stretched his legs, walked

Tim Hindes's graphic design mash-up of the Steelers logo and the Star
of David, at the anti-Trump rally on October 30, 2018

about the house for a bit. When he returned to his computer a few minutes later, the post had five hundred shares. Then a thousand. Then fifteen hundred. By the end of the day, friends had seen it on Twitter. It was
going crazy.

By the next day, Sunday, Hindes realized, somewhat sheepishly, that
he had created the iconic image of the Tree of Life shooting. It was seen
on banners at the Steelers game that day. The actor Michael Keaton, who
grew up near Pittsburgh, shared it on Instagram. People who would
never be able to name any of the victims, who wouldn't recognize the
synagogue's façade if they drove by it, would know the crime by Hindes's
smart, succinct visual. He decided to make it clear that he was giving it
away for free. "I said this isn't mine anymore, this is Pittsburgh's, this is
everyone's. . . . So I posted a link to a quick survey online, where people
could say 'I promise to use it for good not evil.'" He also asked people
to click a box promising that any money they raised with the image—
say, by selling T-shirts—would go to victims' funds. He had no way to
enforce any of this, but it was the gesture he wanted to make. When visitors to the website responded affirmatively, they got a high-resolution
copy of the image emailed to them.

By Sunday evening, the image was in front yards, on doors, and in storefront windows up and down Forbes and Murray avenues in Squirrel Hill. On Facebook and Twitter, it replaced people's faces as their avatars. The simple image proclaimed so much. The words STRONGER THAN HATE shouted out to victims in Boston, Orlando, and elsewhere, saying both *We remember* and *Us, too.* At first glance, you could miss the substitution of the Star of David as the yellow hypocycloid and think you were just looking at the Steelers logo, and that made the second-glance recognition so metaphorically striking: the Jews are a part of the whole, seamlessly integrated but holding on to their own identity. Fitting in but standing out.

"I'm Lutheran," Hindes said. "And actually my heritage is German. I was definitely raised in a churchgoing family. I have gotten away from it recently a little bit, for a number of different reasons. It was mostly around the election"—Donald Trump's election in 2016—"and really trying to stand up for your ideals and thoughts and beliefs that made me wane away from it. It doesn't mean I don't have faith." He tends to feel his faith most deeply in nature. "I am an avid outdoorsman, so I tend to use that as my outlet for my appreciation of the world and greater being. Hiking, kayaking, camping—you name it, I'll try it." Still, as much time as he spends in the hills outside the city limits, he thinks of himself as a native son. "I grew up in Pittsburgh. I never left. I love it too much to leave. It's my city, and God willing I'll be here forever."

———

AS A YOUNG GIRL, Lynn Hyde loved the Jews. Not that she knew any in small Ben Avon, Pennsylvania, fifteen minutes northeast of Pittsburgh, where she grew up in the 1990s. She had no Jewish friends, although she thinks that some of her elementary schoolteachers might have been Jewish; she cannot say for sure. Rather, she met Jews in books. "The diary of Anne Frank was my way in," Hyde remembered. "Because I identified with her. I wasn't Jewish, but I couldn't understand why you would persecute someone who, as far as I could tell, was a whole lot like me." She read through the whole canon of young people's literature about the Holocaust. She read *Number the Stars* and *Jacob's Rescue.* She read *The Devil's Arithmetic,* a historical novel, written in 1988, in which young Hannah Stern, always bored by Jewish ritual, opens the door at her Passover seder—it's customary to open the door for the invisible prophet

Elijah—and is transported back in time to a work camp in Poland in 1942. "It's actually really horrifying," Hyde confessed. After she ran out of YA death-camp lit, she found her way to adult books like *Schindler's List.* "Book after book after book," she said.

Hyde's father was not a religious man, but he did not mind that his wife took Lynn and her younger brother and sister to Bellevue Christian Church, a nondenominational church in Pittsburgh. Occasionally missionaries from Africa would visit to thank the church for its support. Hyde's most vivid memory of church was from fifth-grade Sunday school, when her class painted little blocks for a replica, built to scale, of the tabernacle that the Jews had built in the desert. But she seemed to absorb very little Christian theology there. As a teenager, she began to go with friends to a more liberal, Presbyterian church, which her mother thought was fine. Her attitude, according to Hyde, was basically, "I expect that you will go to church on Sunday. I don't care if you go to church with your friends, if you go to this church or this other church, but you'll go." As long as Hyde lived at home, that was the deal.

"My drifting away started in college," Hyde said. As she made gay friends, she began to question the church's role in their oppression. Her childhood reading had already given her a more expansive view of spirituality, and now she was taking religious studies classes, making Jewish friends, and making friends from other religions or no religion at all. After college, she got a master's degree in dramaturgy and criticism at Brooklyn College, where she made even more Jewish friends. She lived in the Flatbush neighborhood of Brooklyn, where the population seemed to be divided between Orthodox Jews and West Indians. Her world had ceased to have any evangelical Christians in it, but it was filling up with Jews.

In 2010, after five years in New York City, Hyde moved back to Pittsburgh. In New York, she had been meeting men online for years, on sites including Match and eHarmony, and she had been on countless dates that led nowhere. In Pittsburgh, she changed her dating profile to reflect her new locale, and kept trying. Still a whole lot of nothing. But then in 2016 she went on a date with a guy named Jeremy, whom she had met on OkCupid. She had liked his profile from the beginning: he seemed smart and sincere and, in his profile picture anyway, quite cute. But he was over a year younger than her thirty-four years, so she didn't write to him. Fortunately, he reached out—and she was impressed. They had a lot in common, he had clearly read her profile closely, and he used "complete, well-constructed sentences"—hardly the rule in online dating. They went out, and they had a good enough time that they went out again. On their second date, in September 2016, they went to see *Blazing Saddles,* then out to lunch. After lunch, she invited him back to her patio to have a beer. "By this point, I figured that he probably wasn't going to murder me," she said.

It was over that beer that he told her that he was Jewish. "And I remember thinking, *Oh!* Like somehow being surprised." Looking back, she was surprised that she was surprised. Hadn't she always had a thing for the Jews? Hadn't she joked, back when she was living in New York, that she had wanted to marry a Jewish man so she could get all the Jewish holidays off?

And now she had met a cute Jewish boy whom she *really* liked. "After five years in New York, I actually had to move back to Pittsburgh to meet a nice Jewish guy from Long Island."

In the early going, Lynn and Jeremy avoided talk of religion. Jeremy did not seem very religious, but he was not *not* religious. He went to synagogue on major holidays, and his family was on a bit of a collective journey, which seemed somehow significant: his brother had become Orthodox, and his father had lately become a more observant Conservative Jew. Hyde, meanwhile, had no plans to become Jewish—not that Jeremy was asking—but she was happy to have another reason to read about this religion that always seemed to be popping up in her life. She bought and read *Essential Judaism,* George Robinson's guide to Jewish belief and ritual. (That felt better than buying a book called *Judaism for Dummies,* which "actually exists," she noted.) Not wanting to freak Jeremy out, she read it in secret.

Now that she was back into Jewish lit, she couldn't stop. An avid cook, she dove into the rich world of Jewish cookbooks, buying Leah Koenig's *Modern Jewish Cooking,* a raft of classics by Joan Nathan, and more. When she and Jeremy broke up for four months, she had to stop all the Jewish reading—it made her too sad—but when they got back together, her library started growing again. And shortly after they reunited, in March 2018, Jeremy said to her one night, "Well, if I ever had kids—if we ever had kids—I would want them to be Jewish." And

Hyde replied, "Yeah, sure, that's no problem." She was surprised by what she had just said and how easily it had come to her. "Like, it just kind of fell out of my mouth."

She kept reading, books upon books. She read Abigail Pogrebin's *My Jewish Year,* in which the author, a Reform Jew, spends a year learning about every Jewish holiday, from Rosh Hashanah and Passover to the ones that most Jews know nothing about, such as Tzom Gedalia and Tu B'Av. And she kept cooking, making hamantaschen for Purim, blintzes for Shavuot (when dairy dishes are traditional), and a seder meal for Passover.

Even as she did Judaism more than most Jews ever do, she still did not see herself as a Jew or a future Jew. After all, she had grown up Christian, and however far away those Sundays in church seemed, that was her family's culture. No matter how much she learned about Jewish folkways, no matter how many Hebrew Bible stories she knew and loved, no matter how many dishes she cooked, or how well she cooked them, it didn't seem that she could ever *feel* Jewish. Not the way Jeremy did. It was something one was born with, grew up with. She couldn't learn it, and he couldn't shake it.

In 2017, during the Days of Awe, the week between Rosh Hashanah and Yom Kippur—a Yom Kippur when Hyde attended the evening Kol Nidre and Ne'ilah services, and even hosted a meal for friends to break the fast at day's end—the couple had a huge fight over whether they could ever have a Christmas tree in their home. Lynn was an utterly lapsed Christian—"I had not probably for five years put up a Christmas tree!"—but when Jeremy said, in passing, "Well, I can never have a Christmas tree in my house," she was infuriated.

"I said, 'What?'" she recalled. "I said, 'Well, but that's not fair. I'm not Jewish.' I was like, 'So you're just declaring that you could never live with that, but you're not thinking about what any of it means to me.' And he had the whole, 'But it's a Christian symbol!' And I said, 'It's a pagan symbol! And I have ornaments and things from my childhood that make me think of people I love.' And we had this whole back-and-forth about it. And then we kind of let it lie for a little bit. We joke that it was the great Yom Kippur Christmas Tree Argument. Because, like, who argues about Christmas trees at Yom Kippur? But it never really resolved itself."

By 2018 Lynn, in love with a Jewish man and with a rather powerful, unresolved crush on Judaism, decided that maybe she was called to be not a Jew but a *ger toshav*, literally a "resident alien," or, more figuratively speaking, a Gentile among the Jews. (One also hears the translation "righteous Gentile.") This is an ancient category, much discussed in rabbinic literature, that includes non-Jews who agree to abide by the seven Noahide laws, commandments given to the children of Noah, hence to everyone in the world (since, in Torah, we are all descended from Noah and his family, the only people who survived the great flood). These laws include, for example, not committing murder or adultery but above all rejecting idolatry. Thus, a *ger toshav* is somebody who has not converted to Judaism but who does not profess any other, idolatrous faith—not yet a Jew, but definitely not a Christian, Hindu, or anything else. Put another way, a *ger toshav* is a non-Jewish member of humanity who behaves morally. Although at times in history those seeking the status of *ger toshav*—say, to marry a Jew living in an all-Jewish village—appeared before rabbinic courts to ratify their status as commandment-abiding non-Jews, today the term is heard mainly in conversations with people like Lynn Hyde: bookish, theologically curious non-Jews, probably dating or married to Jews, who are wrestling with whether they are called

Lynn Hyde and her husband, Jeremy Burton,
on their honeymoon trip to Israel

to convert or just to hang out with Jews and live fairly Jewish lives. Hyde had read about the *ger toshav,* and it made more sense than anything else. "For a long time, I thought, *Well, that's what I'll do.* Like, who needs to do all the paperwork?" Even though, as she admitted to herself at the time, "it's a lot of work that I was doing anyway."

She and Jeremy live in Uptown, just west of Oakland, which is just west of Squirrel Hill. It's a bit of a nowhere between residential Pittsburgh and downtown, and its blocks of charming old row houses are broken up by commuter lots and downscale commercial strips. There is no Jewish life in Uptown, but the couple had started attending services at Temple Sinai, the Reform temple in Squirrel Hill. The rabbi of Temple Sinai, Jamie Gibson, was well known for his work with interfaith couples, and it was a place where Lynn felt welcome—not just because the service contained plenty of English, and helpful transliterations from the Hebrew, but also because the congregation had no shortage of Gentiles who had joined with their Jewish partners. If ever there was a place that one could lead a Jewish life as a Gentile—live as a *ger toshav*—it was Temple Sinai.

Then October 27 came.

"I remember distinctly so much from that day," Hyde recalled. The couple had gone to services the night before, Friday night, but were at home Saturday morning. "The sirens are mostly what I remember." Jeremy was helping her edit a document for work, and they kept getting distracted by the sirens. "Both of us noticed it—'Gosh, a lot of sirens.'" But they live in a busy area, four blocks from Mercy Hospital, so they figured maybe it was a bad car pile-up. But then their phones "started blowing up" with texts. They had developed a Saturday habit of not checking their phones, but then her laptop screen, synced with her iPhone, registered that his mother was calling. "I'm just like, 'Why is your mother calling me?' And then I picked up. I got my phone and had text messages from my mother, from friends saying, 'Something happened in Squirrel Hill, are you safe?' And so we called his mom back and turned on the TV and watched more local news than I have ever in my adult life—watched, and just kind of sat here in the living room waiting, waiting for more information. And there just wasn't any. It just kept cutting back to the scene in Squirrel Hill."

The next night, like thousands of others, Lynn and her boyfriend

The Soldiers & Sailors memorial event on Sunday evening

attended the memorial service at Soldiers & Sailors Memorial Hall and Museum. The slaughter felt personal. While trying to be mindful that "you don't want to insert yourself into someone else's tragedy," she nevertheless knew that the killer "could have gone anywhere. Like, he was just looking for a synagogue, and if it had been the night before at Temple Sinai, we would have been sitting there." Some days she felt like a Jew, but it was an on-and-off thing. What did it mean that the killer would not have shared her ambivalence?

Within a week, Lynn Hyde had decided to begin studying for conversion to Judaism.

———

ON FRIDAY NIGHT, October 26, 2018, a twenty-nine-year-old Iranian expatriate named Shay Khatiri went out drinking with his friend Sara. He had arrived in Washington, D.C., earlier in the fall, and Sara, whom he knew from an internship the previous summer, had said he could crash at her place, near Dupont Circle, until he found his own. Living in Washington was a big deal. Ever since childhood, Khatiri had felt like an American trapped in an Iranian childhood; he had the soul of a democrat, which in Iran meant the soul of a dissident. He revered the United States, wanted to move to the United States, wanted to give back to the United States. He first moved to the States in 2014, to attend college at Arizona State, and ever since he'd wanted to move to the capital. An acceptance letter from Johns Hopkins University's School of Advanced International Studies gave him his chance. He began his master's program in September, and all fall he'd been feeling high on life. He allowed himself "a few cocktails" that Friday, each one a jab at the ayatollahs whose regime he was committed to toppling someday.

Saturday morning—or maybe it was early afternoon—he awakened on Sara's living room sofa. He thinks he was probably wearing his Real Madrid sweatpants; he also thinks there may have been a movie the night before, after he and Sara got back from the bars. But it was all pretty hazy. He knew he should get moving, sooner or later, but his headache told him there was no rush. As he rubbed the sleep from his eyes, Sara wandered in. He looked up at her, and he knew that something was wrong. Her face "had a brokenness to it," as he would later put it. She told him that a synagogue in Pittsburgh had been attacked. People were dead. They didn't know how many.

Khatiri was sad for his friend, who was Jewish, and he was upset for his beloved adoptive country, the one that he hoped would someday make him a citizen. But he was also heartbroken for the Jews. In Iran, he had heard only the worst things about the perfidious Zionists, bent on world domination, but since coming to the United States, he had come to love the Jews. Over the past decade, he had worked for several American organizations that promoted democracy abroad, and he had noticed that many of these nonprofits were staffed by Jews and got funding from Jewish donors. As a critic of Iran, he had found solidarity with pro-Israel Jews who spoke out forcefully against the Islamic Revolution, who made no excuses for the mullahs who had immiserated his homeland, and who understood the threat that their regime posed to stability in the Middle East. And ever since leaving his home and family, he had been nurtured by Jews. When he thought about his favorite professors and bosses, almost all of them were Jews.

After Sara explained what had happened, Khatiri wanted to do something to help. He told Sara that he wanted to donate some money to the

Shay Khatiri as an enthusiastic college senior on a spring break
trip to Washington, D.C.

synagogue, but she urged him to think better of it—after all, "I was not
in great financial shape myself." He got up, made coffee, and then it
hit him: GoFundMe. He had used the crowdfunding web tool a couple
times before, to raise money when his funds had run dry. Khatiri's first
GoFundMe campaign page, from 2016, begins, "Hi! I'm Shay, and I'm
an international student from Iran attending Arizona State University
majoring in political science and economics." He goes on to explain that
he has an internship at the American Enterprise Institute, but that "the
cost of living and housing in D.C. is really high, especially for an Iranian
who has to pay international tuition, which is twice the amount in-state
residents pay," and who "can't work for money either."* In the accom-

---

* His GoFundMe.com page, set up on May 10, 2016, continued:

    I will use this money for food and housing in D.C. My internship starts on May 16th and goes
    on for almost two months. My rent alone costs more than $1500 for the duration of my stay.
    So the sooner I have this money the better.
        My dream has always been to study foreign policy and work in [the] foreign policy sector.
    AEI's internship is one of the best foreign policy internships in the Country. The selection
    process is very tight and the interns should be very qualified. I am extremely lucky to have
    been accepted. This will be the beginning of my life goal to promote universal human rights
    and [the] American style of democracy around the world and I need your help to do that.

panying photograph, he is wearing a crisp white shirt and a blue blazer, and his red tie is knotted perfectly. Very American. As it turned out, the collective Web had a soft spot, to the tune of $1,500, for a broke Iranian dissident in love with his new country.

And if GoFundMe had helped him out, why wouldn't it come through for Jewish victims of terror? "And I thought if I did something for Tree of Life and it went viral, it could maybe raise something like $50,000," he said. He went to GoFundMe.com and set up the account. "An anti-Semite attacked and killed several attendees to Shabbat services at a Pittsburgh synagogue," Khatiri wrote on GoFundMe. "This fundraiser is meant to help the congregation with the physical damages to the building, as well as the survivors and the victims' families. Respond to this hateful act with your act of love today." He shared the link on Twitter and Facebook.* The first donation, for $100, came in at 1:31 p.m. from one Melody Dorriott, who wrote on the website that "America is about freedom of religion. Everyone should be free to pray in peace." The next donation did not come until 2:53. Then somehow— Khatiri is not sure how—CNN anchor Jake Tapper discovered the fund and shared its GoFundMe link on Twitter. The donations began to pile up. In midafternoon, Khatiri and Sara left her apartment for the Potter's House, a nearby coffee shop. At the coffee shop, he got an email from GoFundMe, which had noticed all the activity, verifying that his campaign was not fraudulent. (A GoFundMe representative also suggested that he use a better picture on the website.) Despite the GoFundMe checkmark assuring people that he was not a con artist, he kept getting emails asking if the site was for real. He would write back assuring them that he would never see the money—it was all going to Tree of Life. People believed him, and the money kept coming.

"After 2:53 p.m.," Khatiri said, "several donations would come in per minute." He had set the original goal at $50,000, but by midnight, it had

---

If you help me, I will forever be thankful to you and I will forever remember your name and your help.

Thank you!

Shay

* Khatiri shared the link with, among many other groups, the Facebook group of *Unorthodox*, a Jewish podcast that I cohost; but I was not on Facebook, and it was weeks before I would hear of Khatiri.

passed $200,000. He kept readjusting the fund's goal upward. The next day, Sunday, at 2:51 in the afternoon, he got a message from GoFundMe that read, "Way to go! You've raised $375,182 from 6,360 donors so far." At 10:21 on Sunday night, the campaign reached half a million dollars. On October 31, at 3:54 p.m.—it was the afternoon when Joyce Fienberg, Irv Younger, and Mel Wax were all buried—Khatiri heard from GoFundMe that his fund had reached one million dollars.

4

The Young

IF YOU KNOW STARBUCKS, you know the big table. It's the one long table, seating five or six or seven people on each side, plus one more at each end, that anchors the room, surrounded by smaller two-tops, stuffed leather chairs in groups of two, at angles to each other, seats at the coffee bar, and high chairs at a bar looking out the window, facing the street. In the Starbucks at the corner of Forbes and Shady, in Squirrel Hill, the big table is set north to south, and one of the ends is just in front of you as you enter the Forbes Avenue door. Sit at one end of the big table, and you are facing north, toward Tree of Life synagogue; sit at the other end, and you are facing south, toward the baristas, and beyond them up Shady Avenue to Beth Shalom, the other big Conservative synagogue, and to Allderdice High School. From this big table, it is a three-minute walk to Rita's Italian Ice & Frozen Custard kiosk, another minute or so across the street to Classic Lines bookstore, another few seconds to the public library, another minute to turn onto Murray and take in a movie at the Manor, and mere seconds to establishments for falafel, shawarma, pizza, burgers, or, for those of age, beers. It is hard to imagine any big table, in any Starbucks, better positioned as a central meeting space, a classic "third space" between work and home, a busy hub to gather and get stuff done—especially for a neighborhood's teenagers. It was at this big table that about ten teens assembled in the early afternoon of October 27, 2018, to figure out what to do.

Emily Pressman often found herself at this big table, but it had not been in her plans for that day. A senior on Allderdice High's debate team, she had awakened at five in the morning to go to a debate tournament in the suburb of Upper St. Clair. She wasn't competing that day, but as the captain, she had gone along "supporting my teams," as she would later put it, with sororal pride. Between the first and second rounds, she was conferring with the younger debaters, when one of the sophomores, seeing a text message, said, "Oh my God, there was a shooting at Tree of Life." Emily lived a block away. Tree of Life was where she had gone to Hebrew school. She snapped into leadership mode, comforting the sophomore and also two Jewish members of her team "who were, like, crying and scared for their lives." She also reassured another friend, a former Allderdice debater who had transferred to a rival school and "was getting no comfort from her team."

It seemed to Emily that out there in the suburbs, a few miles beyond the city limits, at a tournament drawing schools from non-Jewish areas, most people weren't making much of the event. Initially, Emily thought that the tournament would be halted, but then, as the second-round pairings went off, she realized that things would go on as usual. She thought of leaving, but her mother reached her by phone and said, "Don't come home"—it was safer in Upper St. Clair.

Eventually, at about eleven in the morning, Emily left, driving some other Squirrel Hill students home with her. When she got back to her house, a little before noon, she flopped onto her sofa and began watching television. What stood out most, in those early, terrifying moments, was how the reporters kept mispronouncing the name of her street. "I heard them pronounce that this happened 'on the corner of "North Umberland Street."' I'm like, *What the hell? That's not how you pronounce my street name!* And this is the world listening to them saying, *North Umberland.* Then I'm like, *Holy shit. That's where I live!*" The crashing realization that her old synagogue, a block from her house, had been hit, and the world was watching and was getting pronunciations wrong—something about it all made her realize that she had to act, and fast. "I was like, 'I can't sit down.'"

She called her best friend, a fellow senior named Marina Godley-Fisher. "What are you doing right now?" she asked. "'Oh, I'm helping

plan a vigil with some people.' I said, 'Where are you? I'm on my way.'"
Marina was at the Starbucks on Forbes Avenue.

———

BY EARLY AFTERNOON, they were all there: Emily and Marina, Josh
and Kylie, Rebecca and Cody, Peyton and Isabel, a couple others. Some
had found out about the Starbucks meeting through the text group for
Students Demand Action, a gun-control club that had started at Allderdice after the shooting in Parkland, Florida, the previous year. Others
heard just by word of mouth, or rather text to text.

Almost nobody else was in Starbucks—"maybe three other people,"
Emily said. "Squirrel Hill was a ghost town." Up the hill at Tree of Life,
just out of sight from the Starbucks intersection, the police cars and FBI
agents were still swarming, and television trucks were broadcasting to
the whole world.

Inside the quiet coffee shop, the teenagers decided to hold an event
that night at the corner of Forbes and Murray, between the Jewish Community Center and Sixth Presbyterian Church—the main non-Jewish
organization in the neighborhood and, famously, the church that Fred
Rogers, TV's Mister Rogers, had attended. They would convene in time
for sundown, when Jews mark the end of the Sabbath. They began making calls to ask for donations. They needed candles, lots of them. They
needed a stage, and a public address system to amplify their voices. They
needed the police to stop traffic and control crowds.

Soon after the meeting began, Sara Stock Mayo walked in. Mayo's
great-grandparents had settled in Pittsburgh, and her mother had graduated from Allderdice. When Mayo was a young girl, her family had
lived in the neighborhood of Highland Park, but when she was seven,
the family came back to Squirrel Hill. Her first day there, a bunch of
older kids came up to her on the street and invited her to go to the candy
store with them. Her parents told her to go ahead and join them. That
was Squirrel Hill. "There was a lot of freedom to walk around and go
to the library and be independent." She ended up graduating from Allderdice, like her mom. After high school, she went to Israel and worked
and studied on a kibbutz for a year. She came home, went to Syra-
cuse University, then moved to New York City, where she got a degree

in drama therapy. Mayo soon began working as a cantorial soloist for Kolot Chayeinu (Voices of Our Lives), a funky, left-wing congregation in Brooklyn, which set her on a path that was both surprising and not, given her background: her parents were both musicians, but they were not very Jewishly connected, which made this whole religious turn in Mayo's life somewhat unexpected.

When Mayo and her husband, a sportswriter whom she had met in Israel (he, too, is American), were expecting their first child, they decided they couldn't afford to stay in the city. "I came up with this idea that if I wanted my kids to grow up the way I did, with grandparents nearby, maybe we'd go to Pittsburgh." Her husband got permission to telecommute to his job, and in 2001 they resettled in her hometown. At first they lived in Highland Park, but after five years they moved to Squirrel Hill, "for the same reason my parents did—we wanted to be in a more walkable community. . . . We wanted to walk to the movie theater, or synagogue, or grocery store." Her son would soon enroll in Allderdice, where in the fall of 2018 he was a senior, months away from being a third-generation graduate.

By the time Mayo, her husband, and their son and daughter got back to Squirrel Hill, she was at the center of an informal network of liberal and nontraditional Jews living in Squirrel Hill and the other East End neighborhoods, a shadow guild of rabbis, singers, teachers, and lay-people who, by choice or necessity, worked outside mainstream Jewish institutions. Some of them, like Mayo, had been on staff at brick-and-mortar Jewish institutions, had held titles at synagogues; others, like the *kohenet,* or priestess, Keshira haLev Fife, practiced a Judaism (in her case, grounded in earth-based Jewish practice and influenced by *kirtan,* Sanskrit devotional chanting) that was too unusual to fit with the older, more hidebound outfits. They worked with families who couldn't find what they were looking for at synagogues; or they held their own events, sometimes renting space from the synagogues or the JCC, being in them but not of them; or they showed up and offered prayers and songs, as asked. Mayo had worked for a time at Temple Sinai, the Reform congregation in Squirrel Hill (the one that Lynn Hyde, the future convert, attended), but was now a kind of freelance Jew-with-guitar, showing up as needed, providing *ruach,* or spirit, to bar or bat mitzvahs, holiday celebrations, and political rallies. Mayo was also—to use her own words—"the unofficial song leader of Bend the Arc," the liberal Jewish organization that Tammy Hepps and Yael Silk would be working with that night, planning a response to President Trump's announced visit. By the middle of the day on Saturday, it was clear to Mayo, and to others in Pittsburgh's liberal Jewish community, that she, and her guitar, would have a role to play.

"I live nine hundred feet from Tree of Life," Mayo said. "We slept in, and my son came running up the stairs and told us what was going on. I was in shock." She had a terrifying thought: the shooter could come to her house. "So we ran up the stairs, and got in our room and locked our doors until the all-clear. My son, Ziv, has a friend who lives across the street, and he was on social media all morning, like, *The SWAT team is busting in the door, and my brother is really terrified.*" Ziv also had friends who were plugged into the police radio, and he was getting real-time reports from them, too.

As Mayo made calls and sent texts—to rabbis, lay leaders, the informal network that she was at the center of—she gathered that a number of different rallies, vigils, and other events were already being planned. She knew instinctively that she wanted to be part of only one of them. Too many events would diffuse the energy, create rivalries and splits, and inhibit the healing. "I wasn't happy just sitting at home," she said. "Some friends and I who were running programs on spiritual practices were planning on doing something, and heard someone else was doing something. And I thought, *This is a bad idea. We need to funnel this all into one thing.*" She checked in with Rabbi Ron Symons, her old colleague at Temple Sinai, who now worked at the Jewish Community Center, and learned from him that the JCC, having become the waiting room for the families of those caught inside Tree of Life, couldn't possibly host a vigil. She heard about an event the next day at a synagogue in the suburban North Hills area, but she didn't want to wait; the community needed, and she needed, to do something that day.

When she checked in with other Pittsburgh rabbis, she learned that most of them were deferring to the Jewish Federation of Greater Pittsburgh, the umbrella philanthropy, which had already decided to host a large memorial event at Soldiers & Sailors hall on Sunday evening. That would be the citywide event; everyone else was being asked to stand down until the next day.

Mayo got where they were coming from, up to a point. "Listen—when something like this happens, of course you want to be very respectful. We didn't even know the names of the dead yet. We were trying to navigate around people's different cultural responses." And yet she just did not feel right holding off. "The challenge, and the good thing, of not being in an institution is that you don't have people to bounce things off of, but you also don't have people you have to run things by. So you are free to do what you want to do." She felt that she had to act soon.

"I heard a group of teenagers wanted to do a vigil," she said. "And I was connected with the families of lots of the teenagers who were at the Starbucks on Forbes." Once it was deemed safe, she and her husband left their house to take their cockapoo for a walk. As they talked, she told him she was thinking about going over to Starbucks. She knew the students there, and she also knew that they had organized a school walkout after the Parkland shooting. They were serious about activism.

She'd heard that they had already contacted CNN, barely more than an hour after the shooting. "So this was a train that's already going, it's not stopping, and the worst thing we can do is step back and make them do it on their own. They didn't really have the skill set to do that. So I

Emily Pressman (left) and Isabel Smith at the religious service they planned
with other Allderdice High School students at Starbucks

Saturday sundown at the intersection of Forbes and Murray

went into Starbucks and said, 'What can I do to help?'" From Starbucks, Mayo called her husband, who does a lot of community organizing, and enlisted his help. She called her friend Tracy Baton, a Black woman with whom she had worked closely on Pittsburgh's iteration of the Women's March, and drew her into the planning. "I was the person who owned a stage," Baton said. "I knew where to get a sound system. I was friends

with the city's permit guy. I had all that in place." Mayo would make
sure there was at least a guitarist onstage; the teenagers would bring the
rest of the bodies.

In the end, thousands converged at sundown. They brought candles, they heard the students give speeches. Mayo led the crowd in the
Havdalah prayer, to mark the end of the Sabbath, and in a prayer for
healing. The intersection was jammed with Squirrel Hill residents of all
ages: children, teenagers, parents holding babies, old women and men.
Between songs, the most audible sound was the sobbing of the crowd,
heaving as one. The *Post-Gazette* estimated an attendance of "more than
three thousand." It was raining harder by nightfall, and anyone hovering above the intersection would have seen a sea of umbrellas, gently
spreading out in a T at the crossroads of Forbes and Murray, slowly bob-
bing, sheltering the people from the rain above, muffling the sound of
the tears below.

Mayo was sure that she'd made the right call. She was struck in particular by how many non-Jews came. "They were suffering, and they
wanted to feel close to us. No one wanted to feel they were going through
this alone. The kids were spot-on. . . . It was such a beautiful thing, that
after such a horrible thing, there was light, and there was music, and
people wanted to hold each other. People didn't leave. They were standing out there, singing, and local businesses were coming out and giving
people cookies."

It was Emily Pressman, the most religious of the teens, who forcefully argued that the largest, and best, message for people that night was
one that avoided politics. "I knew people in that synagogue. I knew people who died," Emily said. Still, she objected to the idea that the evening's event should focus on gun violence. That didn't feel right to her,
not this soon anyway. "I did not think in the wake of this, this should be
a political activism about guns, about Trump, about anything that way.
This was an act of violence against a religion. That's what this was. So we
made sure that was clear. . . . We said, 'This is Havdalah.'"

5

The Archivist

ON THE AFTERNOON OF Sunday, October 28, Greg Zanis—
having finally seen his eleven white crosses, with Stars of David
affixed to their fronts, pounded into the wet yard of the Tree of
Life synagogue—got back into his truck and began the long drive home
to Aurora, Illinois. As he was driving down Beeler Street, he was spotted by a Pittsburgher named Eric Lidji, on his way to the citywide vigil
planned for five o'clock at Soldiers & Sailors hall, near the University
of Pittsburgh campus. "I saw this white pickup truck drive past me . . .
and it said CROSSES FOR LOSSES," Lidji recalled. The words on the truck
puzzled him. It was such an odd thing to paint on the side of a truck.

Lidji was in a unique position to learn, soon, what Zanis and Crosses
for Losses were all about. Thirty-five years old, Lidji had moved to
Squirrel Hill from Austin, Texas, when he was twelve, sent north to
study at the Yeshiva schools, run by the Chabad movement of Hasidism.
His mother and stepfather soon followed. After Orthodox high school,
Lidji attended the University of Pittsburgh. While in college, he gradu-
ally got less observant—stopped wearing a yarmulke, stopped observing
the Sabbath. An aspiring writer and part-time disc jockey, he graduated
from Pitt in May 2004 and two months later had his first big-time publication, in the July 2004 issue of *The Believer* magazine. His piece, still
available online, is a colorful annotated chart called "The Tale of Backwater Spiritualism: Eight Years of Folk in the Age of Psychedelic Rock,"

in which Lidji traces a musical subgenre that he calls "backwater spiritualism" from Bob Dylan's *John Wesley Harding* album in 1967 through
descendants including Neil Young's *After the Gold Rush,* George Har-
rison's *The Concert for Bangla Desh,* and Joni Mitchell's *The Hissing of
Summer Lawns.*[*]

With a taste of early success, Lidji gave himself a year to find newspaper work in Pittsburgh; when he couldn't find any, he moved to Dallas,
crashed at his father's place, began cold-calling newspapers, and eventually landed a job in Waxahachie, Texas. About a year later, he left for
Alaska, where he got work at the *Fairbanks Daily News-Miner* and then
at *Petroleum News.* In the summer of 2009, Lidji moved back to Pittsburgh, still contributing to *Petroleum News* but looking for other projects. The freelance life was tough, and he began to wonder what else he
might do. In 2012 he started volunteering at the Rauh Jewish History
Program & Archives, a local repository housed on the sixth floor of a
larger museum, the Senator John Heinz History Center. In November
2017 he was promoted to the top job, and the only full-time job, at the
Rauh. He found himself the director of the principal center for the study
of local Jewish history.

So on October 28, when he saw the Crosses for Losses truck drive by,
his curiosity was professional as well as personal. He knew that in the
hours after a mass shooting like the one the day before, all manner of
people would come to town, producing all kinds of artifacts, and his job
was to figure out which ones would matter to history.

The next morning Lidji returned to his office and checked his phone
messages. One of them was from Pam Schwartz, a curator at the Orange
County Regional History Center in Florida. She was the archivist in
Orlando who had collected materials left in the aftermath of the Pulse
nightclub shooting, on June 12, 2016. As Lidji remembered it, "She said,
'If you need any help, let me know.' And I did call her that day, and we
had a really helpful conversation. Because it is paralyzing to go to that

---

* According to Lidji, there were "four hallmarks" of backwater spiritualism: "(1) music determined to combine classic American forms like country, folk, blues, soul, gospel and rock and
roll into a natural whole; (2) lyrical structures created from those religious narratives which connected God with the natural world: the book of Genesis, the Sermon on the Mount, and certain
Eastern faiths among them; (3) a created sense of family with the elders, idols, and influences set
as parental figures and respected contemporaries becoming a fraternal union; (4) the obsessive
need to record large quantities of music paired with the reluctance to release it publicly, a combination that heavily motivated the American bootlegging industry."

Eric Lidji surveying the contents of a time capsule created by the
Tree of Life congregation in 1906, unearthed in November 2019

Trump rally and see a thousand signs, and think, *Ah, how do I even
begin?*" What should he collect? What would people care about a hundred years later, or even a week later?

His talk with Pam Schwartz only confirmed for him that the next
year of his life would be very unusual. He was now part of a cadre of
local archivists charged, by accidents of history, with collecting and cataloguing material created in response to acts of mass violence on American soil. The earliest example that his fellow archivists point to is the
Oklahoma City bombing, in 1995, where "there was a big wall that went
up," Lidji said, a wall that was allowed to remain, where local authorities were "letting people constantly put stuff up." But that was almost
twenty-five years before, and, Lidji was to learn, no set of guiding principles or best practices had emerged. The archivist in Oklahoma City did
things one way, which was not how the archivist did it after Columbine,
nor how it was done in Newtown or Orlando. But in each of these cities, thousands of letters arrived, along with crosses, hand-knit woolens,
homemade dolls, paper cranes, teddy bears, and much, much more.

Other archivists might have been excited to sit where Lidji sat, however inappropriate it would be for them to admit it. Just as there are

journalists who rush to cover the next war or genocide, and meteorologists for whom the months between hurricane seasons are just marking time, there are archivists who don't know how much they love their jobs until they have something truly terrible to record. And maybe if Lidji had lived in another city, or faced a different kind of horror, that would have been him. But this was his childhood home, and these were his fellow Jews. Basically, the killer had come for him and happened to have hit people like him. That tempered the exhilaration that he might otherwise have felt; his sense of purpose had to cohabitate with a sense of intimate loss.

But there was more to Lidji's discomfort with his new role. He was a man of steady habits. He liked predictability. He took his time and worked with care. His temperament was apparent even in his appearance: his dark beard was closely trimmed and well maintained, and to the observer's eye, it never got longer or shorter. He dressed in a versatile uniform that traveled well from synagogue to archive to rock club: khakis or jeans, hemmed just so, and a trim-fit white dress shirt—always white, always with a button-down collar—that was somehow both conservative and fashionable. Lidji had found a job where he could keep his counsel and work alone. He loved the predictability and the sense of control. He could choose his projects, decide what exhibits to mount, and permit himself months, even years, from conception to fruition. Archival horizons were long.

Then there was the very Pittsburgh-ness of Pittsburgh history, with no major eruptions or burning suns. Quick: name somebody from Pittsburgh aside from athletes or Mister Rogers. "The thing I have always loved about the work here," Lidji said, is "that there had never been a major historical moment here, aside from the Pittsburgh Platform"—the major founding document of Reform Judaism, from 1885, announcing the signatories' rejection of what they considered outdated rules like keeping kosher and observing the Sabbath. If the production of a short paper laying out principles for a liberal Jewish movement counts as a city's big moment, well, that's saying something. "We have been able to devote a lot of time to the average person, and do really cool projects, figuring out ways to combine small incremental data into these big composite stories that interest the public but are honoring the lives of everyday people. That's what I found so interesting. That's what I liked the

Greg Zanis's Stars of David, affixed to his signature crosses,
with victims' names inscribed, in front of Tree of Life

most. Now we've gotten not only a big thing, but the biggest of big things,
dropped in our lap."

By the time Lidji visited Tree of Life on Sunday, it was already clear
that Pittsburgh had a new identity, one that would mutate with time.
There would be memorial gardens, pilgrimages, school trips, mentions
in textbooks. The story would become totemic, kitschy, contested. In the
future, Pittsburgh would get lumped in textbooks and high school history classes with other cities where mass shootings had occurred. What
Lidji decided to keep, and what he decided not to keep, would matter.
His work, he knew, was more than just academic. In this case, "the real
task the archive can actually accomplish is to prevent the event from
becoming generic. To maintain the humanity, to maintain the individu-
ality. So that it's not just numbers, it's not just eleven, it's not just names,
it's people, in a community—actual people in an actual community."

Already, however, Lidji was encountering an irony familiar to the
archivists in Oklahoma City, Columbine, Newtown, and all the rest:
while the murdered human beings were each individual, unique, and
precious, the stuff that survivors produce to commemorate them is uniform, predictable, and trite.

Even the most eccentric, highly personalized artifacts can become routine—none more so than Greg Zanis's crosses, handcrafted by a passionate eccentric, but by then an expected part of the posthumous landscape at every mass shooting. If somebody shot up a school in your town, you expected to see those white crosses, and your expectation would be fulfilled. If Zanis somehow didn't make it to town, you could bet that a well-meaning local with a hammer and a can of paint would step up. On the other hand, as predictable as his crosses now were, at least Zanis wrote the names of the victims on each one. Nearly everything else accumulating in front of Tree of Life was utterly impersonal.

Zanis had demonstrated admirable cultural sensitivity in affixing Stars of David to the crosses, but crosses are still crosses.* Just as churches still feel like churches even when the crosses and the renderings of Jesus are covered up—as they would be in Calvary Episcopal Church, a year later, when Tree of Life moved there for its High Holy Day services—a cross of white wood planted on the synagogue grounds, with a victim's name on it, seemed discordant. Nearly everything in the visual vocabulary of mass mourning, already on display at Tree of Life, not just the crosses but the teddy bears and the flowers and whatever else, came from an American Christian idiom, one that many Jews had adopted but that other Jews felt would never truly be their own. A year later, the stars would still be the centerpiece of what tourists saw when they came to Tree of Life: after the yard had been cleared out and flowers replanted outside, Zanis's eleven Stars of David were moved inside glass doors, still visible, staring mutely at buses of curious old people and schoolchildren.

Tammy Hepps wound up having ambivalent feelings about the crosses that she had had a role in creating when she'd shared the victims' names with Zanis. She was profoundly moved. But she was also aware that Zanis had literally put Jewish faces onto structures that were, down to their

---

* Zanis emphasized to me that his sensitivity went beyond using the Star of David. "When I pulled up at Tree of Life," Zanis told me, "this lady came up to me and saw CROSSES FOR LOSSES on my truck, and she said, 'You know, everybody is Jewish here.'" This was after his encounter with Tammy Hepps, a short distance from the shul. "I said, 'You know, we all love God equally.' It started pouring down rain then. I was making the crosses inside the cab. As I got done, I would stand them outside. I was waiting for my comfort dog people. And then as I waited—I don't know how to say this to be polite—but two guys who looked Jewish, with the hats, came up, and I asked them if they would do the honor of breaking the police line and putting them in"—inside the police cordon, on the grass in front of the synagogue. "I didn't want to taint it. . . . I never really carry a memorial into the scene. I carry it up to the scene and hand it off. I need the community to put it there." The two Jewish men agreed, and Zanis gave them the crosses with the Stars of David affixed on the fronts, which they set into the wet earth in front of Tree of Life.

Stones placed by mourners atop a Greg Zanis cross in front
of Tree of Life, November 3, 2018

bones, Christian. "I am sorry," Hepps would later reflect, "that we'll never know what would have been spontaneously created by Squirrel Hill if this focal point hadn't been set up by an outsider."

Lidji, too, saw that the memorial accreting at Tree of Life was, from the beginning, the product of diverse, not always compatible, religious cultures. The Jewishness was there, but to anyone driving by, looking out from a car window, it was hard to see. Because Jews, by tradition, don't build crosses or leave stuffed animals. They leave stones.* Stones arrived almost immediately, placed all over the scene, and Lidji had to decide what to do with them, as with so much else.

"Is there value to cataloguing each of two thousand stones?" Lidji wondered. "On the one hand, yes. Each stone meant somebody who had stopped by and paid respects. But on the other hand . . . is a researcher really going to come and say, 'I'd like to see Blank Stone 284'?"

---

* The tradition of leaving stones on Jews' graves is an ancient one, and nobody is sure where it comes from. Unlike so much else that Jews do, leaving stones at graves is not commanded by Scripture. Some think it has to do with keeping the soul of the dead person in this world, which may be comforting to mourners. Others say Jews leave stones because they are permanent, unlike flowers, and will hold up as markers that somebody has visited. There are other theories. The tradition, it should be said, is to leave the stone at a Jewish gravesite, not where a Jew died, but in Pittsburgh that distinction did not seem to matter.

———∞∞∞———

6

The Body Guards

A RE YOU A Harry Potter fan?" the rabbi asked. It was late
December, two months after the shooting, in the middle of the
day in the middle of the week, not much going on in shul, so
the thermostat was set low. It was cold outside and cold inside. The rabbi
was talking about Harry Potter. "The wand chooses the wizard," he said.
"The wand chooses the wizard."

Daniel Wasserman was pontificating in his confident New Yorkese,
sitting at a round table in *his* social hall in *his* synagogue, Shaare
Torah, the Orthodox shul on lower Murray Avenue. He was gesturing
broadly, with open arms, the proud papa of his community. Something
about his commanding, protective presence made one feel both intimi-
dated and safe; the implicit bargain seemed to be that if you deferred
to him, he'd take good care of you, until the end. That's the most basic
explanation for how death came to define his rabbinate, how he became
the Pittsburgh rabbi known for his willingness to build caskets and to
bury his own congregants, or any Jew whose family came to him, with
his own hands, according to the ancient but mostly forgotten rites. It
was the thing that he felt called to do.

"The wand chooses the wizard," Wasserman said. "As a rabbi, I deal
with people from before they're born till death. And everything is part
of the purview of being part of a community and a family. . . . If somebody needs something in the middle of the night, they call us." To illus-

trate the point, he told a story about a young woman he knew. He was a friend of her parents', and he and his wife found her a nice young man. They got engaged, and Wasserman officiated at the wedding. Soon she had a baby. "One Shabbos morning, I was in shul. She comes with her baby in the stroller, and I happened to be outside. I could tell something was up. She just handed me the stroller and said, 'Jonathan has an emergency appendicitis.' Didn't have to say another word. Because we're family." Wasserman took the stroller, and he and his wife watched the baby the rest of the day. "My wife and I are the surrogate parents, and whatever we can do for people, we do.

"That's part of being a shul," Wasserman said. "That's part of being a community. It's part of being a rabbi. When *Moshe Rabbeinu*"—Moses our teacher—"was saying to God, 'That you told me—*ki somar eylai*—"Carry them in your arms. Hold them to your bosom as a nursemaid would do,"' I'm not aware of anywhere in the Torah that God told that to Moshe." And indeed, there is no record of God explicitly saying that Moses had to take care of his people quite like that. "But Moshe *understood* his role was to carry the Jewish people in his bosom, like a little child. *That's* a rabbi's role: to teach and to be a father and to be a mother and to be a friend when possible. All of those things. So it makes sense that any rabbi is involved in death."

In 1996 Wasserman left a synagogue in Worcester, Massachusetts, to become the rabbi of Shaare Torah, one of Squirrel Hill's two largest Modern Orthodox congregations.* At the time, the main *chevra kadisha* in town, its holy society, or burial society, was run by the other Modern Orthodox synagogue, Poale Zedeck. Wasserman got involved, and within five years he helped reorganize the holy society as a project of the whole Orthodox community, under the supervision of its rabbinic council. (This was just before the founding of Squirrel Hill's non-Orthodox holy society, which Dan Leger was part of, in 2004.) At this point, the society did only *tahara*, the ritual washing of the corpse—it then turned the body over to a for-profit funeral home, which sold the casket and organized the burial. In 2009, however, Wasserman found the gumption to cut the funeral homes out: when a former congregant died in Chicago, Wasserman told the widow that if she could get the

---

* He had first been hired by Shaare Torah the prior summer, in time for Rosh Hashanah services, and commuted for almost a year; he did not move to Pittsburgh with his family until July 15, 1996.

body back to Pittsburgh, he would do the whole burial. The first time his group did the "full service, from death to burial, including pickup and permits and signing the death certificate," was on May 28, 2010.

Soon his new organization, which he called Gesher HaChaim (Bridge of Life), was teaching a small corps of volunteers to do it all. He and one of his congregants, Jason Small, an amateur carpenter (and full-time software programmer at Google), held a casket-building workshop for men in the synagogue. Their small group buried people at cost. Undercutting the funeral homes by several thousand dollars made him some enemies. One time an acquaintance arranged a meeting with a local Jewish undertaker, who tried to persuade Wasserman to stop taking away his business. The rabbi told the undertaker, "You're not a community institution. You are a private business that may do great things, and you have the right to do it any way you want, and you have the right to charge people whatever you want. . . . Just understand that I have no responsibility to you. My responsibilities are to my constituents, to the Jew, affiliated or otherwise." Wasserman tried to explain to this funeral director that the American way of death, with fancy caskets, black hearses, and exorbitant bills, was "a hiccup," one that had come to seem normal only in the last century, when, as death moved out of the home and into hospitals, burial moved out of the home and into professional establishments.

To Wasserman, the funeral industry was the abnormality, whereas Jewish burial was at least as old as the Talmud, which nearly two thousand years ago was making the case for simplicity in burial. The Talmud tells of Rabbi Gamaliel, a wealthy man who nonetheless asked that, when his time came, he be buried like a pauper. It had come to be, the Talmud teaches, that "the funeral expenditures for the deceased were more taxing for his relatives than his death," to the point that relatives "would abandon the deceased and flee." To solve this problem, Rabbi Gamaliel instructed the people "to take him for burial in plain linen garments. And all the people conducted themselves following his example, and instructed their families to take them for burial in plain linen garments." According to the Talmud, Gamaliel's action become a model for all the Jewish people, so that "today, everyone is accustomed to bury the dead in plain garments, even in rough cloth."

Wasserman is unbending on these rules, always doing battle with the prevailing American materialism. Just two days earlier, he said, he had been speaking with a man preparing to bury his wife. "He said, 'Is there any way we can use a different casket? Because I don't want my son to think we don't have money.' I said, 'First of all, the answer is no.' But then I gave him the whole *drasha*"—sermon—"about 'Why are you worried about what people think? What you're going to do is the greatest honor for your wife, to have a community bury her, with simplicity and dignity, and you're worried about what people think? Deal with *that*. Don't ask me to have a different casket, because I won't do it. I just won't do it.'

"I tell people, 'I do not apologize to anyone for saving thousands of dollars because we're nonprofit, but that's not the reason we do it. The reason we do it is because the community should bury its own.'"

In 2009 Wasserman, having failed to make the city's funeral directors see things from his point of view, found himself under investigation by the state's Bureau of Enforcement and Investigation, an arm of the Pennsylvania Department of State, for "practicing as a funeral director without a license." The state kept up its investigation of Wasserman for over two years, and in August 2012 he sued the state in federal court, alleging arbitrary and discriminatory enforcement of the law—which, according to Wasserman, nowhere made religious burials illegal—and violation of the rabbi's constitutional rights under the First and Fourteenth amendments. That December the case settled and the state issued a memorandum of understanding that clarified the permissibility of religious burial.

"This memorandum explicitly clarifies Pennsylvania law, and guarantees that individuals engaged in performing the ceremonies, customs, religious rites or practices of any denomination or sect are excluded from the definition of 'funeral director' in Pennsylvania law, as has always been the case," Wasserman said in a statement at the time. "This includes churches, meetings, mosques, synagogues, temples or other congregations of religious believers engaged in handling, transporting, preparing and disposing of deceased human bodies. No longer will the filing of scurrilous complaints and other attempts of the 'death industry' to control and co-opt non-profit, religious funeral practices and rites be allowed to stress and curtail our religious expression."

———

NONE OF THE ELEVEN PEOPLE killed at Tree of Life attended Wasserman's synagogue. They were Conservative and Reconstructionist Jews, not Orthodox. For the most part, they weren't observant enough to have been allowed into an Orthodox holy society. Wasserman would not have accepted Daniel Leger's conversion as legitimate, overseen as it was by a non-Orthodox rabbi, and therefore he would not have accepted that Leger was a Jew. Wasserman had met some of the victims; two of them had in fact attended his shul from time to time. As for the others, he may have known them or their families slightly—would have nodded at them at the Giant Eagle supermarket on Murray Avenue. But, to put it simply, these were not his people. They crossed paths as Squirrel Hill Jews, but they were different kinds of Squirrel Hill Jews.

And yet Wasserman felt, in the aftermath of their murders, that he and his kind could be of use. Unlike most members of Tree of Life and the other two congregations attacked, Wasserman had a small army of Jews practiced in the art of death care, and so he sent his people to act as *shomrim,* guards of the dead—those who stay with the dead bodies, in the morgue and before they are transported to funeral homes. They made sure that the *metim,* the corpses, were never left alone.

Wasserman's volunteers arrived outside Tree of Life on Saturday afternoon, and they stayed—with reinforcements coming to relieve the original guards every so often—all night long, in the rain, until the wee hours of Sunday, when the medical examiner began to remove bodies from the building. Then they drove alongside the bodies, following them to the morgue. "In the chaos after the Pittsburgh shooting," Emma Green, a journalist for *The Atlantic,* wrote on the Tuesday after the murders, "an Orthodox rabbi, Daniel Wasserman, stepped in to oversee the care of the bodies. He coordinated with the FBI and the Allegheny County medical examiner to make sure that the investigation was handled with religious sensitivity: that it was fast, that the autopsies were minimal, that the community was able to maintain a presence throughout the process." Wasserman was there when the bodies were removed, and "he organized a spreadsheet for volunteer *shomrim* who would guard the bodies: One slot for every hour until an undetermined time, when the dead would finally be released for burial."

According to Green, Wasserman ensured that the morgue workers knew that volunteers would be coming by throughout the night, getting as close to the bodies as they could, which in this case meant using a small room off the lobby, usually reserved for grief counseling. The room was, Green wrote, no bigger than "a spacious walk-in closet." In that room, keeping the dead in mind, the guards recited Psalms.

"They read the Psalms in order, one after another, with each person making sure the next guard knew where the readings had left off," Green wrote. "Everyone had a different way of praying. One man stood facing the wall and rocked slowly from one foot back to the other. Another woman paced as she read, whispering the Hebrew words under her breath. A young couple came in and sat catty-corner to each other; they split up the numbered verses, odds and evens, and occasionally checked in to see how far the other had gotten. Each person brought a prayer book, some as big as textbooks, others the size of pocket dictionaries. Outside of occasional logistical discussions or buzzes of a cellphone, the room was quiet. Some sort of machinery—maybe the lights or the heating system—whirred in the background. Every once in a while, a door opened and slammed."

By Sunday evening, all but two of the bodies had left the morgue for funeral homes, but the *shomrim* would stay until the last body had been taken away. "A little after 8 p.m.," Green wrote, "an officer came to check on whether people would be there throughout the night, since the last of the bodies were almost ready. Yes, answered the woman holding down the guard. Volunteers would be there all night. . . . Over the course of three hours, officers came in several times to check whether the guards needed water or help with anything. They brought updates on the bodies, asking someone to text the rabbi to make sure he knew what was happening. Wasserman said that the officials involved in this investigation have been very concerned about religious sensitivities. At one meeting, he hugged an officer in thanks. When the rabbi left the room, the officer began to cry."

————

THE FUNERALS DID NOT begin until Tuesday. The period from death to burial had gone on too long. The Jewish dead are supposed to be in the ground as soon as possible, and as I said earlier, they are often buried the next day. It can take longer if, for example, the dead person was traveling and the corpse has to be flown home. But a Jew knows that if somebody dies, you had better hurry if you want to make the funeral. It's not unusual for a child traveling abroad to miss his own mother or father's funeral. But in this case, the bodies had to be processed by the medical examiner, the police, and the FBI. They had to be inspected, examined, probed for evidence, evacuated of bullets, and stitched up where they were pierced and torn. And they had to be given the *tahara*, the ritual washing done by a holy society.

Monday night, six men from the New Community Chevra Kadisha gathered at Ralph Schugar, Inc., a funeral home in Shadyside, just north of Squirrel Hill. These six represented about half the male membership of the holy society; it was all the men who could come that night. They were there to wash the first of five men's bodies they would prepare for burial that night and into the next morning. As difficult as the night would be, they all knew that the most painful work would come the next morning, with the *tahara* of their friend Jerry Rabinowitz. He had been in the holy society, had done more than a hundred *taharas* with these men, preparing other Jewish men for burial. In the morning, his turn would come.

The New Community Chevra Kadisha had been founded in 2004 as a non-Orthodox alternative to the holy society that Rabbi Wasserman ran. In 2003 a small group of liberal Jews, mostly members of Dor Hadash, had gathered to talk about the fact that if a family wanted its loved one to get a *tahara* before burial, the holy society run by Orthodox Jews was the only option. While the Orthodox society would perform *tahara* on any Jew, they required their members to maintain traditional observance. "We were interested in becoming a part of the Orthodox *chevra*," said Malke Frank, who was at that first meeting. "But they didn't want us. We weren't Orthodox, we weren't Jewish enough, no Shabbat"—meaning they did not all strictly observe the laws of the Sabbath. The group decided to start something of their own.

So they got going. Jamie Gibson, the senior rabbi of Temple Sinai, in Squirrel Hill—the rabbi who would later work with Lynn Hyde on her conversion—was a major booster (and he gave them a suggestion for their name, which they took). Ron Symons, another local rabbi, who would later work at Temple Sinai and then at the JCC, joined their new society almost right away and never left. David Zinner, who lives in Maryland and coordinates a national network of non-Orthodox Jewish holy societies, came up to Pittsburgh to give workshops in how to do a *tahara.* There is no Orthodox monopoly on the right way to do a *tahara,* he told them, because *halakhah,* Jewish law, does not in fact prescribe one way to do it. And the existing holy society, led by Wasserman, did allow the members of the new society to observe their *taharas,* to watch and learn.

In 2007 the New Community Chevra Kadisha performed its first *tahara.* As with its Orthodox counterpart, men do *tahara* for male bodies, women for women. Over the years, the organization grew to about thirteen men and thirteen women, who in 2017 performed about eighty *taharas.*

With no specifically commanded rites, the organization had to develop its own traditions for *tahara.* In an essay written in October 2019, Jordana Rosenfeld, a newcomer who, along with many others, was inspired to join the society by its work in the aftermath of the shooting, described its practices.* The back of the funeral home chapel "resembles a large garage; its eastern wall rolls open to allow hearses to back up to an industrial cooler like the ones at the bakery where I used to bake sourdough bread," Rosenfeld wrote. "Around the corner from the cooler is the preparation room—cold, stuffy, and small—where we find the *meitah,* the deceased"—the masculine for body is *met,* the feminine *metah,* or *meitah*—"lying on one of two tables that look like porcelain but probably aren't, her whole body wrapped in a sheet.

"We gather outside the preparation room to greet each other and read the *meitah*'s obituary. Often, one or more of us has a personal connection to the *meitah* or her family, which we momentarily acknowledge. We ask the *meitah* for forgiveness if we 'fail to act according to [her] honor, even though we act according to our custom.' We enter the prep room and remove the sheet. . . .

"We place a handkerchief over the *meitah*'s face, as she is *nireh v'eyno ro'eh,* one who can be seen but who cannot see. We cut off her hospital gown and dunk washcloths in buckets of warm water at our feet. We drape her in a clean sheet, only uncovering parts of her body in order to wash them. We comb her hair, taking care to collect any strays in a linen pouch that will be buried along with her. We remove nail polish, we clean up excess bodily secretions, we wipe off any shmutz left behind

---

* As of 2020, the New Community Chevra Kadisha had thirty-seven female and twenty-seven male members, but that list "may not be current," member Allen Baum told me.

by medical tape. We turn the *meitah* on her side to wash her back—two people steady her by holding her body close, while someone else cradles her head in their hands. As we finish the washing, we recite a line from Song of Songs: '*Kulakh yafah rayati umum ein bakh.*' 'You are beautiful, my beloved friend, and there is no flaw in you.'"

All the victims at Tree of Life received *taharas* before their burials; five of the eleven, on five male victims, were performed by the New Community Chevra Kadisha. (The others, presumably, were given *taharas* by the Orthodox holy society, or by Jewish undertakers trained in the practice, but it's hard to get confirmation, precisely because the holy society's work is supposed to be anonymous.) None of the women in the liberal holy society had a *tahara* to do. Three of the *taharas* would take place at Schugar's, the Jewish funeral home in Shadyside, while two, including Jerry Rabinowitz's, would be at D'Allesandro Funeral Home, in the North Side Lawrenceville neighborhood, the next morning.

The women could still help, as guards, watching over the bodies. This was the work that Wasserman had organized his holy society to do over the past two days, as the bodies lay at the medical examiner's office.

————

SINCE SATURDAY MORNING, Reform rabbi Ron Symons, who had been with the newer holy society since its founding, had not stopped. A former pulpit rabbi, since 2015 he had worked at the Jewish Community Center, so he had been on-site at the JCC on Saturday, when it was the hub for families waiting to hear if their loved ones were alive. He had worked all day Sunday and then Monday, too, when the JCC decided it would open for business as usual. On Monday he left the JCC at five in the evening to attend a meeting that the city's Jewish federation was holding to bring rabbis up to date on everything: security, media, funerals, shivas (a traditional family week of mourning at home), bodies. That meeting made him late for the first two *taharas*. When he finally arrived at the funeral home, he rushed into a back room to get ready for the third.

Then, as Symons was changing into clothes that could get wet with blood and fluids and human waste, something unexpected happened. "There was a knock on the door," Symons said. Then came a woman's voice, speaking through the door. "She said, 'Don't worry, I'm not gonna hurt you.'"

Symons was, he recalled later, "freaking out." Eleven members of his community had been murdered less than three days earlier, shot by a stranger who had barged through the doors of a Jewish gathering place. Now here he was, gathering with other Jews to do sacred work, and a stranger was at the door. He didn't know what to think. He went to find one of the funeral directors on staff that night, who removed the folding chair that had been propped under the doorknob for extra makeshift security. Together, tentatively, they opened the door. A little old woman was looking up at them. She was holding her hands up to her face, and they were clutching a thousand dollars in cash.

"This," the woman said, gesturing with the money, "is for the married couple." She meant Sylvan and Bernice Simon, the couple killed in the same Tree of Life chapel where they had been married sixty-two years before.

Standing next to the rabbi, the funeral director asked the woman what her name was.

"No name," the woman replied.

The funeral director asked if she could give the woman a hug.

"No hug," the woman said. She turned and walked away—"just disappeared into the night," Symons said.

Symons and the funeral director closed the door and jammed the chair back into place. Then they looked at each other and hugged. "We just embraced each other for five minutes," Symons said, amazed "that there could be such goodness after such darkness."

Symons finished changing his clothes and joined other members of the holy society for the final *tahara* of the night. During a *tahara,* they recite a line from the prophet Hosea, in which God says that the people Israel "shall blossom like the lily" and that the people's branches will spread wide. "His beauty shall be like the olive tree's," the verse continues, "His fragrance like that of Lebanon." When Symons got to the part about the olive tree, he began to sob. That prophetic promise—that the Jewish people would increase in number, take root, blossom, thrive— seemed so distant. All he could see was death.

"For all my liberalism," Symons said, "all my talk that antisemitism is part of a greater hatred, this was an attack on *us*." The killer was symptomatic of a greater cancer, that of bigotry and white supremacism, but for the moment Symons couldn't think about the larger questions of

American politics. "He went after *Jews*. And it wasn't just that he went after Jews . . . he went after Jews that I know." Eventually, he composed himself and went on with the *tahara*. When that was finished, and the body was sewn into its shroud, he went home.

Tuesday morning Symons was back at it, at D'Alessandro's. There were two bodies, one of them Jerry Rabinowitz's. With a dozen men present, they had to take turns, three or four at a time. Everybody wanted to touch Jerry one last time. And once again that line just got to him: "His beauty shall be like an olive tree's . . ." In Torah, it refers to all the people of Israel, so it referred to Jerry.

When they were finished with the *taharas,* and the funeral directors were ready to move Jerry's body to the hearse, Symons changed his clothes and went back to the JCC, where Jerry's funeral was to be held at eleven in the morning. At the JCC, Symons found himself in the new and unexpected role of "funeral director," as he put it. Jerry's wife, Miri, had suggested the JCC for her husband's funeral. None of the funerals could be held at Tree of Life, which was still a crime scene, and the JCC had a room big enough to handle the crowd (or, as it turned out, most of the crowd). For Symons, who couldn't shake the fresh memory of tending to his murdered friend that morning, the work was overwhelming. The largest room in the JCC had a capacity of 350, and Symons knew they would have to livestream the audio to mourners in overflow spaces. Chairs had to be found and set up in rows. Somebody had to remember to reserve chairs for immediate family. As Symons ran about, corralling maintenance workers and checking items off his list, somebody came up to him and said that Ellen Leger wanted to see him.

Symons found Leger and gave her a long hug. "How's Dan?" he asked, knowing that her husband was still in serious condition in the hospital. "All right," she said. "We'll see." Ellen asked him if she could see Jerry's widow, Miri, and Symons said that he would see what he could do. He went upstairs to the room where the Rabinowitz family was gathering before the service. "I found Miri," Symons said. "She was surrounded by her friends. I tapped her and said, 'Ellen wants to see you.' And so she said, 'Of course.' I brought her out, and Ellen was there, and they embraced. It was probably the most painful thing I'd ever seen in my life."

7

❧

The Funerals

J ERRY RABINOWITZ'S FUNERAL BEGAN at eleven in the morning on Tuesday. He was the first of the eleven victims to have a funeral, and his body had not been left alone since the moment he was removed from Tree of Life. More than one thousand people came to the funeral. Many men in the audience wore bow ties, in honor of Rabinowitz's signature accessory. Saul Silver, a local cardiologist who had known Rabinowitz since the late 1980s, came straight from work, in his own white lab coat. He told a reporter that Rabinowitz was an unusually compassionate physician, the kind who treated AIDS patients humanely at a time when many doctors were scared to touch them. "He would give 'em a hug and shake their hand without gloves," Silver told the *Post-Gazette*. "That was Jerry."

Michael Kerr, a gay former graduate student at the University of Pittsburgh, told *The Daily Beast* that, until he went to Rabinowitz, he "never knew what it was like to go to a doctor who wouldn't shun you or treat you with stigma around the issue of sex." A few months after his AIDS diagnosis, Kerr had swallowed a handful of pills. Rabinowitz sat with him and told him not to give up. "There's going to be medications that are going to come your way," Rabinowitz said. "So you need to hang in there." Rabinowitz made no promises, but he offered hope. According to Kerr, "He never said, 'It will be OK' or 'Don't worry.' He had lost patients. But he showed me I was being cared for, and he appreciated that I was scared. . . . He had everyone's backs."

When the funeral was over, Jerry's body was taken outside and put in a hearse to be driven to Homewood Cemetery, less than a mile away. As the mourners were dispersing to their cars, to go alongside the hearse to the graveyard, Ron Symons saw something he had not expected: "I saw that there was a whole line of Orthodox Jews standing by the hearse." A couple of them approached and asked if he had made arrangements for them to walk with the hearse. "And I said, 'What are you talking about?' And they said, 'Did you tell the police we're walking, because, you know, that's what we do?' And I said, 'Okay, I'll tell them.'"

Walking with the hearse wasn't part of his tradition as a Reform rabbi, but Symons did as he was asked. He approached the policemen outside the JCC, who said they had no problem if the men in black hats walked in the middle of the street, accompanying the hearse. Symons told the Orthodox men they had their permission, then turned to walk away, his work there finished at last. "I figured I did what I needed to do for Jerry, and I would see to other community events," he said.

"But as they started walking, my feet just started going with them." He fell in line with the Orthodox men. As they walked down Forbes

Jews escorting the hearse carrying Jerry Rabinowitz's body to Homewood Cemetery

Larry Perl, of nearby White Oak, Pennsylvania,
watching the funeral caravan enter the cemetery

Avenue, "the entire community stopped. Like, it wasn't just traffic that stopped." Shopkeepers and customers emerged from stores and saluted. "It was beautiful," Symons said. "It felt like a New Orleans funeral without the music. It was one of the most spiritual things I ever did."

————

JERRY RABINOWITZ'S FUNERAL WAS still under way at noon, when a thousand other mourners packed the sanctuary at Rodef Shalom, the large Reform temple in Oakland, just over the Squirrel Hill border. They had come for the joint funeral of Cecil and David Rosenthal, the two brothers killed at Tree of Life. There were Jews and non-Jews. There were politicians, clergy, and athletes—the Rosenthals' sister Michele had worked in the Pittsburgh Steelers' press office, and several players turned out for her brothers that day. Brett Keisel, a defensive lineman, was one of the pallbearers.

Before the funeral, the caskets holding Cecil and David were rolled down the central aisle of the sanctuary, and a procession of eight firefighters, wearing their dress uniforms, proceeded to the front, stopped at the caskets, and saluted. One of the firefighters, Mike DiBattiste— "Debo" to his friends at the 18 Engine firehouse on Northumberland

Street—had known David for twenty years. He thought of David, who for years came into 18 Engine on Saturdays before synagogue, as a friend.

"Back when I first got here in '97, he knew all the guys by name," Debo recalled later. "He loved to banter with us, and he'd give it back to us"—occasionally dropping f-bombs, just like the firefighters he looked up to. "He'd have breakfast with us. . . . He just wanted to be one of the guys. And he was." Around nine on Saturdays, they would often be cleaning up, and David would grab a broom himself. Even when he didn't help out, he liked to supervise. "'No loafin'!' he'd say."

In recent years, as some of the firehouse old-timers retired or left for other units, David's Saturday attendance at 18 Engine had become spottier. Often he wouldn't come for weeks at a time. But in the fall of 2018, he'd started coming back. The morning of October 27, Debo was at a funeral a couple miles northwest of Squirrel Hill. In fact, most of the regulars, the guys David would have known, were off duty that morning. When Debo, sitting in the funeral, began to get text messages about the shooting, he started doing the calculus about David, whether he'd have stopped by 18 Engine, how long he might have stayed, whether he'd be on his way to Tree of Life, whether he'd be there already . . .

"As I was leaving the church," Debo said, "I thought of David right away. I was hoping he wasn't there, but knowing he probably was." Then he had a more hopeful thought. "Sometimes we made him late." But what if David had stopped in, then left because his regular pals weren't there? "I think, *If I had been working, would he be here? Would he have been late that day?* You always think all these crazy things."

It was Debo's idea to do something special for "the boys," as everyone called the Rosenthal brothers. He decided they should make David an honorary fireman. So Monday night, the night before the funeral, Debo and several others from 18 Engine went to the shiva at their sister Michele's house. At the shiva, they met Joy and Eliezer Rosenthal, the boys' parents, who had flown up from Florida to bury their sons. Debo gave the Rosenthals an honorary firefighter's badge and a Jewish translation of the Hebrew Bible. They had got the Bible from their union office, where there was a store of Bibles, in Christian and Jewish versions, to be given to family members at firefighters' funerals.

The firefighters stayed about an hour. Shortly before seven o'clock, they had to return to the firehouse because a local troop of Girl Scouts

The bar mitzvah of Jonathan Berkun—here with his father,
Rabbi Alvin Berkun, congratulating him—at an age when
he was friends with the Rosenthal brothers

was coming to bring them cookies (homemade cookies, not Girl Scout cookies). In the days after the killings, people were bringing them food all the time. The firefighters would say, "You want to bring this to the police, no?" It was police officers who had been shot, after all. But people wanted to help those whom they saw as helping them; firefighters, in their uniforms, would suffice. At 18 Engine, they understood the need they met, and they accepted the food.

At the funeral on Tuesday, after the firefighters saluted, the rest of the procession moved on, and people sat down. Jeffrey Myers then took the pulpit for the first of five funerals, for seven total congregants, that he would hold that week.

"I'm Rabbi Jeffrey Myers, the rabbi of Tree of Life," he said from Rodef Shalom's large stage, the caskets of the brothers before him. "We gather here today, sharing our sorrow." He lamented losing "two of the sweetest human beings you could ever meet, Cecil and David Rosenthal."

Myers invited up to the *bimah* Jonathan Berkun, the rabbi of a large Conservative synagogue in Aventura, Florida. Berkun had grown up at Tree of Life, where his father, Alvin Berkun, had become the rabbi in 1983, when the son was ten years old. That fall, thirty-five years earlier, as

Jonathan was first getting acquainted with his new synagogue community, he had fallen in with these two older brothers with special needs,
Cecil and David Rosenthal. David was almost twenty, Cecil older still,
but they were good playmates for Jonathan. The morning of the shooting, Jonathan was at his own shul, leading services, when he got word.
His thoughts went to all the people he knew would be there early on
Shabbat. That was a group that definitely included the Rosenthal brothers. But it also could have included his father.

As it happened, the elder Rabbi Berkun had skipped shul that morning because his wife was not feeling well. Once he heard about the
shooting, he put on his old police chaplain jacket and made the two-
minute walk from his house to Tree of Life, from which he had retired in
2005. He couldn't get close to the action, so he hovered outside the police
lines, talking to people, comforting whomever he could. Then he went
home, where he found that his wife's condition had worsened. He took
her to the hospital, where she was admitted with a serious infection.

In Florida, Jonathan, the younger rabbi, faced a tough decision. Like
Jews everywhere, those in his congregation were scared; nobody knew
when or where another attack would come. They needed each other—
and they needed their rabbi. But Jonathan felt that he had to be with
his dad, his ailing mom, and his hometown of Pittsburgh. So two days
later, on Monday, he flew to Pittsburgh, his Steelers yarmulke on his
head. After landing at the Pittsburgh airport, he went to buy a bottle of
water in the terminal. "The saleswoman was so friendly," he wrote later
that day, "that I quipped how I had forgotten how nice people are in this
city. . . . 'It's been a tough day for us, sir,' she responded with a tear in her
eye." He took his water and went to the car rental garage, where the
employee who helped him said that he couldn't understand how something like this could happen. Before he got into his car, Jonathan and the
man from the rental agency hugged.

And now here he was, at the *bimah,* helping the new rabbi bury the
men who had helped him make mischief in shul when he was a boy. Once
in the pulpit, he began to sing "Mizmor l'David," "A Song of David,"
the introductory words of the twenty-third Psalm, the one we know in
English for its next line, "The Lord is my shepherd; I shall not want."
When Berkun finished singing the whole Psalm in Hebrew, Myers took
the pulpit again and said, "There are two *mitzvot,* two commandments,

associated with the Jewish funeral. One is the proper burial, conducted a little bit later today. The first is to offer words of tribute and praise in memory of the deceased."

Then came the tributes to "the boys." A letter from the Catholic bishop of Pittsburgh was read aloud, followed by a short eulogy from Diane, one of the boys' two sisters. When she was finished, she called on her husband, Michael, the boys' brother-in-law, to say some words.

"David was very social in some respects," Michael said, "but at the same time a bit private and shy. Phone calls with him always started with, 'Hey Michael, the police are looking for you.'" The Rodef Shalom sanctuary laughed, the first break in the morning's sadness. "To which I would always playfully reply, 'No, David, the police are looking for you.'" He described David's love of the police and other men in uniform—his favorite toy was his police scanner, which he carried with him wherever he went. "David was an intensely hard worker. . . . His jobs were always related to cleaning, and he was fanatical about keeping things neat and in order. If you were sitting in a chair and you put your glass of water down for a minute and you turned your head, it would be gone."

Along with the police, firefighters, and cleanliness, his other great

Cecil and David Rosenthal's funeral at Rodef Shalom,
the Tuesday after the shooting

love was women. "David loved women," Michael said. "I'm sure the bulk of the ladies here today were at one time or another asked by David, 'Are you married?' Followed by 'Wanna go to Hawaii?' During our annual family holidays, he would always suggest, 'Let's go out and have a beer, meet some girls.' I agreed that this sounded like lots of fun." At their annual trip to the flea market, David always asked for a pair of mirrored sunglasses, state trooper style, and a new bottle of cologne. "Had David not been handicapped, I think he would have been a movie star or a celebrity."

Cecil, meanwhile, was "the consummate politician . . . a social-ite. He knew everyone's business." Cecil always "knew if your mother was sick or if your grandmother had died." They called him the Town Crier. "How many times did Cecil stop one of you on the street to tell you about someone's pending marriage or pending divorce? . . . If you wanted local news gossip, Cecil was your source. When Cecil answered the phone, he would thunder, 'Hello DEAR!'" Then he would get down to business, asking about the kids, the dog, everything. "And of course, 'When are you coming to Pittsburgh?'"

One time, Michael remembered, somebody had died, and the family decided not to tell the boys, so as not to upset them. It didn't work. "Somehow," he said, "Cecil managed to find out about the funeral service and managed on his own, by a combination of walking, riding the bus, or hawking a ride from someone, to find his way to the service to pay his respects. I still remember him strolling in, not wearing his usual suit and tie, and carrying the bag of trinkets and papers that always accompanied him.

"I can guarantee that he is looking down upon us now, asking, 'Are you proud of me?'"

8

The Trump Visit

I F ALL YOU KNEW about Squirrel Hill was that it was an urban neighborhood, that would be enough, in today's America, to know with reasonable certainty that its residents voted overwhelmingly for Democrats. That's simply the way it is in the United States now. One of the most important political developments of the last quarter century is the Great Sorting: Democrats have moved to be near Democrats, Republicans near Republicans. In 1992 Bill Clinton carried almost half of the country's 3,100 counties, while in 2016 Hillary Clinton carried fewer than 500—and still won the popular vote, because Democrats have packed themselves so tightly into urban areas. Liberals and Democrats increasingly say they want to live in denser, walkable areas, while Republicans prize larger houses with more land around them. And as political identities have polarized, so have the cultural traits that increasingly go along with them. The journalist Dave Wasserman has made a fun game of mapping election results onto food preference, and he found (to take one example) that "in 2012, Obama won 77 percent of all counties with a Whole Foods and just 29 percent of all counties with a Cracker Barrel."

And as with Whole Foods, so with Jews and immigrants—they're all stand-ins for liberal voting patterns. So if you knew that Squirrel Hill was not just an urban neighborhood but also a historically Jewish urban neighborhood, whose Jews had largely stayed when other white ethnic populations moved to the suburbs, then your certainty that its population was liberal should ramp up even more. And if you knew that it has lately become more diverse, welcoming large numbers of Asian immigrants who, along with the Jewish population, send their children to a high school that is over one-third Black, then you could pretty much push in all your chips: *These people vote blue.*

And you would be right. Ward 14, which almost maps right onto Squirrel Hill, gave Hillary Clinton over 80 percent of its votes in the 2016 election. But it would be a mistake to read too much into that level of support for the more liberal candidate. To be sure, Squirrel Hill resembles other urban, liberal neighborhoods in lots of ways, and someone relocating from the Upper West Side of Manhattan, Silver Lake in Los Angeles, or Jamaica Plain in Boston, and looking for a slice of home in Pittsburgh, might choose to live in Squirrel Hill. But Squirrel Hill is very much its own place, too, and a new arrival from those neighborhoods might be surprised by how conservative it feels.

It's more religious, for one thing. Houses of worship play a big part in its sense of identity, even for people who don't attend them. And not just synagogues but Sixth Presbyterian, Mister Rogers's old church (and, at the time of the shooting, still his widow's), Calvary Episcopal in the nearby Shadyside neighborhood, the Roman Catholic cathedral in Oakland, the Unitarian society, and others. Not everyone belongs, but everyone respects belonging. And a large sector of Squirrel Hill society is very obviously observant: the Orthodox Jews. And they are, politically, a relatively conservative bunch. While they may be comfortable voting for Democrats in local elections, they tend to be slightly more skeptical of Democrats in national elections. Democrats are pro-choice, which many Orthodox Jews are not, and Democrats are seen as less friendly to Israel, which worries the Zionists in the Orthodox community.

Partly as a result, in the 2016 election, some Jewish neighborhoods in Wards 14 and 15, which cover the East End of Pittsburgh, showed substantial support for Donald Trump. In Ward 14, District 27, Trump got 26 percent of the vote, and in District 28, which covers the little enclave of Swisshelm Park, he got 34 percent, the highest in the ward. Next door in Ward 15, which embraces most of the more Orthodox neighborhood of Greenfield, south of Squirrel Hill, Trump got 28 percent in District 7, 26 percent in District 10, and 36 percent in District 11. These numbers are not huge, but they suggest that even the most liberal

Squirrel Hill voters—like those in District 13, where almost 92 percent of ballots cast were for Clinton—live near, and are socially entwined with, plenty of Trump voters.

And if these liberal voters travel around greater Pittsburgh and Allegheny County, they will encounter lots of Republicans. If you take the urban core of Pittsburgh out of Allegheny County, you're left with an aging white population that likes to hunt—and even if you leave Pittsburgh in, you still have a city where the liberals live next to, and are interspersed with, conservative neighbors. Observers of Pennsylvania politics tell an old joke about how Pennsylvania is Philadelphia on one end, Pittsburgh on the other, and Alabama in between. That's a bit of an exaggeration, but it gets at something real. For a blue state, Pennsylvania—as recent presidential elections have shown—is not all that blue. Its population is the eighth oldest in the country, with 18.2 percent of its residents over the age of sixty-five, and old people are more conservative than young people. It's over 76 percent white (it's the nineteenth-whitest state in the country), and nearly all its nonwhite people are concentrated in two metropolitan areas, on opposite sides of the state. It has very gun-friendly laws—no permit needed to carry a gun in your home or place of business—and a strong hunting culture.

In fact, as absurd as it sounds to those who see Pennsylvania as part of the Northeast, western Pennsylvania shares more of a soul with West Virginia, its neighbor to the south, than it does with Philadelphia. This is coal country, and the *Pittsburgh Post-Gazette,* which is still the big daily newspaper for some subscribers in West Virginia (and used to be read by far more of them), covers the energy industry closely. Some Pittsburghers have country houses in the West Virginia hills. People from western Pennsylvania hunt in West Virginia, and vice versa. The Jewish community has a special tie to West Virginia: generations of Pittsburgh Jews have attended Emma Kaufmann Camp in Morgantown, West Virginia, which is run by Pittsburgh's Jewish Community Center, the one where Jerry Rabinowitz's funeral was held.

One analysis of the 2016 election pointed out that Pittsburgh, if taken as a metropolitan statistical area, went barely for Trump. "With 50.2 percent of the vote in the Census-defined metropolitan statistical area," the urbanist website *CityLab* wrote, "Pittsburgh was the second-largest metro area where Trump won a majority, topped only by Dallas–Fort

Worth. Tampa–St. Petersburg–Clearwater and Phoenix-Mesa-Scottsdale are the only larger metros where he garnered a plurality of the vote."

And so when President Donald Trump announced on Saturday evening, in Murphysboro, Illinois, where he had traveled for a speech, that he would visit Pittsburgh, the Jewish residents were split about what to do. They were split not so much on Trump himself—again, most Squirrel Hill Jews didn't vote for him—but on how to receive the presidential visit. They were divided in a way that liberal Jews in other neighborhoods would not be. First, because in Squirrel Hill's close-knit Jewish geography, even anti-Trump Jews were likely to know, feel warmly toward, and even love a Trump voter, and second, because Squirrel Hill is a fundamentally traditionalist place, not radical or even particularly countercultural. It's the kind of place where someone who drives two miles once a week to the Whole Foods in the East Liberty neighborhood still makes a point of buying some of her staples at the Jewish-owned Giant Eagle supermarket on Murray Avenue. People respect the old ways, the old stores, and the old synagogues, and that respect extends to the office of president.

Hence the variety of responses. Activists like Tammy Hepps and her colleagues in Bend the Arc began to plan a march; they would soon find themselves negotiating with groups farther to the left who argued for more defiant action than Bend the Arc was prepared to undertake. Still others had reservations about Trump's coming—believed that he was grandstanding, regretted that his visit would take attention away from the week of funerals and mourning, wondered why he didn't wait a week or two—but weren't prepared to take to the streets. Most local Democratic politicians came out against a presidential visit. Then again, some believed that a presidential visit was entirely appropriate; after all, how would it look if the president *didn't* come? Others might have preferred that the president not come, but so long as he was coming, Jewish tradition, and basic manners, dictated that he be received hospitably; this seemed to be the position of Jeffrey Myers, the rabbi of Tree of Life. And then there was a small faction of admirers who were excited to meet the man they had voted for.

There was one more factor driving people's response to the presidential visit, a feeling less easily articulated than voting preferences but just as powerful: their varying responses to antisemitism. Even before the shooting, American Jews sensed that they were becoming a little less safe, and a little less beloved, than they were used to being. Many Jews, especially those who were engaged with synagogue life, who read local Jewish newspapers, or who had a lot of Jewish news in their Facebook feeds, had been aware for the prior five years that the Western world seemed to be entering one of its cyclical periods of antisemitism.

Beginning about 2015, violent antisemitism had been on the rise in countries like France and Germany. The violence ranged from low-level street thuggery to the most brutal violence, like the 2015 murders of four Jews in a kosher market in Paris, or the 2017 home invasion and murder of a sixty-five-year-old Parisian woman, a retired doctor who was beaten to death and then thrown from her balcony. It was often perpetrated by Muslims against Jews. But what troubled many American Jews more, as they looked across the Atlantic, was not the specific acts of violence but the governments' seeming impotence to protect the Jews. Antisemitic violence, Jews know, is nearly as old as Judaism and will never go away entirely, but Jews have been reassured by a recent development in the contemporary West: governments, instead of fomenting, tolerating, or participating in the brutalization of Jews, have been their protectors. That is one reason why the past few years had been a little unnerving for Jews who paid attention to trends in Europe. A new generation of right-wing populist leaders, two of whom had come to power in Hungary and Poland, others of whom had strong support in Germany, France, and elsewhere, were not sympathetic to Jews. They were trying to downplay their countries' culpability for the Holocaust (witness Andrzej Duda in Poland, or the Alternative für Deutschland leaders in Germany), or blame Jewish financiers for economic travails today (Viktor Orbán scapegoating George Soros in Hungary, for example). In France, the desire not to inflame tensions between Jews and Muslim immigrants led to the authorities' reluctance to treat brutal crimes against Jews as antisemitic. In Great Britain, Labour Party leader Jeremy Corbyn was widely viewed as hostile to Jews, in part because of his sympathy for radical Islamists (he characterized Hamas as being "dedicated [to] long-term peace and social justice") but also because of snide comments he had made about Jews, such as the time he said that certain Zionists, despite "having lived in this country for a very long time, probably all their lives . . . don't understand English irony"—basically, weren't proper Brits.

The rising temperature of antisemitism in Europe was largely invisible to most Americans. But to engaged or observant Jews, it was pretty hard to miss. And again, the seeming abandonment of Jews by government figures was, in its way, worse than, say, the attacks on Jews by North African immigrants in France. Jews had come to rely on governments to protect them. If that assurance was going away, maybe they had real reason to be scared.

Hence it was a relief—not unexpected, but still gratifying and reassuring—when the police, medics, FBI agents, and firefighters, the whole apparatus of the state, rushed to the defense of Pittsburgh's Jews. As melodramatic as it sounds, there was a feeling that whereas once upon a time world governments rounded up Jews, and whereas today they can seem indifferent to their plight, here in America the state was still on Jews' side.

"We obviously are so grateful it wasn't any more tragic than it already was," said Mollie Butler, a resident of Squirrel Hill, the day after the shooting. "And that's because of our first responders. That's because of our great police officers here in the city." She had brought her children to Tree of Life to give home-baked cookies to the police still on duty there. "The kids heard the sirens at our synagogue down the block, and we just told them, 'That's the sound of people saving your life.'" Later that

Outside the Rosenthal brothers' funeral

day she told her children that while "a crazy man did a terrible, hateful thing, and there are terrible, hateful people everywhere," she and her children were nevertheless lucky. "We live in a place where our policemen care about us, and they come right away."

Obviously, not everyone in Pittsburgh, or even in the city's Jewish community, felt so affectionate toward the police. Still, Trump's visit has to be understood in the context of the gratitude that many Jews felt that weekend, when they saw the forces of law and order muster to save their lives. On October 27, 2018, America—the America of Donald Trump—tried to protect its Jews from a madman.

———

BUT THEN AGAIN, what if Donald Trump's America had created the madman? Liberal Jews could not overlook Trump's refusal to condemn the white nationalists of the Charlottesville rally the previous year, and they believed that he suborned antisemitic conspiracy theories. Besides, whether or not the president was himself an antisemite, antisemites seemed to think that he was an antisemite. What if the shooter was not mad but a rational actor who—intoxicated with a racist and antisemitic ideology for which the president seemed to have some sympathy, and emboldened by murderous groups who felt that they had an ally in the president—had done what he felt had to be done?

That was the position taken by Tammy Hepps and her fellow members of Bend the Arc: Jewish Action, the left-leaning Jewish social justice group. Founded in 2012 as a merger of two smaller groups, Bend the Arc was unusual in that it had nothing to say about Israel. Other organizations on the Jewish left, like Jewish Voice for Peace and IfNotNow, publicly opposed the Israeli presence in—they would say occupation of—the West Bank, and that issue dominated their public profile, no matter what other issues they tried to engage. To be identified with one of those organizations was to be identified with the anti-Zionist cause. Bend the Arc, by contrast, was a vehicle for liberal American Jews to work for liberal American causes: gun control, immigration, expanded health care, progress for people of color, and queer rights. So after the 2016 election, progressive Jews in Pittsburgh chose to affiliate their new, local group with Bend the Arc.

In other words, the Pittsburgh chapter of Bend the Arc basically existed to fight Donald Trump. And Trump, its members felt, had to answer for the Tree of Life shooting. To Trump's critics, it didn't take a genius to make the case. *Lord, the shooter connected the dots himself!* Tammy Hepps thought, when she read about what the shooter had written on social media, about immigrants, how they had to be stopped. "That message of his—this is perverse, I know—was a *gift*. He said, 'This is where I am getting this idea from, and why I am doing this thing.' We didn't have to make the argument. He said it outright." The statement she had helped write, in which Bend the Arc insisted that Trump renounce white nationalism before visiting Squirrel Hill, had gone viral in liberal circles. On Sunday night, Nancy Pelosi had included Stosh Cotler, the national head of Bend the Arc, along with the group's Pittsburgh leaders, on a conference call to talk about the shooting. From Tammy Hepps's keyboard to the Speaker of the House's ear.

Packed into Bend the Arc's statement was a map of how deftly the left has to maneuver to get its message out. On Sunday morning, at Yael Silk's house, still wearing borrowed pajamas, Hepps had managed to tone down a stridently anti-Trump statement and build a case aimed at a broader audience. In the draft developed overnight, by a Google Docs committee of Bend the Arc national staff and local organizers, the clear implication was that Trump was not welcome in town. Hepps rewrote the statement to allow for the possibility that Trump could be welcome, in theory: "President Trump, you are not welcome in Pittsburgh until you cease your assault on immigrants and refugees." And so forth. The *until* was important to Hepps, who wanted the statement to convey a spirit of optimism—*maybe*, she wanted say, *maybe he'll see he has gone too far.* Of course, there was almost no chance that Trump was going to make a clear denunciation of white nationalism—he had resisted such calls before—and certainly not on Bend the Arc's say-so. But Hepps wanted to signal an openness to cooperation.

"I have always felt I am one of the more centrist members of the group," Hepps said. Her Jewish world was more observant, and also somewhat more politically diverse, than the world that some members of Bend the Arc lived in. She had a good number of Orthodox friends; she was an admirer of Daniel Yolkut, the Orthodox rabbi of Poale Zedeck, and attended his classes from time to time. Her point was this: anyone was welcome, as long as they rejected white nationalism. The president, lefties, righties, the Orthodox—anyone.

———

INCLUDING NON-JEWS. Gentile allies were everywhere in the days after the shooting.

Tracy Baton, for example. She was chair of the local Women's March committee, the Pittsburgh branch of the organization that arose after the first anti-Trump Women's March, in January 2017. And Baton, who had done yeoman labor for the teenagers, played a powerful role as a Black Gentile ally for Tuesday's march, too.

Baton, who was fifty-five years old at the time of the Tree of Life shooting, was used to being the "Shabbos goy," as she joked, using the old-fashioned term for a non-Jew paid to perform tasks forbidden to Jews on the Sabbath, like turning on lights or putting a flame under the teakettle. Baton was a Shabbos goy metaphorically—she had helped Jews with their political work, been a local fixer and connector in the progressive community—but her mother had been a Shabbos goy literally, having worked for an Orthodox family that ran the only kosher catering business in Harrisburg, where Baton had spent her early years. The matriarch of that family, Dolores, used to come over to Baton's house to watch the soap operas with her mom.

When Baton was seven, her family relocated to Pittsburgh, and Baton briefly attended Allderdice High School before graduating from McKee Place, a small "hippie school" in the Oakland neighborhood that has since closed. Baton stayed in Pittsburgh, became a social worker, and joined the 14th Ward Democratic Club. People on the left like to talk about intersectionality, how we are all the sum of multiple identities, but Baton pretty much *is* intersectionality. "I am Black, queer, and Mennonite," she said, proudly. Her grandson is Black and Jewish. And in the logistical planning for Tuesday's march, there she was.

"I said, 'He is coming in twenty-four hours'"—President Trump, that is—"'and y'all are at funerals, and cleaning bodies and cleaning for funerals, so we have to do this.'" As the Jews were enfolded in their grief, and tending to the obligatory rituals of mourning, it was the job of Gentile allies to support them.

In addition to offering her contacts and her procedural know-how, Baton advised the other Gentiles on how to be good allies to the Jews. When she saw a Facebook post from Tom Prigg, a suburban politician who had lost a Democratic primary for Congress in May, announcing an anti-Trump event, Baton shut that down. "I got on the phone and said, 'Take that down, that is not your lane. You are not Jewish and not from Squirrel Hill, and that is not your lane.'" Prigg took down the post—though, as he later told me, he actually has Jewish ancestry: two of his great-grandparents fled Austria before World War II.

———

ACCORDING TO ONE REPORTER on the scene, *Air Force One* touched down on Tuesday at Pittsburgh International Airport shortly before 3:55 p.m.[*]

"As President Trump's plane lands outside Pittsburgh on Tuesday afternoon, a crowd is already gathering at the intersection of Beechwood and Forbes in Squirrel Hill, just a few blocks away from the Tree of Life Synagogue," read an account from a different reporter, for the *Pittsburgh Current,* a weekly newspaper. "It's a diverse crowd. There are seniors, college students and children. Some heads wear yarmulkes, some wear hijabs and others sport the pink cat-eared hats of the Women's March. Some chat about the funerals they attended this morning. Some only know of the victims what they have read.

"All of them have two things in common. First, they are grieving. . . .

"The second thing they all have in common is that they do not want President Trump to come to Pittsburgh. But, he is here. And so are they.

"The street rapidly fills with people. Many of them are holding homemade signs that express why they feel President Trump is unwelcome. NEONAZIS ARE NOT 'VERY FINE PEOPLE,' one sign reads. WE DO BRIDGES NOT WALLS, reads another."

The marchers filed "past Squirrel Hill homes decorated for Halloween. The crowd is full of images. On signs and on shirts, there are Stars of David, Pride flag rainbows, cardigan-clad Mr. Rogers, yellow bridges and that angry, orange face." They concluded the march on the steps of Sixth Presbyterian Church. "We started this event on Beechwood Boule-

———

[*] At 3:55 Julian Routh of the *Post-Gazette* tweeted a video of the president getting off the plane.

Squirrel Hill residents protesting President Trump's coming to town on October 30

vard, which is where Mr. Rogers used to live, and now we're ending this event at the church where Mr. Rogers used to pray," Jaime Forrest, one of the Bend the Arc organizers, said. "Pittsburgh is, as so many people say, the friendliest city in the country, and we are all steadfastly determined to keep it that way. Love thy neighbor—no exceptions."

Tammy Hepps stepped forward with Rachel Kranson, another Bend the Arc organizer. They stood in a semicircle of women, including Keshira haLev Fife; Sara Stock Mayo, the song leader who had been so instrumental in helping the students plan their Saturday-night event; and Cantor Julie Newman, who within the year would be hired as a music leader for the grieving congregation Dor Hadash. "For the past three years," Hepps said, her words directed at the president, "your words and your policies have emboldened a growing white nationalist movement!" Around her, protesters listened silently, holding signs that read MR. ROGERS' NEIGHBORHOOD IS NO PLACE FOR HATE and SOCIAL-IST STUDENTS—A STUDENT MOVEMENT FOR THE 99 PERCENT. An old woman in a purple parka sat in a wheelchair, holding up a handmade cardboard sign reading I FULLY DENOUNCE WHITE NATIONALISM.

"Song sheets are distributed through the crowd," the *Current* reported, "so that all of the attendees can join together in song as they

(Left to right) Sara Stock Mayo, Sasha King, and Tammy Hepps
at the anti-Trump march

begin to march in the direction of the synagogue where Trump is due to
visit along with the First Lady, his daughter Ivanka and son-in-law Jared
Kushner." Led by the guitar and voice of Mayo, the people sang "Ozi
v'Zimrat Yah," "My Strength and God's Song," and Menachem Credi-
tor's beloved Hebrew melody "Olam Chesed Yibaneh," "I Will Build
This World from Love." The lyrics continue: "And you must build this
world from love . . . And if we build this world from love . . . Then God
will build this world from love."

This account, in a small, left-leaning paper, describes the march as
Bend the Arc would have it remembered: peaceful, cooperative, with
a diverse crowd of attendees "who number in the thousands." Hepps
heard it was a crowd of five thousand. *The Washington Post* put it at
two thousand. The *Post-Gazette,* whose owner, John Block, was widely
thought to be a Trump supporter (correctly, as Block confirmed to
me) and was frequently at odds with his liberal newsroom employees,
played down the protest, describing it as a bit of a minor distraction to
the Trump visit: "Shortly before Mr. Trump arrived at the synagogue, a
crowd grew at Northumberland Street and Shady Avenue. Traffic slowed
more than usual. Police told people to get out of the street and onto the
sidewalk. . . . Tensions spiked at this intersection as marchers coming

from Beechwood Boulevard met police with sirens blazing, and at least one man was wrestled away by officers." The article was solicitous of the marchers but focused as much on their gratitude to the police as on their disdain for Trump: "As the march proceeded down Northumberland, singing softly its prayer as before, they passed the Zone 4 police station. That was when they broke into a loud and sustained ovation of clapping and cheers for the public safety workers. 'Thank you! Thank you! Thank you!' "

———

WHEN THE SHOOTING OCCURRED, Tova Weinberg, Squirrel Hill's most famous matchmaker, was already in the process of leaving town. In 2014 she and her husband, a pulmonologist, had sold their home of thirty-three years, three blocks from Tree of Life, and moved into a condominium on the same block as the Jewish Community Center. They were downsizing in preparation for their long-planned move to Jerusalem, where they had owned an apartment since 1991. Three of their five children and nineteen of their twenty-five grandchildren lived in Israel, and, as Modern Orthodox Jews, Tova and her husband had long aspired to end their years in the Promised Land. Tova was living out of boxes, slowly disassembling her apartment; she would leave for good that January.

In Israel, her husband would continue his work as a doctor—in 2019 he would found the first adult cystic fibrosis clinic in the Middle East—and she would continue to work for SawYouAtSinai, the dating site that she had cofounded in 2003. SawYouAtSinai was never as famous or as popular as JDate, the uncontested online champion of Jewish lonely hearts, but it had carved out a substantial niche, especially among Orthodox and other tradition-minded Jews. Meanwhile, she was still in Pittsburgh, still going to Poale Zedeck every Shabbat, which is where she was when Rabbi Yolkut announced from the front of the room that there was a shooter at Tree of Life.

Like Tammy Hepps, Jonathan Perlman, and so many others, Tova Weinberg had her own synagogue, and then she had her bigger community, the whole neighborhood. For example, Joyce Fienberg, one of the victims, attended Tree of Life, but she had an Orthodox niece who had taught for many years at Hillel Academy, the Orthodox day school where Weinberg sent her five children. To some in the Orthodox community of Squirrel Hill, Joyce was an honorary member, and when Weinberg heard what had happened at Tree of Life, her thoughts went to Joyce. And then they went to "the boys": "Cecil and David were the greeters on Murray Avenue!" Weinberg said. *Everybody* knew them. So despite being firmly ensconced in the Orthodox world, Weinberg knew three members of Tree of Life.

Actually, she knew four. After dark, when Shabbat was over, Weinberg's husband, Joel, got a text message from a friend: "Is Jerry at your house?"—Jerry Rabinowitz, the doctor, liberal Reconstructionist Jew, and, as it turns out, friend of the Weinbergs'. "Because Jerry sometimes, from shul, he comes to our house—he's a doctor, with Joel, they're colleagues." This was around six-thirty—sundown was at 6:22 p.m. in Pittsburgh—and the names of the victims still had not been released, even though bits and pieces had leaked out; at this point, Miri Rabinowitz knew that her husband had died, but the rest of Squirrel Hill did not.

So on Tuesday, when Trump and the march against Trump came to Squirrel Hill, Weinberg did not feel like a passive onlooker. Few of the Jews in Squirrel Hill did, of course; everyone had a stake. Since Saturday, their neighborhood had been at the center of the known universe, and now the most famous man in the world, the widely loved and loathed president, had arrived. Weinberg was in an unusual position, being a friend of the Fienberg family and of Jerry Rabinowitz *and* being a bona fide Trump voter. She was excited to get close to her president, and even to have a little fun with his critics.

"This whole Trump visit, you had a lot of people—these liberals, very, very liberal," Weinberg said, bemused. "I like liberals, I like right and left . . . but not such *extremes*." She couldn't understand why the liberals were so upset about the president coming. After all, she said, the first responders, like the police and firefighters, "they wanted him!" And "the people in the hospital—they would have liked to see him, you know? But no one thought about that."

So when Tuesday afternoon came, Weinberg took matters into her own hands. "It was a beautiful day," she said, "and I decided I'm going to ride my bike, and antagonize everybody, because that's what I like to do! I see a group of my friends—well, not my friends, but people from the health club, with a sign that says FUCK TRUMP!" Weinberg walked over to the man who had the sign hung on string around his neck. "I said, 'Good for you. I am so proud of you! You wear your homosexuality on your chest, and it's so wonderful that you want to sleep with the president! Good for you! Good for you! You're attracted to him.'"

She got back on her bicycle and rode over to another street corner where protesters were massed. "I see this woman—I see her often, a very snobby Jewish woman with her dog. And I said, 'What's all the hoopla?' She said, 'President Trump is coming.' She said, 'I wish I had a revolver. I'd shoot him.' I said, 'Is that nice? Is that nice? Eleven people just got killed. Are you out of your mind?'" She walked past protesters from the left-wing Jewish group IfNotNow, "very negative people about Israel," and wondered what their problem was. She saw a Presbyterian minister, a woman, carrying on about how Trump was "ruining the shiva." Weinberg smiled at the woman, completed her circuit, then bicycled home.

———

THE PRESIDENT ARRIVED OUTSIDE Tree of Life forty-five minutes after touching down at the airport and well after the protests were under way. He came with a small entourage including his wife, his daughter Ivanka, and her husband, Jared Kushner. Jeffrey Myers, the synagogue's rabbi, greeted the family outside the synagogue and brought them inside, where they stayed for eighteen minutes. The rabbi had agreed to receive the president and meet with him, a decision that angered some of his congregants and pleased others. The most common response I heard was something like, "What could he do? A rabbi has to meet with everyone." Myers never said what he and Trump discussed, but Trump's spokeswoman, Sarah Huckabee Sanders, said that they lit eleven candles and shook hands with FBI investigators. According to later reports, the president never saw the crime scene. They emerged just after five o'clock, and the rabbi led the Trumps to the eleven white wooden Stars of David delivered two days earlier by Greg Zanis. There they were joined by Ron Dermer, Israel's ambassador to the United States. Following the Jewish custom of using small stones to honor the dead, the president placed a stone on one of the Stars of David. It was a gray and quiet afternoon, and the only sounds were the flashes and clicking of cameras. Melania Trump took a small white flower off a tray she was holding and placed it

Jeffrey Myers, the rabbi of Tree of Life, with the Trumps
after taking them inside the synagogue

on one of the crosses to which a Star of David was affixed. It was a conspicuously non-Jewish thing to do—Jews don't typically place flowers on graves—but it seemed to fit the moment.

From the synagogue, Trump's party went to UPMC Presbyterian Hospital, several minutes away, where he visited with Tyler Pashel, a police officer who had injured his knee responding to the shooting, and met with two police officers who had been discharged already. Some reports suggested that he looked in on police officer Tim Matson, who was still in intensive care. Afterward the president met with Margaret Durachko, Richard Gottfried's widow. She "wanted to meet the president and let him know that people wanted him there," spokeswoman Sanders told the press.

After the visit to the hospital, Mr. Trump's motorcade left, and he departed on *Air Force One* at seven-thirty p.m.

———

TO THOSE OUTSIDE Squirrel Hill, the afternoon came and went, a bit of local color they heard about on television: plane lands, president and his party make visits, photos are snapped, all in time to make the local news.

But to those in its path, a presidential visit is like a violent windstorm: electrifying, terrifying, cinematic, then gone, leaving scarcely any sign that it was ever there, just a little debris in the road and your mussed-up hair. To the anti-Trump marchers, the visit was a moment of epochal unity, when divisions on the left closed up, when religious symbolism and political conviction merged into a fluent language of protest, dignified and powerful. To the few conservatives watching from the sidewalks, the march was a big nothing, an immature tantrum by leftists who couldn't see that Donald Trump was a great friend to Israel and the Jews, a man brave enough to stand up to the antisemitic mullahs in Iran, and the proud dad to a daughter who had converted to Orthodox Judaism.

And for one Squirrel Hill resident, a University of Pittsburgh sociologist named Joshua Bloom, the Trump visit meant going to jail. The entire day, in all the waves of protest under the banners of various groups, he was the lone person arrested. The way he tells it, it was nothing he had planned.

On Saturday morning, Bloom had been doing the dishes when his twelve-year-old daughter's phone started "blowing up" with text messages, including one from her friend who lived across the street from Tree of Life, "who is hearing that machine-gun fire and seeing all these people with, you know, military weapons outside the window."

Bloom felt two emotions at once.

First, there "was just this feeling like I had to protect my kids. . . . I'm feeling like they're Jewish, and *here's this guy*," Bloom said. "You know, when they started reporting things, one of the early things was this thing about 'All Jews must die'"—not the shooter's specific words, but yes, the general idea. But Bloom also felt that this attack was part of structural trends that went beyond the Jews. All presidents bring corporate executives and military men into their cabinet, but none before Trump had espoused such an illiberal governing philosophy. "Fascism," Bloom said, "combines xenophobic authoritarianism with strong finance and military political leadership." The "xenophobic authoritarianism" was Trump's specialty, and that was never good for Jews or other outsider peoples.

As Trump's visit approached, Bloom kept tabs on how liberals and leftists were responding. He had friends in Bend the Arc, he read their statement, and he liked their framing: Trump was welcome, but *only* if he renounced white nationalism. It was the right thing to say. And yet the more Bloom thought about it, the more he felt that words were only a beginning.

"I just felt like the statement was really right—and I also just felt like the statement wasn't enough," he said. "And so what I decided to do, what I really wanted to do, was to just stop him from getting to the temple. . . . That statement from Bend the Arc said, *You know, you're not welcome.* I was like, *Yeah, you're not welcome, and you can't come!* You know? Like, just saying this to him symbolically, but then having him do his photo op with his son-in-law at the temple, with the rabbi?" To Bloom, that just seemed grotesque.

Bloom talked with some friends about organizing a sit-in at the four intersections around Tree of Life, so that there was no way the presidential motorcade could approach the synagogue. What if he could get a mass of people to move right into the intersections, sit down, lock arms, and refuse to move? They would go limp, and the police would have to carry them away one by one. Even if they were all cleared out eventually, they'd eat up enough time that maybe the president, always on a tight schedule, would have to skip his visit. And even if he got through, the images of uniformed police officers clearing out hundreds of Jews, praying and singing liturgical melodies like "Oseh Shalom"—"Make Peace"—would ricochet around television and the internet, offering a visual lesson in who was for peace, and who for violence.

But after talking it over for a bit, they gave up on the idea. "It was just logistically too hard, in too short a period of time," Bloom said. They couldn't get that many people willing to risk arrest, not without days of organizing and planning.

When the day came, Bloom walked over to Tree of Life, just to be there. Outside the synagogue, he joined a crowd of hundreds of people; it was the mourners and onlookers. For the moment, there were very few protesters there.

After four o'clock, as Trump's motorcade was moving from the airport toward Squirrel Hill, the crowd outside Tree of Life began to swell. The police, who at first had just let the crowd be, began to move in, informing people that they had to move away from the intersection. When the police got to him, Bloom was in a state: "crying and meditating," as he remembered it, still mourning his abortive plan for a mass act of civil disobedience, trying to figure out what, if anything, his presence meant. As the police informed him that he had to move out of the intersection, he couldn't think of anything to do but capitulate. Without a word, he began trudging along the sidewalk, away from the synagogue.

Immediately, Bloom was overwhelmed with regret. *"Actually letting myself be removed?"* he thought. "Because I felt like, you know, *I'm ceding this ground to Trump?"* After about a minute, he and hundreds of others parked themselves at the intersection of Shady and Northumberland, yards from the firehouse where David Rosenthal used to shoot the breeze on Saturday mornings before services. Bloom was kicking himself. Why had he let the police move him along? What if he had stood his ground—would others have stood with him?

The Bend the Arc protesters were still some blocks away, but more people were arriving in the vicinity of Tree of Life, and, unable to get close to the building itself, they were being sluiced off toward the crowd on Northumberland. Cars were rolling by, slowing down to catch a look, plus the noise drew more curious onlookers. The police weren't pushing people any farther down Shady Avenue, so Bloom found himself in the middle of an impromptu town square. Angry at Trump—and at himself—he began to talk to the crowd. "So the crowd grew," he recalled, "and I was talking with the crowd about, you know, how it wasn't *okay*— that here we were, this was our neighborhood, and we're Jews, and we were pushed out, so that Trump can come and do a photo op for his politics."

As Bloom kept speaking, the sound of the Bend the Arc march got closer, and soon the march was in sight. The marchers—walking slowly, singing in Hebrew—flowed into the intersection at Northumberland, joining Bloom and hundreds of others in a single mass of mourners, united in grief and in antipathy for the president.

When the Bend the Arc marchers merged into the crowd waiting at Northumberland, the organizers handed out small pieces of black paper. "The crowd is instructed to lift them up in unison, and then to tear them apart," the *Current* reported. "This is Kriah, a Jewish tradition and a ritual of mourning. Kriah, or keriah, is a Hebrew word that means 'tearing.' The tearing of one's clothes is an expression of grief and anger that is traced back to the patriarch Jacob, who tore his garments when he believed his son Joseph was dead." At the intersection, the only sound

Keriah, tearing black strips in mourning

from the crowd was the paper ripping. The ripping felt good: they had made noise, taken action, and let Trump—and the world—know how they felt.

Bloom was frustrated. "We had done what we could do," he said, with a note of defeat. Out of ideas, he decided he would just walk home. And then, from up Shady Avenue, from the direction of Tree of Life and the direction the marchers had come, he saw the lights and heard the motorcycles of the presidential motorcade.

Now he was baffled. Wherever Trump was heading next—the hospital, as it turned out—there were multiple ways out of Squirrel Hill. All Bloom could figure was that Trump and his people "were just trying to exert their muscle, you know? . . . Just to add insult to injury, they decided to push the motorcade right through these thousands of people. . . . I was standing right there at the corner of Shady and Northumberland, and these motorcycles and those sirens—*Whee-ee!*" The police began yelling, "Get out of the way, get out of the way!" "And all these peaceful protesters, they're right there," Bloom said, "thousands of us, you know?"

It was just too much. The intrusion of Trump's black motorcade, snaking through Squirrel Hill, a phalanx of police and quasi-military

Josh Bloom getting arrested

and Secret Service, with their black sunglasses, their weapons, and their little earpieces—it didn't look the way America should. Bloom was still beating himself up for his decision half an hour earlier to leave the intersection in front of Tree of Life, and he was damned if he was going to be shoved aside by police again. "I was thinking, *Get out of the way—are you crazy?*" No way was he going to do it. "So I just sat down. That's all, you know? I was just like, *No, I'm not. I'm not getting out of the way.* So I sat down, and that was it."

The police arrested Bloom and placed him in the back of a paddy wagon. He was alone. They had prepared for large-scale disorder, but it had never come. Instead, they just had sociology professor Josh Bloom. By and large, the police were pretty decent, Bloom said. He had talked with a couple of them earlier in the day, and they'd had pleasant exchanges. Like everyone in Squirrel Hill, Bloom was mindful of how police had rushed toward danger on Saturday. They took him to jail, where he spent the night "with thirty guys in the cell who were just in for whatever, for drugs and guns."

Bloom was released in the morning and never charged. He was glad he'd done something. "I didn't feel like I could sit on the sidelines," he said.

9

The Symbols

Almost immediately there were signs of the attack everywhere, visual echoes. To remember the victims, people were making art, icons, representations, and putting them in windows, in trees, in shops, on doorsteps. For example, on November 2, 2018, the day of Rose Mallinger's funeral, Squirrel Hill residents stepping into the newsstand on Forbes Avenue would have seen something very unusual on the cover of the *Pittsburgh Post-Gazette.* There, at the top of page A1, the premium space for presidential elections and Steelers victories, ran a headline in Hebrew.

It was the first four words of the Mourner's Kaddish, the prayer Jews recite in honor of the dead. By tradition, the prayer is recited daily during the year after a Jew has lost a parent; those who have lost a spouse, sibling, or child recite the Kaddish, with a quorum of ten, for thirty days after the death.* After the first year, one says the Kaddish for the loved one on each anniversary of the death, according to the Hebrew calendar. In the year after the Tree of Life shooting, Jews across the country said Kaddish daily for the eleven dead in Pittsburgh. Traditions teach that saying Kaddish nudges the departed soul into the world to come (Jews don't gener-

---

* Some say eleven months, not a year. Most follow the Hebrew calendar, in which months are different. And as a final clarification, the Kaddish is not only for mourners; it's an important prayer that is recited communally any time there is a quorum of ten. But one of the recitations in each prayer service is set aside for mourners in particular to recite, and that is the Mourner's Kaddish, which is often just shortened to "the Kaddish" or "Kaddish."

The *Post-Gazette*'s Hebrew headline

ally talk about Heaven, and Jewish theology is hazy about what comes after death), but the prayer really functions to soothe those left behind. It's one of the few prayers that even secular Jews may recognize; it has been part of the worship service for about a millennium. The practice of mourners reciting Kaddish also functions to marshal community: since the Kaddish may be recited only with a quorum of ten, Jews call on each other to show up to prayers if a mourner might be present.

So to see the beginning of the Kaddish—*"Yitgadal v'yitkadash shemei rabba"*—as a headline, in a Hebrew typeface, was moving for Jews who knew what they were reading, and visually arresting for everyone unaccustomed to seeing headlines in anything but the Roman alphabet.

The headline was the idea of *Post-Gazette* editor David Shribman, a veteran newspaperman who had taken over the Pittsburgh daily in 2003, after a long career at *The New York Times, The Wall Street Journal,* and *The Boston Globe,* where in 1995 he won a Pulitzer Prize for his Washington coverage. Shribman is a Jew of the proudly interfaith persuasion: he married a Catholic woman and had two daughters; the family always belonged to a temple but also celebrated Christian holidays; and one of the daughters is now a Reform rabbi. He also had a deteriorating relationship with his boss, *Post-Gazette* publisher John Block, a quirky, pocket-watch sort of man who resembles the banker in the board game Monopoly and whose Jewish family has owned the paper for three generations. Block, whose mother was not Jewish, attended boarding school at Hotchkiss before matriculating at Yale, and he had no relationship to the local Jewish community, which was untrue of the editor he employed. It was well known in the newsroom that Block—who, as noted earlier, unlike nearly all the journalists he had hired, was presumed to be a Trump voter—had taken to second-guessing his editor-in-chief.

It was in the middle of the night on Wednesday, turning into Thursday morning, that Shribman, who had hardly slept since Saturday, had the idea for the headline in Aramaic. (The Kaddish is written in Hebrew script, but the language is actually Aramaic, the early Middle Eastern language spoken by Jews in Palestine, including Jesus.) When he got into the office Thursday morning, he learned that the *Post-Gazette* was not equipped to print what he had in mind. "We don't have a Hebrew font," he said. "So I called Rabbi Gibson"—Jamie Gibson, the rabbi of Temple Sinai, the Reform temple on Forbes Avenue in Squirrel Hill, where Shribman was a member—"and I said, 'I need the first four words of the Kaddish in Hebrew.'" Shribman explained what he had in mind, and then Gibson emailed him the lettering, using the Hebrew font on his own computer.

Shribman still was not sure if he should run with the headline, fearing some people might be offended. Later he remembered that on Thursday he asked several other people—he couldn't remember who—who told him, "You can't do that." But he was slowly becoming convinced that his instincts were right. On Thursday night, he had dinner at the Milky Way kosher restaurant with Gibson and two rabbis visiting from out of town. They were encouraging of his idea, and after dinner he went back to the office, where the newspaper's design director, Diane Juravich, had already prepared a mockup of the headline. Shribman was so jazzed that he did something he almost never did: he gave advice to the designers. "I said, 'No, I want it a little bit bigger, a little more white space,' and we fooled with it. It was the most hands-on thing I had done in years." His managing editor, Sally Stapleton, chose the picture to go below the headline, a photograph of funeral-goers huddled graveside under umbrellas. Shribman approved the page, then sent it to the presses. He did not show it to the paper's owner.

Friday morning Shribman was at the St. Clair Hospital branch in the suburb of Bethel Park. His doctor had sent him to be screened for cancer, so he was in for tests, which came back negative. But while he was there, "being zapped and stuff," he checked his phone and saw that his headline had caused a sensation. CNN.com covered it, as did the online publications *Vox, HuffPost,* and *The Daily Beast,* the Washington, D.C., publication *The Hill,* Israel's daily *Haaretz,* and many more. The website of the Jewish *Forward* wrote that "the course of history occasionally brings a front page that proves impossible to forget. *The Chicago Tribune's* premature, incorrect declaration 'Dewey Defeats Truman' on November 3, 1948; *The New York Times's* 'U.S. Attacked' headline on September 12, 2001; the ubiquitous 'Nixon Resigns' headlines on August 9, 1974. For many, the *Pittsburgh Post-Gazette's* front page of November 2, 2018, has entered those ranks."

Nobody complained. As far as Shribman could tell, nobody was offended, "not a soul." On the internet, a few religious Jews and Hebrew-speakers noticed that the headline got the last letter of the last word, *rabba,* incorrect, substituting an unvoiced *heh* for an unvoiced *alef*— a mistake in the Hebrew that Gibson had sent to Shribman. Shribman was unfazed. "It was an innocent mistake," he said. "I got only two calls. Some Orthodox guy and some other Orthodox guy."

But Thursday evening, while still working on the next morning's paper, Shribman had gotten a message that the publisher wanted to see him. After he finally put the Friday paper to bed, he went into John Block's office. Shribman had already planned to step down as editor in August, after which he would be paid for a one-year sabbatical, as a kind of bonus. But now Block told Shribman to start his sabbatical early, on January 1 (which Shribman's contract allowed Block to do, according to Block). Shribman's editorship would be over, for good, in two more months. To this day, neither man will talk about the timing of Shribman's departure. I was told that Shribman's contract prohibited him from disparaging his employer, and all Block would say was that there was a "need for change" in the newsroom and that he needed "more of an inside-the-office editor as opposed to an outside-the-office editor, a celebrity editor." Block said that Shribman "was off doing other things most of the time."

Block had not much appreciated reading Shribman's op-ed column in *The New York Times* the day after the shooting, a raw, poignant essay that had been widely circulated on social media. In the *Times* piece, a love letter to his adoptive hometown, Shribman, a Squirrel Hill resident, wrote of Pittsburgh's history of tolerance, how welcoming it had been to waves of European immigrants, and remarked that "in the eternal mix of irony and tragedy that is the human story, an anti-Semitic rampage at the Tree of Life synagogue has inflicted deep wounds on perhaps the least anti-Semitic city in the country." But publishing on the *Times* op-ed page the day after the shooting seemed to sum up everything that made Block uncomfortable about the editor he had hired: the need for celebrity, the desire to have his work read by big-city sophisticates. (Shribman also wrote a regular column for the Toronto *Globe and Mail*.) "I didn't like the idea that he was constantly grandstanding for other media outside his remit for us," Block said.

Shribman had good reasons to run the piece in the *Times* and not in the paper that he edited. For one thing, it would reach a vastly larger audience. What's more, as a paean to Pittsburgh's virtues, the column was not intended for Pittsburghers themselves—it was a reminder to the rest of the world that the city was so much more than the worst thing that ever happened there:

"More than a third of this city is Catholic," Shribman wrote. "The bishop always interrupts his Midnight Mass processional—stopping at the seventh row from the altar every Christmas Eve—to give a hug to the rabbi whose synagogue is down the street from the cathedral. There are six kosher food establishments in a two-block area of town. Yet the city's signature sandwich is an unkosher mess of meat and creamy coleslaw, with fries mashed atop the glop.

"The garment of choice every Friday before a Steelers game is a black-and-gold Ben Roethlisberger or Antonio Brown shirt. Hours later, at sundown, the streets are full of Jewish men in the black garb of the Orthodox and the observant on their solemn march to Sabbath prayers."

By Thursday evening, as he was closing the paper, Shribman may have already suspected that his tenure was coming to an end. His relationship with Block had been rocky for years, and this would be as good a time as any for Block to make a switch, especially in what promised to be the biggest news year in Pittsburgh history. Despite his preppy pedigree, Block thought of himself as a man of the people, in opposition to the coastal, Ivy League–egghead type. Would Block have bridled at seeing a foreign language in seventy-point type? It was cosmopolitan, he might have thought, too hoity-toity; what would it do for the guy in the pub from the steel mill family? Or for one of their many readers in West Virginia? In theory, Shribman could do what he wanted with the headline; the newsroom had editorial independence from the business side of the operation, all the way up to the owner. In practice, however, running such an unusual A-1 headline, and refusing the boss the courtesy of having a peek, was a monumental screw-you to the big guy.

Asked about his decision, Shribman said only, "I didn't show it to anyone for fear that there would be pressure to kill it . . .

"I left the office knowing that the morning paper would have that Hebrew headline," said Shribman. "I felt that I had done my duty for Pittsburgh, that I had done my duty for the *Post-Gazette,* and that my work here was complete."

———

LATER ON THE DAY that the headline ran, Danielle Kranjec put her two children to bed at their home in Squirrel Hill and drove the short distance to the Hillel Jewish University Center, the hub for Jewish students at Pitt and Carnegie Mellon (as well as several smaller schools in the area). Her title was "senior Jewish educator," but Kranjec, a practicing Jew who had done graduate studies in medieval Jewish history, was the closest thing the students had to a campus rabbi; she was warm and funny and seemed younger than her thirty-nine years. Students looked to her.

It had been a difficult week for Jewish college students everywhere: away from home, often unsure about their own safety, trying to make Gentile friends and roommates understand why these murders felt so personal. They felt misunderstood, and perhaps guilty, for having been so close and survived. They felt as if they should show solidarity with their fellow Pittsburgh Jews, yet they had no idea how to do that. The center of Squirrel Hill was a five-minute drive away, but few Pitt or Carnegie Mellon undergraduates had ever taken in a movie at the Manor or bought shoes at Little's; their lives were on campus, in the classrooms, dormitories, and fraternity and sorority houses, and in the college bars in the Oakland neighborhood. If Jewish, they were probably not observant; if observant, they prayed at Hillel or at the campus Chabad house. They had never heard of Tree of Life.

Kranjec had to step into this gap, counseling, consoling, and hugging Jewish students who came to see her. In general, her Carnegie Mellon students were faring better. It was a smaller and more nurturing school than Pitt, its next-door neighbor, and its administration had acted immediately to show how seriously it took what had happened. The new president of Carnegie Mellon, Farnam Jahanian, had been formally installed the day before the shooting, and he canceled all the celebratory activities scheduled for the remainder of the weekend. He also canceled all the homecoming activities planned for alumni, including the football game, and the provost and many faculty showed up for a student vigil at seven o'clock that night.

Meanwhile, over at Pitt, many Jewish students felt lost. Afterward they would point to the symbolism of the football games: Carnegie Mellon had canceled its game, but Pitt had gone ahead with its home game against Duke. Drew Medvid was with the Pitt marching band—he plays mellophone—on the bus to Heinz Field when they all began to get texts about the active shooter at Tree of Life. Immediately "everyone wanted this game to be canceled," he remembered. At the game, there was a moment of silence for the victims (how many, nobody knew yet), but otherwise it was business as usual: "The coach didn't say anything, the marching band director didn't say anything." And the members of the band were not given permission to leave, which bothered Medvid, who is not Jewish but whose girlfriend was. "Jewish students begged to go home," he said, but they were ordered to stay.

The next day at band practice, the whole band was required to don hastily printed T-shirts that said, of course, STRONGER THAN HATE, per Tim Hindes's design. But students hated Pitt's STRONGER THAN HATE shirt. Although it bore a small Star of David above the school's name and the legend STRONGER THAN HATE below, the design was so reliant on the Pitt name, in Pitt's famous cursive typeface, that it just looked "like another piece of Pitt swag," as Kranjec later put it. Medvid recoiled from wearing the shirt. "I tried to refuse, but I couldn't," he said. "It was very much pushed on us."

By Thursday night, then, Kranjec was tired and dispirited. She wanted to be home with her husband and children. But she had said she'd show up at the challah-baking session being run by Challah for Hunger, a student group that sold bread and donated the money to fight hunger. The president, Emma Shapiro, had designated the event "Braiding Together Against Hate." She had solicited donations from students to sponsor a loaf of challah for "a family in Squirrel Hill." And now here Kranjec was with a team of students, late at night, baking. Before she left for the night, Kranjec posted a picture on Facebook of boxes and boxes of fresh challah, with the caption, "575 loaves of challah boxed and ready to go out to the community . . . smells like *ahavat chinam*"—baseless, boundless, unmerited love.

Challah for Hunger had promised that loaves would go to Squirrel Hill families, but students didn't know Squirrel Hill families. So they left it to Kranjec, who lived in Squirrel Hill and seemed to know everybody there. At about eleven p.m., she loaded a box of challahs into her car and drove back toward her neighborhood. She stopped at the Zone 4 police station. "All of the officers are changing shift and loading into their cars, and I get out and I thank them and I hand them these loaves of warm, delicious, fresh challah," Kranjec recalled. She then pulled up in front of the house of Alan Mallinger, who lived on her street—his mother was Rose, one of the eleven victims, whose funeral was the next day, and his sister, Andrea, had been wounded. "And I see that everyone is gathering, and all the lights are on. And I don't want to bother them, but I get out of the car and I knock on the door and I hand six loaves of warm challah to the family."

The next day, Friday, the last day of funerals, she spent the morning "driving from house to house, leaving challah loaves anywhere that I know I can." She left a challah on the front steps of Jonathan Perlman, the New Light rabbi who had narrowly escaped the killer, and his family. She brought a challah to her friend Kristen Keller, a librarian active in the Jewish community. She brought some loaves to her mother-in-law, who gave one of them to her neighbor Joe Charny, a Tree of Life member who had escaped the shooter.

"In some ways, delivering the challah felt like the smallest, most insignificant thing," Kranjec said. "In some ways it felt like the most important thing, the only thing I could be doing." After giving loaves to everyone she could think of, she had ten left. She saved them for Saturday morning, when she loaded them into her daughter's stroller and brought them to her synagogue, Beth Shalom, where she knew there would be a crowd the Sabbath after the killing.

ON THE MORNING of the shooting, Melissa Lysaght had got to the Starbucks she managed at five-thirty, in time for the six o'clock opening. When she unlocked the doors, it was just she and one "partner," as employees are called, working the counter. By the time of the shooting, there would be five employees in the building, doing the Starbucks thing, with that signature customer-is-right attitude that Starbucks, as much as any American company, has perfected. Satisfaction was high at this Starbucks, and like most Starbucks, it had a loyal group of regulars. On October 27, some of the regulars would be missing: it was a Saturday, and the Orthodox would be away, at least until Shabbat ended at nightfall.

Lysaght, thirty-nine years old, had grown up in Kittanning, a small town forty miles northeast of Pittsburgh. Baptized Episcopalian, she had mostly attended a Presbyterian church growing up, but now was seldom in church. She had started working at Long John Silver's in 1995, when she was still in high school, and in 2011, after sixteen years with the company, she was itching to leave—"It wasn't the company it had started out to be." Having grown up in a town with no Starbucks, Lysaght did not know much about the chain, but an uncle who followed the stock market had heard good things about its corporate culture and recommended that she check it out. She began working for Starbucks in 2011, and in 2016 she was asked to manage their important store at Forbes and Shady, the more visible of the company's two locations in Squirrel Hill.

At Starbucks, Lysaght got to know Jews for the first time, since many of them were and are frequent customers. The Orthodox have questions about which drinks and food items are kosher; she tries to get answers for them, and they are always educating her. "There are still a lot of things I have questions on, as far as what do you do on this holiday, do you fast or not do this?" she said. "There is still a lot I don't understand. And I definitely got an education to realize how much antisemitism had been around, how long it has been around. It's just mind-blowing to me."

Her telephone off, Lysaght learned about the attack on Tree of Life when she heard the sound of sirens outside her store. When she looked outside, she "observed vehicles racing north on Shady Avenue" and "noticed an ambulance darting across Forbes," according to an account she gave the *Jewish Chronicle*. Then one of her customers came inside and said, "Something must have happened on the corner of Shady and Wilkins." Within minutes, customers were staring at their phones, reading news briefs and getting texts. They began chattering about Tree of Life, the shooting, an active shooter on the loose. Lysaght called her district manager to ask what she should do. He told her to do whatever she thought best.

Lysaght consulted with her crew. "We didn't know where the shooter was," she said. "There were rumors he was in between Wilkins and Murray Avenue." She went from table to table, talking to customers who were looking at their laptops and phones, reading alerts and news stories. "I let them know I was locking the door on Shady—I said, 'Hey, we don't have all the details, but I am going to be locking the side door. If you don't feel safe, you are welcome to come in back.' Our store is such a fishbowl, with windows on the street." She had decided to leave the main door on Forbes open. More people were coming in than leaving.

It was a tough day for Lysaght and her staff, as they wondered "who we might not see come through our doors again." But staying open quickly proved to be the right move. Customers came, all morning and into the afternoon, when the students from Allderdice High School sat around the long table near the Forbes door to plan their vigil that night. If the Jewish Community Center became the de facto hub of the Jewish community for the next forty-eight hours, the Starbucks on Forbes became a secular satellite, a place where Jews and Gentiles—where Squirrel Hill—came to mix and drink, debate and decompress.

Late in the afternoon of the shooting, at about four-thirty, as the crowd was thinning out, and the students were deep in the planning for their event, Lysaght left to drive home. In the car, she sent a text to her husband's cousin, Nicole Flannery, a former art teacher in the Pittsburgh public schools, asking if she wanted to paint something meaningful in the big windows facing Shady Avenue. Lysaght knew that many pedestrians walking to Tree of Life to pay their respects would go right past the Starbucks. This was a chance to make truly public art. Lysaght gave her only one instruction: Flannery should include the words *kindness, love,* and *hope* in her design.

Flannery, who describes herself as "not a very strict Catholic," knew that it would be a daunting task. The attack was so terrible, and then there was the creepy fact that the alleged shooter was a fellow Baldwin native, somebody who attended her high school a few years before she got there. "I knew it was going to be important to her, the store, and the community," Flannery later told a reporter, "and I need to do this in a respectful way and I need to do it right."

First Flannery prayed. Then she went to Google. Looking for appropriate Jewish or biblical images, she found the Star of David; the tree of life, which is a metaphor for the Torah, or the Hebrew Bible; and the dove, which Noah sends out in the book of Genesis to see if the flood has receded—three images, one for each of the tall windows. She decided to put a heart around each of the symbols—"it was almost like a hug of a heart around each one," Flannery said. And finally she decided to render the words in both English and Hebrew. A former student of hers connected her with Danny Shaw, a local Orthodox Jew, who helped her with the Hebrew lettering. Flannery began painting the windows at five in the morning on Sunday, November 4, and she finished on the morning of Tuesday, November 6. In the final display, the Star of David inside

The iconic Starbucks windows Nicole Flannery painted

a heart got the legend *love,* in a curly cursive, along with *ahavah,* in Hebrew lettering; the tree inside the heart was captioned *kindness* and *hesed;* and below the dove were painted the words *hope* and *tikvah.*

As she painted, passersby were "knocking on the window or giving me a thumbs up," Flannery told the *Jewish Chronicle.* She wrote on Facebook that she "asked God for guidance during this entire process" and that "He was there with [her] through it all." Speaking with the *Chronicle,* she remembered one man who "was just walking by, going wherever he was going, and he just turned to see, because here I am painting. He stops and he looks, and he put his hand on his heart. . . . [He] started crying, and he had to walk away. . . . I think at that moment I realized this is God working through me, for whatever reason, and I just feel so blessed and so honored to be able to do that."

———

THE PAINTINGS ARE STILL in the Starbucks windows. They have become part of the Squirrel Hill artscape. A generation from now Allderdice students will sit down at the big table with their drinks, look at the reverse images, as seen from inside the store, and notice that there is Hebrew in the window, even though some of them may not know why. The STRONGER THAN HATE posters, with Tim Hindes's design based on the Steelers logo, seem to have taken up permanent residence in local shop windows. Right now they share space with assorted variations on a theme, like lists of the eleven who died and signs proclaiming opposition to racism, Islamophobia, and homophobia. But when all the others have been taken down for window washing, the Steelers-inspired poster will most likely get put back up. Like the Starbucks window, it is now part of Squirrel Hill.

Other visual motifs were omnipresent at first but disappeared with the seasons. The hand-knit Stars of David, which didn't go up until November, were somehow the most touching. In the month after the shooting, people from around the world heeded the call of Jewish Hearts for Pittsburgh, a Facebook group created October 30, and crocheted, knit, cut out of paper, or otherwise crafted small Stars of David with hearts in the middle, which were hung by string from trees, street signs, and doorknobs all over Squirrel Hill and beyond. The winter after the shooting, there were days when you could look up in the trees and see large snowflakes falling around the Stars of David, like some sort of heavenly wintry mix.

Jamie Lebovitz grew up in Squirrel Hill and now lives in the suburban South Hills. She volunteered to help distribute the stars, which had been collected by Ellen Broude, one of the Facebook group founders, who lived outside New York City and was driving the stars to Pittsburgh. On a day in mid-November, Lebovitz met with other volunteers in a room lent by Chatham University, across the street from Tree of Life. Lebovitz had helped create a list of places around Greater Pittsburgh where they could hang hearts; she wanted to get the artifacts, and their message, beyond just Squirrel Hill. She wanted to hang them from statues in downtown Pittsburgh. She wanted to hang stars from the Christmas tree at the ice-skating rink at PPG Place downtown. These were not just for Jewish Pittsburgh. "I went to the top of Mount Washington"—the hill that rises above the banks of the Monongahela and Ohio rivers—"and put one on top of the fencing over the overlook. . . . We wanted them to be seen."

Lebovitz decided that all the famous men made into statuary should get a Star of David. "I wanted to attach them to statues. I joked with some of the women, 'I know I'll get in trouble!' I tied one on Art

A homemade Star of David hanging from the H
on the Forward Avenue sign

Rooney's hand in front of Heinz Field. I attached one on Roberto Clemente's finger in front of PPG Field." Rooney was the founding owner of the Steelers; Clemente, the legendary Pittsburgh Pirates outfielder. "There was a statue representing the police dogs—I attached one onto the dog. I wanted to do the Mister Rogers statue, even though I didn't know where I could hang it from, but it was closed for repair, so you couldn't get near it."

As the sun began to go down, Lebovitz still had some stars left. She put them everywhere she could, gave them out to everyone who seemed they could use a star with a heart in the middle. "I saw a homeless woman in a wheelchair," Lebovitz said. She was a woman without legs whom Lebovitz had seen before, "a regular" among the beggars in Squirrel Hill. "She saw me, I said hello to her. I gave her five bucks, and a Jewish star."

10

The High School

T HE SATURDAY OF THE SHOOTING, most of the students who gathered in the afternoon at the big table at Starbucks were Jewish. The one student who did not identify as white was an interracial Allderdice High senior named Isabel Smith, known as Izzy. She lived in one of the nicest sections of Squirrel Hill, a ten-minute walk from Tree of Life, and she is from a classic Squirrel Hill overachiever family: both parents are doctors, her brother was at Yale, her sister at Northeastern. In less than a year, she'd be off to Oberlin. Her aunt, Tracy K. Smith, is a former poet laureate of the United States.

When Izzy heard about the shooting, she was attending an Urban League event for young Black women at the Penn State campus in McKeesport, just outside Pittsburgh. "Probably around ten, ten-thirty, or eleven, I started getting all these texts from people, like, 'How are you doing? Are you okay? Do you know what happened?' And I had no idea what had happened." One of the other students with her said that there had been a shooting at a church in Squirrel Hill, but Izzy soon learned that it was at Tree of Life. But then she couldn't figure out which synagogue was Tree of Life—"because, I mean, there's a lot of synagogues around Squirrel Hill." When she finally placed the synagogue in her mind, she realized it was the one she drove past every morning on her way to school. She began texting with her friend Marina Godley-Fisher, who told her that there was a meeting at Starbucks. When the conference ended midday, Izzy and some other students boarded a bus to return them to the Urban League offices downtown, whence they would proceed home. Since Izzy couldn't get to Starbucks for another few hours, she began calling around, seeing who would donate what for the Havdalah event that night. She got Squirrel Hill Flower Shop to offer flowers, and she reached management at the Giant Eagle supermarket, which said it would give something like 250 candles, far fewer than they ended up needing.* "We had grossly underestimated, but people brought their own supplies, which was great." When she got home, she immediately walked over to the Starbucks.

Izzy, who has Christian heritage but was raised with no particular religion, was close with a lot of white students. She was a top student, active in a wide array of clubs, the kind of compulsively busy student leader who commanded respect, and affection, across subcultures, cliques, microgroups, and racial divisions. Some of her best friends were Black, and some of her close friends, like Emily Pressman, were Jewish. She found the Saturday-evening Havdalah service, which she had helped plan, to be "inspiring," in particular because there were "a lot of people who weren't necessarily a big part of the Jewish community there."

At the same time, she couldn't help but notice, as a half-Black girl, that the deaths of eleven elderly Jews became an urgent, inescapable community-wide trauma in a way that the deaths of more Black boys and men, spread out over the year, didn't seem to. That recognition did not diminish her compassion for her Jewish friends, nor did it lessen the grief she felt as a human being and—this was big—as a Squirrel Hill native. But she had additional feelings that some of her white friends might not feel, or feel as deeply.

As it happened, the Black Student Union at Allderdice High met on Monday afternoons at three o'clock, after school, so they met the first day back after the shooting. As usual, they were in a classroom with their adviser, Michele Halloran. It was a tense meeting. "There were a lot of mixed feelings within the group about what had happened," Izzy recalled. "I mean, this past year, multiple Black teenagers in Pittsburgh died." In general, the students at the BSU meeting fell into one of two camps. "One was support, like, 'The Black community has felt this a

---

* In the end, Smith said, the other organizers said the flowers weren't necessary, and people brought their own.

thousand times, so we can definitely relate to almost exactly how this is feeling for them. So we should just come together and support them.' But also there was this other side, one of 'There have been instances where Black teenagers have been killed.' . . . It felt like the school didn't focus a lot on that, or make it as much of a school-wide thing, when it was a poor Black person as opposed to the white Jewish community that we live in."

And then there was a middle position, which in truth probably described the feelings of most of the students at the meeting. These students "were upset about the shooting, but they were still feeling frustrated . . . that a lot of students didn't jump to action" after the deaths of Black people the way they had when Jews were murdered.

Looking back later, Izzy had no regrets about standing with her Jewish friends and fellow Squirrel Hill residents. "I was at peace with the way I reacted." Just as "you don't have to be Black to stand up for Black people," you don't have to be Jewish to stand up for Jews. Still, the empathy should flow in both directions—so why had there been so little outrage from her white friends, the previous June, when Antwon Rose II, a seventeen-year-old African American from East Pittsburgh, a borough outside the city, was shot by a police officer? "I didn't see a lot of people pursuing things on social media, sharing flyers for protests, or simple things like that," Izzy said. "It just didn't feel like they cared as much."

———

ALLDERDICE PRINCIPAL JAMES MCCOY has the advantage of looking like the principal of our American dreams. He's tall, crew-cut, muscled. Speaks softly, carries a big . . . you get the idea. He wears his authority the way a varsity captain wears his jacket. He is white, fair, and male, but there is a Hispanic male version, a Black female version, multiple other versions on television, in the movies, in pop culture, and maybe in the hallways of whatever school you attended. They were teachers and coaches first, and they got promoted up the chain because they had the unusual ability to carry calm with them, backed up by a little menace. When they poke their head into an unruly classroom, the children fall silent.

McCoy is the first to say that he has "a plum job," and he knows how lucky he is to have got it as a young man. On the morning of the shooting, he was thirty-seven years old and in his second year as the principal of Pittsburgh's most famous public high school, over two hundred thousand square feet of light, bright yellow brick, atop a hill on Shady Avenue, watching over the neighborhood like a wise professor. If it was not the powerhouse school that it was fifty years ago, when it had three thousand students and had to run on three shifts, it was still fifteen hundred students strong, powerfully diverse—half white, a third Black, the rest Hispanic and Asian and much else—academically robust, the city football champion, and, for Pittsburghers of the last century, legendary.

Allderdice has its famous alumni, for sure, like writers Nathaniel Philbrick and Howard Fineman, and Murray Chass, who covered sports for *The New York Times;* two mayors of Pittsburgh; and numerous athletes. Broadway star Billy Porter attended Allderdice (although he graduated from another Pittsburgh high school, in 1987), and in recent years few high schools anywhere have produced as many important rappers: Pittsburgh Slim, Beedie, Wiz Khalifa, and the late Mac Miller. The edition of *The Foreword,* the Allderdice student newspaper, that carried news of the shooting at Tree of Life also ran a story about alumna Frances Arnold (Class of 1974) winning the 2018 Nobel Prize in Medicine for her work in the directed evolution of enzymes.

Allderdice High School in 1967

But locals' affection for "'dice," as the current generation of students has nicknamed it, has less to do with its famous graduates than with the unfamous ones. It opened in 1927, just as Squirrel Hill was solidifying its status as the city's premier Jewish neighborhood, and since then it has been a touchstone for the Squirrel Hill Jewish diaspora: anywhere in the world, if a Pittsburgh Jew meets another Pittsburgh Jew, she can say "Allderdice?" and chances are good the reply will come back, "Of course! What year were you?"

And unlike other elite city high schools—New York's Stuyvesant High School and Bronx High School of Science, for example, or Philadelphia's Central High School—Allderdice has always been a neighborhood school. Entrance was never by examination or teacher recommendation. It wasn't built for gifted children citywide; it was built for the girls and boys in its geographic zone. And while that zone has grown more diverse, and while the school has added some magnet programs that bring in students from elsewhere in the city, its status as a neighborhood school has meant that for decades it's been Pittsburgh Jews' hometown school.

McCoy didn't know many Jews growing up in Penn Hills, just outside the city. He was a big athlete at Penn Hills Senior High School: a defensive tackle on the football team, a catcher on the baseball team, and a shot-putter on the track team. As an undergraduate at the University of Pittsburgh, he took up rugby—and sometime in his second or third year, he realized he wanted to be a teacher. After college, he taught history and social studies for ten years, then got onto the administration track and worked his way up through positions at different schools, before getting the call to 'dice. "I think other people saw it in me before I did myself," McCoy said, reflecting on his path to the principalship. "They thought I'd be a good administrator. And I feel like it's something my personality was better suited for. It's been enjoyable. Stressful for sure. I feel like I'm aging rapidly."

The morning of October 27, 2018, he was at a park with his wife, their young daughter, and his mother-in-law. Allderdice was going to play for the city football championship later that day. When he got the call about the shooting, he didn't yet know which synagogue had been hit, and his first thought was that it could be the one right down the street from Allderdice. (That's Poale Zedeck, which, of course, wasn't hit.) As it turned out, the cheerleaders were already inside Allderdice, and the girls' basketball team was practicing in the gym. The first thing he did was call the coaches and tell them to stay put, not let anyone out of the building.

Then McCoy faced the frustrating reality that he couldn't go be at his school; as long as he thought the shooter might be within a few hundred yards of the school building, going anywhere near Allderdice would be madness. But soon he got the all-clear. "It wasn't too long before we found out that it was a different synagogue," McCoy recalled. "And then I headed straight there." He talked with supervisors, including an assistant superintendent, and sent an email to all Allderdice families, telling them that the football championship game had been canceled, and that he would be in touch with details when they became available. He then wrote to a few staff members, including his assistant principals and some faculty, telling them to be at the school Sunday morning.

On Sunday he met at the school with about a dozen of his top people, and the line he laid down was that the shooting at Tree of Life was not to be the main topic of conversation in classes on Monday. Teachers could mention it, but then class had to proceed as usual. "We're not an all-Jewish school," he said later, explaining his thinking at the time. "We have people from all over."

In other words, while this event was a tragedy for some students, for others, it wasn't. And even for students who were deeply shaken, reliving the events in French or geometry class might not be what they needed. That's what he told his administrative team on Sunday morning, and what he then relayed to the whole staff at a meeting before school on Monday. For the students who needed to talk about the massacre, there was Room 114, a first-floor room where counselors were available; any student could leave class at any time and go to 114. But meanwhile, in classrooms, teaching would go on.

This was not an easy decision at the time, and few decisions in the aftermath of the Tree of Life shooting provoked more second-guessing. It used to be that there was no playbook for what to do when a terrorist comes to shoot up your school; now there are protocols, with lockdown drills and alarms and acronyms—principals and security guards all know about ALICE (which stands for Alert, Lockdown, Inform, Counter, Evacuate), an "active shooter response training" trademarked by a for-profit company called the ALICE Training Institute, which charges schools and other organizations to tell them how to respond in the highly unlikely event that they face a shooter. (The institute's online store sells squishy red "training balls" with the ALICE logo, as well as the ALICE "I'm not scared . . . I'm prepared!" kids' activity book; until recently, it sold ALICE polo shirts for thirty dollars, baseball caps for ten, and packs of laminated wallet cards with ALICE concepts printed on them, fifty cards for twenty-five dollars.) But while there are protocols for what to do while under attack—many of them dubious, unproved, and basically unprovable—there is no consensus on what to do the next school day. The protocol at a Catholic high school, which would likely involve a lot of prayer, would look nothing like the protocol at a surf school, or a thousand-person insurance company, or a national park. McCoy was dealing with teenagers at a diverse urban high school, gingerly divided by racial and economic lines, some of whose teachers knew victims or their families. It was the traumatized teaching the traumatized.

"So, you know, you had people who thought we should drop everything, and with every single student talk about it," McCoy said, shaking his head with bafflement, even months later. "But we also recognized, you know, we didn't want to retraumatize students and people who wanted to come back to school to get a sense of normalcy. Because for the last two days, I'm sure that's all they'd been hearing about." Some students would need to talk, while others would need *not* to talk. There were students who "kind of just wanted it to get back to normal."

"Not everyone was probably happy with every decision we made," McCoy said. "But we feel we did the best we could."

———

MICHELE HALLORAN IS WHITE, she grew up in a mostly white town outside Pittsburgh, and her schools were nearly all white. They were entirely Gentile, too, at least as far as she was aware; looking back, she could not remember any Jews, but she also could not remember there *not* being Jews, because she wasn't looking for them. Her world was white and Christian (or lapsed Christian). "When I came to Allderdice, that was a huge cultural shock to me," she said. "For a lot of reasons."

Halloran had been teaching at Allderdice most of her career. She'd done a stint years ago, then gone to other schools, then returned to 'dice in 2010. In her years as a teacher, she had become an avid multiculturalist. She began teaching classes on Black history, and eventually she became the adviser to the Black Student Union; the 2018–19 school year was her fourth consecutive year with the club. "This all happened at a crazy time for me, in terms of those two populations intersecting at Allderdice," she said, referring to Blacks and Jews. The Monday after the shooting, Halloran found herself moderating a painful discussion among Black students about how much they should care about the murder of eleven Jews—but she had been thinking about Blacks and Jews, at Allderdice, well before that. "One of the things that comes up inevitably, every year, is most of the white kids are in the gifted-level classes, most of the Black kids are not, and how do we change that?" In her Advanced Placement classes, she got mostly white students, and a disproportionate number of them were Jewish. At the same time, as a teacher of African American studies, and as an adviser, at a school with almost no Black teachers—as of 2020, Allderdice had thirteen Black educators on staff, including counselors and assistant principals, but only two Black full-time classroom teachers—Halloran was, in a big way, the Black students' main advocate.

Monday morning, Halloran got the word that the shooting was not to be the main topic of conversation in class. "They didn't want us to really have conversations about it, for fear the teachers weren't experts in knowing how every kid in the room was going to react." Still, as an experienced teacher, one with close relationships with students of all races, Halloran felt comfortable, even compelled, to say a few words. "I took a couple of minutes at the beginning of each class to talk briefly about it. Even for me, the emotion of it was really raw." At one point, she realized that a couple years earlier she had taught the grandchild of one of the victims. "It was a blur trying to make it through that day."

———

GIAVANNA GIBSON, the Allderdice senior class president, grew up in Greenfield, a small neighborhood, less than a square mile, a little south and west of Squirrel Hill. It's more racially mixed than Squirrel Hill, less affluent, less professional-class, and part of it always fed into Allderdice. Recently, the Chabad movement of Hasidic Jews has established an outpost in Greenfield, where it's easier to get a big house for a large family. Many of Greenfield's Jews walk to synagogue in Squirrel Hill every

Saturday, and the Tree of Life attack felt very near. For some of Gia Gibson's fellow African Americans, not so much.

Thinking back, Gia assumed that she first learned about the attack "either through social media or the news." She thinks she "saw it on Snapchat or Instagram, a hashtag." But "none of my friends texted me about it," she said. And when she returned to school on Monday, she encountered Black friends who did not even know that eleven Jews had been shot. In their social media feeds, it wasn't a thing. "There is such a huge disconnect," she said.

She, too, attended the Black Student Union meeting, as its president. And because of her dual presidencies, Gia felt she had "not only to comfort Jewish friends and Jewish peers, but also make sure there is a bridge between the Black and Jewish community." This was a delicate mission, and at times it required submerging her own politics. Because the truth was, from what she was seeing, a Jewish tragedy counted more. "I try not to let my personal opinions go into business, you know? But I felt kind of angry how . . . the administration *did* react more, and the community *did* react more. And the Black community, especially, is losing lives every day. . . .

"I will give it to Allderdice that it's so diverse. But when it comes to classes, and it comes to learning, there is a huge divide. There is such segregation in classes. We have CAS and AP"—Centers for Advanced Study, or honors, and Advanced Placement, for college credit—"which are faster-paced, and then we have PSP"—Pittsburgh Scholars Program—"which is a slower class. And the majority of PSP students are Black. And the majority of AP and CAS are white. So Black and white students—you can look at lunch tables, they don't know each other." Gia said that Black girls were more likely to get "dress-coded," disciplined for dressing too provocatively, even though "the white girls tend to dress a little more provocatively." White students were less likely to get suspended, she said, even when they brazenly flouted rules. "At prom, a group of kids came in completely wasted and did not get in trouble at all. Black kids get suspended and expelled for weed, and the white kids are constantly high or drunk at dances or school functions."

How many of these indignities are real, how many are perceived? In the 2018–19 school year, 12.4 percent of Black students in the Pittsburgh public schools were suspended at some point, compared with 4 percent of white students and 4 percent of Hispanic students. School administrators might offer explanations different from the students'. But no matter the climate at Allderdice and in the public school system, it's easy to appreciate how Gia felt about the Tree of Life shooting. "Right around the time Tree of Life happened," she said, two Black people in their sixties, Vickie Lee Jones and Maurice E. Stallard, were shot in a grocery store, the Kroger market in Jeffersontown, Kentucky. The killer, according to police, was Gregory Bush, a white man with a history of mental illness. Minutes before entering the Kroger that day—October 24, three days before the Pittsburgh shooting—Bush had tried to enter a Black church, but the doors were locked. So he went to the Kroger, where he found Jones and Stallard.

Of course, when nine Black people were killed at a Charleston church, that was news. In mass shootings, there seems to be some threshold of about five or six dead, at which point it goes national. A slow drip of one or two homicides at a time doesn't always make the news. "That was on the news for thirty seconds," Gia said about the Kroger killings. "And Tree of Life consumed our lives."

—⊗⊗⊗—

II

The History

IN OTHER AMERICAN CITIES with a sizable Jewish population, the Orthodox would likely have their own enclave, the secular Jews would be scattered around town, and most of the Jews, certainly the non-Orthodox ones, would have gone to one suburb or another. But as of 2018, Squirrel Hill was home to a quarter of metropolitan Pittsburgh's fifty thousand Jews, and the adjacent neighborhoods, including Greenfield, Oakland, Point Breeze, and Regent Square, were home to another quarter. These East End neighborhoods are all geographically tiny, connected by sidewalks and roads; it's not as if one has to cross a river or take a bus to get from one to the other. And more than half the Jews in the entire metropolitan area have elected to live there for about a century.

Such a Jewish community exists nowhere else in the United States. In other cities, Jews who lived in city centers migrated to the edges, then kept going, out into first-ring suburbs and then—looking for more land, lower taxes, better schools, or perhaps greater distance from nonwhite people—to outlying suburbs ten, twenty, or fifty miles from where their great-grandparents had settled. In other words, most Jewish neighborhoods are typically American, in that they change, with each wave of arrivals displacing the last. But around World War I, Jews came to Squirrel Hill and never left. The question is why.

———

SQUIRREL HILL WAS NOT the original Jewish neighborhood in Pittsburgh. Between the 1840s and the 1880s, the original Jewish settlers, mainly from Bavaria and other German-speaking regions, clustered in Allegheny City and other neighborhoods north of downtown. But once the mass immigration of Yiddish speakers from Eastern Europe began, in 1880, the Hill District quickly became the center of Pittsburgh Jewish life. *The Jewish Experience in Western Pennsylvania: A History 1755–1945,* a book that my family had long owned because of some brief references to Moses Oppenheimer, my great-great-grandfather, contains a charming description of the Hill District in its turn-of-the-century Jewish heyday. It "swarmed with activity," as "peddlers passed with packs on their backs to go door to door. . . . Horsedrawn wagons rumbled by, and when they stopped, the drivers were overheard arguing in Yiddish as to who had the best horse." At the corner of Reed and Crawford, "a renegade Jew gave a speech urging Hebrews to become Christians. Jews ambling by shook their fists in anger and cursed him."

After a day at public school, boys rushed to Hebrew school or gathered in the streets to play ball. Vendors' wares spilled out of their store-

The Hill District, circa 1927

fronts and onto the sidewalks. "Cloths of every color were haphazardly piled in front of one shop," while another store sold secondhand clothing. Stalls offered beets, carrots, cabbage, potatoes, horseradish, all "popular items at the Jewish dinner table." There were butchers and kosher restaurants, nickelodeons and theaters. Bookstores sold newspapers in Yiddish and books in Yiddish and Hebrew.

There were bookies and numbers-runners, Jewish pimps and Jewish prostitutes. One local rabbi threatened landlords with excommunication for renting apartments to working girls. No sooner did the Hill District become the Jewish neighborhood than clergy, doctors, and well-meaning settlement house workers, eager to improve, sanitize, and lift up the poor, began sounding the alarm about its unclean—physically and morally—conditions. The Hill District was crime-ridden, not to mention crowded, loud, and smelly. "The Jewish people are furnishing more, alas, a good deal more, than the average rate of immorality in this community," read one 1910 report prepared for a local Jewish women's group. "Shocking housing conditions are to a very great extent responsible for this." The Hill District was what was called a slum (except by those who called it home). So no sooner did Jews populate the Hill District than those with a few shekels to rub together wanted out. Seeking a more wholesome existence, or just better plumbing and a quarter-acre yard, they moved east, getting farther from the grime of downtown.

Nevertheless, even as Jews of some means left the Hill District, poor and working-class Jews were content to stay in their urban ghetto so long as it was theirs. A real exodus began only when non-Jews moved in. At first it was Italians and other immigrant populations, but before long Blacks "began penetrating the Jewish area," as *The Jewish Experience in Western Pennsylvania* puts it. "From 211 individuals in 1900, the population of blacks in the Lower Hill District rose to 6,146 by 1910 and ten thousand by 1920 when, as a result of displacing white immigrants in the area, they comprised 40 percent of the population."

Jews were scared of Blacks, for all sorts of reasons. Jews were still arriving from Europe, and many of the new arrivals had never seen a Black person before ("I thought that perhaps in America people became black," one new immigrant said). As they Americanized, Jews adopted the pervasive American racist beliefs about Black people's supposed stupidity, laziness, criminality, and sexual immorality. And then, of course, there was the basic fact of the real estate market, the self-fulfilling prophecy of white flight (even as Jews were not yet considered "white"): when Black people moved in, property values went down—and the knowledge that they went down led more people to sell, and quickly, which depressed values even further. The majority of Jews in the Hill District were renters, but they, too, perceived that the neighborhood was changing. Prohibition took its toll, as the Hill District became the neighborhood of speakeasies. It also was becoming a thriving center of Black culture and entertainment, but that held little appeal for most Jews.

The Jews moved east. For some time, the well-off Jews had been moving to nearby Shadyside, Oakland, and East Liberty. In 1890 several (non-Jewish) investors had chartered the Squirrel Hill Land Association, which began developing housing in Squirrel Hill—where, as it happened, the streetcar line arrived just three years later. The trip from downtown to various points in Pittsburgh's East End—parts of Squirrel Hill and the adjacent neighborhoods—had taken two hours by horse-drawn trolley; with streetcars, that time was cut in half. In the 1850s, Squirrel Hill had been spared factories because the trains of the era couldn't handle its slopes, especially when the trains were filled with coal or mass-produced goods. But the trolleys, filled only with people, had no problem with Forbes Avenue, and the neighborhood itself was "where people moved, if they could afford it, to get away from the smoky pollution that cloaked the city," as one local history puts it.

Initially, the population taking advantage of the relatively bucolic Squirrel Hill was principally Gentile. But after World War I, Jews got the memo. Once Jews established a foothold in Squirrel Hill, it became irresistible for those who could afford it, and Jews drained out of other neighborhoods: in 1924 twenty-three thousand Jews still lived in the Hill District, 46 percent of Pittsburgh's Jewish population, but by 1940 there were only forty-five hundred left. They were pushed by the same anxieties, about race, crime, and property values, that sent Jews fleeing urban centers around the country; at the same time, they were lured by the appeal of a close-by neighborhood with cleaner air, bigger houses, front yards, and new driveways for new cars. These are the reasons Jews left the Lower East Side of Manhattan for the outer boroughs, the reasons the Jews of South Philadelphia moved up to Strawberry Mansion.

But in these other American cities—as in Cleveland and Detroit—the

Squirrel Hill in 1911, when it was still sparsely populated

Jews moved on *again,* a little bit after World War II, then more completely in the 1960s, '70s, and '80s, for the suburbs, citing the same kinds of concerns the generation before had. Indeed, this is what happened in East Liberty, the Pittsburgh neighborhood that, after Squirrel Hill, was the biggest recipient of Jews leaving the Hill District. It's not a Jewish neighborhood anymore. Squirrel Hill still is.

———

SO, TO REPEAT THE QUESTION: Why did Squirrel Hill, once Jewish, stay that way? Everybody has a theory, which means that nobody really knows.

Many of the theories betray a genial Squirrel Hill chauvinism. Historian Barbara Burstin teaches at Pitt and has written four books on the history of Pittsburgh Jewry. She lives in Squirrel Hill and is generally thought to know more about the neighborhood than anybody else. When I asked her why Squirrel Hill's Jews never left for the suburbs en masse, she more or less threw up her hands. "Squirrel Hill has really a lot to offer, so why would you leave?" she said. "There simply was not that kind of push, that kind of panic almost, to get out. Because you had nice homes, within the city limits, very convenient. So I don't have this all-encompassing kind of theory. This was a community that was attractive, has been attractive for over a hundred years, and after World War II continued to be attractive." People had always liked it, and they kept liking it.

Burstin, however, was willing to venture some smaller, more provisional theories. For one thing, she said, some of the most elegant suburbs were thought to be restricted, with covenants in some houses' deeds that forbade sale to Jews. There is actually no concrete evidence of these covenants, but they were widely presumed to exist, and communities that did not formally exclude Jews may still have been hostile to them. By the early twentieth century, metropolitan Pittsburgh was spreading to the west, out along the Ohio River. "However," the historian Amy Shevitz writes, "many of these towns resisted and manipulated development to preserve their semirural character." As townships like Sewickley transformed from weekend and summer colonies into bedroom communities, the "character" that town fathers wanted to preserve was genteel, and Gentile. Jews got the message. "In the 1920s, perhaps as few as a dozen Jews lived in nearby suburban Bellevue, Avalon, or Ben Avon, on the Ohio. Because of this residential sparseness, there were no synagogues at all in this area. The few Jews who moved into Sewickley in the 1950s were swimming in distinctly inhospitable waters."

The eastern suburbs and the South Hills were more welcoming to Jews (and even Sewickley became friendlier, in time). Even so, Squirrel Hill did not empty out. Another reason, Burstin volunteered, was that "you did not have real estate agents like you did in Boston—you know, panicking." She was referring to real estate agents' practice, in many communities, of hastening Jewish relocation—and other forms of white flight—by scaring them into selling. In many cities, at the first sign of any nonwhite people moving into a neighborhood, real estate agents would tell Jews to get out before the market crashed entirely. Whites would sell (at a panic-induced discount), Blacks would buy (at an inflated price), and in the residential churn the real estate agents took nice commissions. In Squirrel Hill, that panic never hit and was never ginned up by real estate agents. As a result, local banks never soured on the neighborhood; there was no redlining of Squirrel Hill, no refusal to grant mortgages.

In other neighborhoods, government policy, too, drove Jews away. In the 1930s, as increasing numbers of Blacks were moving into East Liberty, a bustling, ethnically diverse neighborhood with large numbers of Jews, the Home Owners' Loan Corporation, a now-defunct federal agency, was undertaking a survey of over two hundred cities "to document the relative riskiness of lending across neighborhoods," as one article about redlining puts it. "Neighborhoods were classified based on detailed risk-based characteristics, including housing age, quality, occupancy, and prices. However, non-housing attributes such as race, ethnicity, and immigration status were influential factors as well. Since the lowest rated neighborhoods were drawn in red and often had the vast majority of African American residents, these maps have been associated with the so-called practice of redlining, in which borrowers are denied access to credit due to the demographic composition of their neighborhood."

One government map of East Liberty noted its strong business climate, calling it "the shopping center for the entire East End District," with "chain stores and mail order houses located there." Larimer Avenue was "the shopping center for [the] Italian population." It had "good transportation" and was "near employment." And yet. The neighborhood had a "lower class populace," infiltration by "relief families" being "very heavy"—and with 30 percent infiltration by "the Negro."

The description "Infiltration of: Italian—negro" in a neighborhood summary of East Liberty, produced for the federal government in 1937

After the maps were published, banks paid attention, and the housing stock of East Liberty, already in "poor condition" according to the government survey, declined even further. In time, more white people moved out. The neighborhood became poorer. In 1960 the city council approved a redevelopment plan that was supposed to rescue East Liberty, but the plan proved disastrous, one of the worst urban renewal blunders in a country full of them. Within a decade, the city's Urban Redevelopment Authority had bulldozed more than twelve hundred homes, in the process relocating thirty-eight hundred people, to build new apartments planned around a large open-air pedestrian mall. The mall never caught on, the city never built a promised highway connecting East Liberty and downtown, and the endless construction was devastating to the neighborhood's legacy shopkeepers. "Small businesses fared the worst," the *Post-Gazette* wrote in a 2000 story on what went wrong in East Liberty. "Forced to wait through six years of construction work and unable to get much help with relocation costs, more than 280 merchants probably closed their doors, one study estimated."

Among those merchants were numerous Jews, who, having seen bad city planning wreck their family businesses, decamped for the suburbs. Some of the Jewish institutions held on—the B'nai Israel congregation stayed in its landmark synagogue building on North Negley Avenue, with its Romanesque rotunda and ornamented drum, until 1995, long after most of its congregants had left the city—but East Liberty ceased to be a center of Jewish life.*

The fate of East Liberty points toward a painful truth, one that everyone who spends any time with the history of Squirrel Hill ends up con-

---

* That was not the end of the story, of course—neighborhoods are nothing if not changeful (Squirrel Hill coming closer than any to being an exception). No sooner was East Liberty counted out than it rose again: since about 2000, it has grown into the city's hipsterville, with coffee shops, restaurants, coworking spaces, and—the cherry on top—Google's Pittsburgh outpost, in the Bakery Square development (so named because it inhabits the old Nabisco factory), as well as a major big-box shopping destination, the site of the city's Home Depot and its Whole Foods market. It also helped East Liberty that the city's educational institutions were all growing. In 2009 the Oakland neighborhood, where Pitt has both its main campus and its huge hospital and medical complex, had a class A office space vacancy rate of zero. Both Pitt and Chatham University, a small Squirrel Hill school, began renting space in East Liberty.

But the new East Liberty, whatever it is, is not a Jewish neighborhood—and as gentrification critics would point out, it's less of a Black neighborhood every day. It's some new hybrid, a very pleasant place to walk, work, and spend money but pretty soulless. East Liberty may be a healthy neighborhood again, but only after a descent into poverty, a spell of nefarious, racist redlining, a well-meaning urban renewal manhandling, and the loss of nearly all its multigenerational families and businesses. None of that happened to Squirrel Hill.

fronting, at least for a moment, even if they'd rather not: wherever large numbers of Black people moved near the Jews of Pittsburgh, the Jews left—and the only reason it didn't happen in Squirrel Hill was because Black people never came. That's because Squirrel Hill housing prices were a little higher, just out of reach for most Blacks; because the housing stock was a little better—bigger, well-built—and thus white residents were less inclined to sell; because the banks never redlined Squirrel Hill; and because government never built large-scale affordable housing there.

And there is this: Pittsburgh just doesn't have that many Black people. In some cities, most white neighborhoods emptied out for the suburbs, one by one, as they were "taken over" by Black and Brown people. According to the 2010 census, about 23 percent of Pittsburghers are African American, and only 3 percent are Hispanic. A full two-thirds of Pittsburghers identify as white. Cleveland, by contrast, is 49.6 percent Black, Chicago is 30.1 percent, Boston 25.3 percent, Detroit 78.6 percent. They all have bigger Hispanic populations than Pittsburgh, too. As a result, when Black Pittsburghers did what typical Americans do and periodically uprooted themselves in search of a better neighborhood, they did not move into very many Pittsburgh neighborhoods. And Squirrel Hill was among the neighborhoods where hardly any of them went.

It bears saying that Squirrel Hill has never been all Jewish or even mostly Jewish. Squirrel Hill, while remaining the indisputable center of Jewish Pittsburgh, is by Pittsburgh standards actually extremely diverse. In fact, it is one of the most diverse places in very white western Pennsylvania. In 2018 Squirrel Hill North was about 72 percent white, 19 percent Asian, 4 percent Black, and 4 percent people of two or more races. Squirrel Hill South, the area south of Forbes Avenue, was almost the same, but with slightly fewer Asian American residents and slightly more white people. The number of Asians and Asian Americans living in Squirrel Hill is growing—as recently as 2013, Squirrel Hill North was only 11.7 percent Asian—and the number of mixed-race residents doubled in five years, from 1.9 to 4 percent. While these percentages would not scream diversity in a multiracial city like New York or San Francisco, in Pittsburgh they are unusual.

Racial considerations aside, with so many suburbs offering better public schools, lower taxes, and more acreage, it's remarkable how many Pittsburgh Jews stick with Squirrel Hill—especially when one considers that, outside of Orthodoxy, most American Jews don't put a premium on living near synagogues, a kosher market, or even other Jewish people.

––––––

IT'S WHEN YOU LEAVE aside the question of what would make Jews want to leave, and focus on why they affirmatively choose to stay, that the theories get really creative. One longtime Squirrel Hill resident suggested to me that something about being located between two large parks, Frick and Schenley, created the psychological conditions for staying put. Was it just that the parks were beautiful and welcoming, with the golf course, tennis courts, and botanical gardens in Schenley Park, and the sledding hill and scenic Nine Mile Run stream in Frick Park? "No," he said, "the thinking is that there was something psychological, like being between the two parks, and on the elevated land of the hill of Squirrel Hill, [that] gave people a sense of safety. They felt safe there." University of Pittsburgh professor Adam Shear said that some of his fellow Squirrel Hill residents believed that the morning commute through the Squirrel Hill Tunnel had dissuaded people from moving to the eastern suburbs. (He dismissed that theory: "Bad traffic here would be a pleasant day in Boston.")* As part of the Squirrel Hill Project, a yearlong scholarly investigation that he supervised at Pitt, Shear collected oral histories from Squirrel Hill residents, many of whom had a theory about the neighborhood's Jewish character. Shear knew that a lot of Pittsburgh Jews had left the city in the 1950s and '60s to move to suburban Monroeville. "The Westinghouse research park was out there," Shear said, "and there was a good number of, you know, Jewish former GIs, [now] Westinghouse engineers, who were settling for their family life in the '50s. And Westinghouse was out there, and maybe you wanted to buy a house in the suburbs, because it's the '50s, and that's what you do." But in researching the history of Squirrel Hill, Shear encountered more than one Jew who said his family had left the suburbs to return to Squirrel Hill. " 'It's really weird,' " Shear recalled one of them telling him, " 'I was

* And Howard Rieger, whom we are about to meet, dismissed Shear's dismissal: "Shear never had to go to the eastern suburbs or return during rush hours. The traffic on the Parkway at the Squirrel Hill Tunnel is insane by any standard and completely unacceptable to most Pittsburghers."

born in 1958, and my parents lived in Squirrel Hill. . . . When I was three, in 1961, we moved to Monroeville. But then when I was eight, in 1966, we moved back to Squirrel Hill.' So there may be some slice of the population that got out there and said, 'You know, this suburban life is no good. Squirrel Hill was paradise.'"

Another theory relied on Pittsburgh's retro quality. When Shear first moved to Squirrel Hill, somebody told him the apocryphal Mark Twain joke about how "if the apocalypse comes, I want to be in Pittsburgh." Why? "Because it will happen there ten years later." As it turns out, Twain probably never made that wisecrack about Pittsburgh (or about Cincinnati, which is another form the joke often takes). Nevertheless, Shear found in the joke a nugget of truth: Pittsburgh *is* behind the times, sometimes in ways that are salutary. What if, Shear wondered, the white (and Jewish) abandonment of cities, which in other cities was such a fait accompli by the 1980s, simply had not quite hit Pittsburgh with full force by then? Given that in the 1990s crime began to fall across the country, a fall that abetted a new romance with urban living, maybe there simply wasn't time enough for Squirrel Hill to crater out. In other words, what if, by the time the bad news about cities arrived in Pittsburgh, the good news was already coming around again?

Well, it's one theory. Shear had yet another. The steel industry for which Pittsburgh was famous was never really concentrated in Pittsburgh; the mills were in outlying towns such as Donora and Braddock, which had small Jewish populations. Some of the Jews worked for the steel companies themselves, but more of them were merchants or professionals—accountants, lawyers, doctors—serving the Gentile populations. What if, in the postwar era, these steel town Jews decided, as they earned more money and were able to buy automobiles, that they didn't want to live in rougher towns like Braddock, with sootier air and fewer people like them? "So if you were a Jewish businessman," Shear mused, "a first- or second-generation immigrant in one of these towns . . . maybe you wanted to move to Squirrel Hill so [your children] could be in a bigger Jewish community and go to a better high school?" Shear wondered if there was "a paradox of the geography of Pittsburgh and the steel industry" that in the mid-twentieth century drew Jews out of less pleasant industrial towns and into the more elegant and educated Squirrel Hill.

But ultimately Shear, like everyone else who wonders what makes Squirrel Hill special, threw up his hands. "There's almost no way to study this!"

––––––––

THIS TALK ABOUT SQUIRREL HILL being unique is not just anec-dotal. Pittsburgh was a pioneer in surveying its local Jewish population, so there are finely grained records of where Pittsburgh Jews lived going back almost one hundred years. The first Jewish community survey was in 1938, and the next one was in 1963, by which point the commercial district around Forbes and Murray was at its peak: you could buy challah at Silberberg's, kosher meat at one of several butchers, a bar mitzvah suit at one of several haberdashers, shoes at Little's (still there on Forbes Avenue, a quick dash from the Starbucks), a mezuzah for your doorpost, a corned beef sandwich—everything you could ever want to live Jewishly. You could get a newspaper in Yiddish or a conversation in Hebrew. That year, 1963, the surveyors counted 40,090 Jews in Greater Pittsburgh, of whom 22,104—just over half—were in Squirrel Hill. Just over 6,000 more were in other east side neighborhoods around Squirrel Hill. In other words, nearly three-quarters of Pittsburgh's Jews were in the East End. In 2017 the most recent survey of Pittsburgh Jewry estimated that there were about 49,000 Jews in Greater Pittsburgh, with about 26 percent in Squirrel Hill, and another 31 percent still within the city, primarily in the East End.* As I said earlier, Jews were never a majority in any of these

---

* In this study, the authors define "Squirrel Hill" as ZIP codes 15217 and 15232, which is basically Squirrel Hill plus Shadyside. Matthew Boxer, one of the study's authors, said to me in an email: "We know from experience that asking people what neighborhood they live in doesn't always work in a community study, even in places with very well-defined neighborhoods. Rather than take up a lot of time on an already too-full survey asking a question we weren't confident would give us clear data, we decided early on to rely on ZIP codes. We also knew that we couldn't have too many geographic regions—as I'm constantly telling my graduate students, statistics is literally a numbers game that requires sufficient data in each category for reliable analysis. We consulted with the community study committee about which ZIP codes to include in which regions, and we decided to define Squirrel Hill as ZIP codes 15217 and 15232. The latter, as noted above, is actu-ally Shadyside, but the committee agreed that Shadyside was more similar to Squirrel Hill than the 'Rest of Pittsburgh' category to which it otherwise would have been assigned, so we made the adjustment. The US Census Bureau estimates that there were 39,301 people living in those two ZIP codes in 2017 (from American Community Survey five-year estimates for 2017).

"Note, though, that our report says that although 26% of Jewish households lived in Squirrel Hill, 30% of Jewish individuals lived there. . . . From a total Jewish population estimate of 49,200, that would make the estimate for what we included in the Squirrel Hill region closer to 14,700. In turn, that would suggest that just a bit over one-third of the total population of the two ZIP codes was Jewish."

neighborhoods. Rather, they held steady as a substantial minority. The 1960 U.S. Census found 17,874 heads of household in Squirrel Hill, and by the United Jewish Federation's count, 6,407 of them—35.8 percent—were Jewish. In 2017 the Jewish population of Squirrel Hill and the adjacent Shadyside (which really functions as an extension of Squirrel Hill and includes another, some would say rival, shopping district), was about 14,700, or 37.5 percent. Broadly speaking, the Jewish part of Pittsburgh went from being just over a third Jewish in 1963 to being . . . about exactly the same today.

Amazingly, the Jewish population held steady even as the Forbes and Murray shopping district lost many of its "Jewish" stores. By the early 1980s, there were no more classic Jewish delis in Squirrel Hill: Weinstein's was damaged by a fire and closed down in 1969, and Adler's went a few years later. The neighborhood fish store closed. Once upon a time, the gas station had been Jewish-owned, but the old Jacobson service station was now owned by Giant Eagle, the larger, less personal (if still locally owned, by Jewish families) supermarket chain. Many more Jewish food purveyors had opened and closed over the years—greengrocers, fruit stands—but by the 1970s they seemed only to be closing. And most distressing of all to the window-shoppers and *flâneuses* who adored the Squirrel Hill stroll, the clothing stores, once so thick on the ground that one could speak of the Squirrel Hill fashion district, had disappeared: gone were Adele's, Bartlett Furs, the Coach House, Grace Miles, Mister Mart . . . nearly all these businesses had been Jewish-owned and, to a great extent, Jewish-patronized.

During these years, as the kosher butchers and bakers closed in Squirrel Hill, they closed elsewhere in Pittsburgh, too. As that happened, the Jewish populations of other neighborhoods, like East Liberty and Stanton Heights, emptied out, leaving as their stores did. Squirrel Hill Jews didn't.

————

BUT WHILE SQUIRREL HILL'S STABILITY owes a great deal to chance, it has also been the fruit of intention: when many Americans turned on city life, Squirrel Hill leaders made a collective decision to stay and bolster the neighborhood they loved. In 1972 business and neighborhood leaders formed the Squirrel Hill Urban Coalition, a nonprofit organization that lobbied the city on a range of issues, from infrastructure improvements, like widening sidewalks and updating the sewer system, to fighting off development that would have changed the character of the neighborhood. In the 1980s the coalition helped stop the construction of a ten-story high-rise apartment building on Northumberland Street, which would have been visible from the beloved public golf course in Schenley Park. The coalition also fought efforts to relinquish management of the golf course to a for-profit company. When the city decided to close down Wightman Elementary School—my father's elementary- and middle-school alma mater—the Urban Coalition acquired the building and turned it into a well-used community center.

These neighborhood efforts were not specific to any one ethnic or racial group. But the Jewish community felt a special stake in Squirrel Hill, and it had a visionary leader who was determined that his community would remain anchored there. Howard Rieger's first sighting of Pittsburgh was in 1980, when he was still the director of operations for the Jewish Community Federation of Cleveland and a colleague suggested they take in a ballgame in Pittsburgh. "I remember looking at Pittsburgh across the river and thinking, *I have this weird feeling someday I am going to live there*," Rieger said. The next year he was hired to be head of what was then called the United Jewish Federation of Pittsburgh.*

In his new role, it immediately became clear to him that Pittsburgh had an unusually stable Jewish population, and that this stability was both a blessing and a bit of a curse. "What I came to find was a really *decent* community," Rieger said. "But what also struck me was that, because the nature of the community hadn't moved, had been in the same place forever, every one of the physical facilities [was] really out of date, run down, in need of something." Some of the looming projects were obvious: the small, aging Squirrel Hill branch of the Jewish Community Center, which had its main branch in Oakland, had to be replaced. The Jewish elementary and high schools had inadequate buildings, too. Other challenges weren't as apparent but affected the quality of life nonetheless. For example, Jewish Family and Children's Service,

---

* He was the CEO, even if his title did not reflect it at first. Here's Rieger: "For what it is worth, my first title at the UJF was executive vice president. At some point a lay leader insisted that I should be the president and he should be the chairman. Titles!"

the federation's social work agency, was in the same building as the federation's main offices, so a couple seeking help for a troubled child or a senile grandparent had to walk past the offices for Jewish fundraising.* Nothing terrible, but not ideal, either. "It was a bad arrangement," Rieger said.

At nearly all these institutions, there was talk about whether to renovate, rebuild on the same location, or leave Pittsburgh altogether. Although Squirrel Hill was still desirable, many Jews had moved to the South Hills; those new to the area, with no stake in Squirrel Hill's historic legacy, were especially prone to choose the suburbs. And considering that office space was cheaper outside the city, maybe the federation should move its headquarters? The Orthodox community was staying put in Squirrel Hill, so their schools would, too. But what about the non-Orthodox school, Jewish Community Day School? It needed a new building, and it could use some decent playing fields, too, the kind that one finds in suburbs. And a new Jewish community center was a once-in-a-century investment; if there was a strong feeling that Jews would be leaving for the suburbs over the next few decades, maybe the infrastructure should be built there.

Rieger didn't see things that way. Moving the community institutions to the suburbs "seemed to me completely illogical," he said. "I had lived in Cleveland, and there is no Jewish presence in the municipality of Cleveland, even though it had a huge presence into the 1950s. I saw what suburbanization can do to a community. My mother grew up in Detroit, in a community that has migrated three times already. I knew it was a bad way to go." And so Rieger spent the next dozen years persuading Pittsburgh Jews that there was a better way. First, everyone agreed to build a new, bigger JCC in Squirrel Hill; it was completed in 1988. Then through endless meetings with school principals, agency heads, city politicians, donors, and just plain old Jews, he rallied support for what became the Renaissance Campaign, a $45 million effort to shore up Squirrel Hill as the center of Jewish Pittsburgh.

The Renaissance Campaign, which launched in September 1993, was ridiculously ambitious. The initial prospectus listed three goals. First, there would be "a new building in the heart of Squirrel Hill," across

---

* In 2017 Jewish Family and Children's Service would change its name to Jewish Family and Community Services, about which I write elsewhere in the book.

from the Jewish Community Center, that would house Jewish Family and Children's Service, the non-Orthodox day school for kindergarten through eighth grade, offices for the JCC, and offices for the Holocaust Center. It would be one-stop shopping for elementary education, social work, Holocaust education, and more. The second item on the Renaissance list was "comprehensive services for the aging," including housing, nursing care, rehabilitation, and so forth. Finally, the project would help fund the expansion and improvement of both Orthodox schools. All of Jewish Pittsburgh was being asked to foot one comprehensive bill, from nursery school to nursing home, across the spectrum of Jewish observance, within walking distance of the JCC's exercise rooms and swimming pool and preschool and art gallery.

And it worked. Not exactly as the original plan envisioned, of course; to move the ball down the field, Rieger and his team had to make many adjustments over the next decade. They improvised as they went. In 1993 the original plan proposed the site of St. Philomena's, a defunct Catholic church and parochial school, as the new home of the Jewish Association on Aging, which would include a nursing home on the site. But some objected to its use as a nursing home—one Jewish neighbor feared that "outsiders" would populate the nearby bus stop, by which he seemed to mean nonwhite nurses and health aides. Rieger ended up forging a compromise: the federation would take over the property as planned but would give it instead to Community Day School. The Renaissance Campaign donated $3 million to help with the renovation, which took nearly a year and was interrupted by the use of the site to film *Diabolique*, starring Sharon Stone as the mistress of a Catholic school headmaster. In September 1996 the students of Community Day School began the year in their newly outfitted building, on the seven-acre campus of the former church, school, and rectory of St. Philomena's. The social work agency got a new building, too, constructed alongside an assisted-living facility, all just a block away from the JCC. The Yeshiva schools, run by the Chabad sect of Orthodox Judaism, and Hillel Academy, a Modern Orthodox school, completed major renovation and building projects in 1994 and 1995, respectively.

It was an astonishing feat. After about a decade of thinking and listening and planning, Rieger and his allies launched a capital project in 1993 that, within three years, ensured that the Jewish infrastructure, from preschool to assisted living, would be in Squirrel Hill, in bigger, brighter buildings than they had had in decades. This meant that the people would stay, which also meant that they would continue to have babies in nearby Shadyside Hospital or in their Squirrel Hill homes. When they died, they would grieve and sit shiva in the houses of Squirrel Hill. They would hold funerals in the neighborhood synagogues. They would have a community center, too, and a grocery store and a firehouse where the firefighters knew their names.

—∘⊱⊰∘—

12

The Visitors

T RAUMA TOURISTS," the locals called them, when their cynicism, or their fatigue, got the better of them. These out-of-towners were certainly well-meaning. Catholics stopped by Tree of Life, leaving little angels and crucifixes on the lawn, propping up condolence cards that promised that the victims had already met Jesus in Heaven. Bob Ossler, a retired Chicago firefighter and part-time Baptist minister living in Florida, arrived in Squirrel Hill the Monday after the shooting. According to one newspaper account, "When Bob Ossler heard about the shooting in Pittsburgh, he knew exactly where he needed to be: the city's Squirrel Hill neighborhood, scene of the deadliest attack on Jews in U.S. history. 'My purpose in life as a minister is to go out there and greet people and offer comfort and prayer and be a listener,' said Ossler. 'I want to bring comfort and love.'" He had previously traveled to Ground Zero in Manhattan, to New Orleans in the aftermath of Hurricane Katrina, and to Parkland, Florida, to offer comfort to students at Marjory Stoneman Douglas High School. At Tree of Life, "he stood outside speaking with the people there. 'I saw people just sitting there stunned, just frozen—stunned and awed by what happened,' said Ossler. 'I would just listen to people share.'" When the reporter asked him how he processed "his own feelings of grief," Ossler replied that he planned to pray and would "offer Communion at his church on Sunday." And not only that: "He was also helped by the presence of therapy dogs at the Pittsburgh airport, with whom he played before his flight out on Wednesday. 'I held two dogs,' he said. 'It was great—I felt like a kid again.'"

Therapy dogs were everywhere in the week after the shooting. There were the five dachshunds brought to Pittsburgh by Anne Rosenberg. There were the three "canine advocates" who belonged to the Center for Victims, a Pittsburgh nonprofit that detailed the pooches to the Jewish Community Center the Monday after the shooting, and to select Jewish events over the next year. The canine advocates receive intensive training to work with traumatized people, and the Pittsburgh police and the children's hospital use them for, among other things, helping soothe children describing sexual abuse. While some dogs, like the canine advocates and Rosenberg's dachshunds, have had special training, a "therapy dog" can be any dog whose owner says his dog is therapeutic—the vests that the dogs wear onto airplanes, with plastic sleeves holding official-looking certificates, are not legally recognized—and well-meaning dog owners, from around Pittsburgh and from homes farther afield, had their animals out in public after the shooting, offering them up to pet and snuggle.

One executive at a local Jewish philanthropy told me that, in the

Therapy dogs in Squirrel Hill the week after the shooting

weeks after the shooting, he and his buddies kept a list of the most egregious trauma tourists, whom they distinguished from well-meaning, but ultimately misguided, people who "just wanted to help." "The trauma tourist," he said, "is the college student who drove to town, attended a vigil, then back on campus wrote a blog post about how his life was forever changed, and took hours of a Hillel professional's time to process his grief. The clown is something different. Not sure what to call it. The clown has genuine skill/value but niche application. She wants to really help and is gladly waiving her ten-thousand-dollar fee and asks the federation only to organize a group of left-handed, color-blind kids, ages six to eight, on forty-eight hours' notice—and by the way could use help to find a hotel room. The former has a level of distaste, the latter is more annoying. The overlap is that they take up valuable time and resources."

The "clown" to which he was alluding was probably Nimrod Eisenberg, the Israeli "medical clown" who flew into Pittsburgh late Sunday night. A medical clown is a performer who specializes in bringing merriment to hospital wards; Israel has a strong tradition of medical clowning, which many doctors there believe helps patients heal. Eisenberg, who was born in 1974, calls himself "one of the pioneers of professional medical clowning," and that seems to be true. A juggler, puppeteer, and street performer, he got a college degree in medical clowning from the University of Haifa, and since 2003 he has clowned all over the world, working with the Red Cross and other relief agencies. Like Bob Ossler and Greg Zanis, he hurries to sites of mass suffering—he has clowned in Africa, and in 2015 he clowned for victims of the Nepal earthquake. And he "has the distinction," according to his promotional literature, "of being the first medical clown drafted for reserve duty" in the Israeli army.

Eisenberg stayed in Pittsburgh for seven days, splitting his time between two families who offered to put him up. Over the course of the week, he went everywhere people would have him. In the suburb of Mt. Lebanon, he spent an hour playing with an eleven-year-old boy on the autism spectrum, a child whose mother had been "severely influenced by the attack."

Visitors could be an imposition: scores of people arrived, trying to help, but ended up needing attention themselves, asking school principals to find them classes to talk to, asking local Jews to house them.

Some of these visitors had special requests, too, such as kosher meals or lodging within walking distance of synagogues. And for all the small acts of kindness that a medical clown could do—Eisenberg played with children at the JCC nursery school, clowned at a synagogue on Shabbat—it is fair to ask whether such well-meaning visitors were right to accept the community's hospitality, in the same week that Squirrel Hill was burying eleven men and women.*

Nina Butler is a former principal of Hillel Academy, one of two Orthodox day schools in Squirrel Hill, and a member of the Orthodox holy society. She was one of the *shomrim* who kept watch over the bodies at the medical examiner's office, comforting the departed souls with prayers. The Saturday evening of the shooting, after the prayers concluding Shabbat, she went to stand outside Tree of Life, where she learned for the first time that Cecil and David Rosenthal were among the dead. Butler and her husband, Danny, have two grown sons with the same disability that the Rosenthal brothers had. Soon after she got home, her telephone rang. It was Daniel Yolkut, her rabbi at Poale Zedeck synagogue. He said that his phone was ringing off the hook, and he was having trouble fielding all the calls from out-of-towners who wanted to help.

"He said, 'Nina, do something about all these people calling me.' So I created a really basic Google form." The form asked questions like, "How many are in your group?" "When do you plan to arrive?" "When do you plan to leave?" and whether the visitors needed kosher food, synagogue service times, and information about the funerals. After she created the form that night, she sent it to Yolkut, who liked it and shared it with Daniel Wasserman, the leader of the holy society and the rabbi of the other large Modern Orthodox synagogue in Squirrel Hill. Wasserman liked the form, too, and so they shared it with the email group of the Rabbinical Council of America, the national body of Modern Orthodox rabbis. By Saturday night, Butler was suddenly the coordinator for "every shul and every school" that wanted to send people to Pittsburgh.

Before long, Butler's form had been filled out by forty-two different

---

* Eisenberg acknowledged that his services may not have been entirely welcome. At the JCC day care, he met with a group of children whose "level of tension was superhigh," he told me. "It was clear. They were very sensitive to what is different today, why is there a clown today? They were suspicious about why is this clown even here! It was very clear to me that what is happening right now is not just their normal response to a clown." In other words, in a time of heightened anxiety, the children were less receptive to a clown, not more.

groups that wanted to visit, mainly synagogues and high schools, from New York, New Jersey, Maryland, Los Angeles, and elsewhere. A woman from Israel had no immediate plans to come but wanted to offer her services: "My name is Rena Ariel. I live in Israel and lost my daughter Hallel in a terror attack 2 years ago. She was 13.5 years old. If you need any help speaking to groups or schools, we are here." Many people were planning to bring groups to the funerals and to visit families who were sitting shiva. The tone of the replies varied; some seemed to understand that they might help best by staying away, or by sending food or money, while others were intent on coming: "_____ here," one man wrote, "formerly of Harrisburg, now Memphis, TN. I'm so sorry to reach out to you regarding this horrible tragedy. My shul would like to find some way to embrace the families of the victims. Is there a way for us to sponsor a shiva meal/meals? Can you think of any way we could be helpful from afar?"

"We are a group of rabbis from Baltimore who would like to visit as many *aveilim*"—mourners—"as possible. Wednesday is the best day for us, but if you think that is not a good idea or if you can provide any direction as to how we can maximize our short time in Pittsburgh, it would be greatly appreciated. Thank you."

"We're contemplating bringing a group of Columbia/Barnard students. We may have some flexibility on dates so I wanted to see if there were particular days/times/shivas/funerals at which visits would be more appreciated before solidifying any details on our end. Thank you for organizing this!"

"Just a general sense of if our presence there would be supportive and welcomed, and the best time to come."

"Please can you send me the names of those in hospital and the addresses of the hospitals. Thank you."

Very quickly, Butler realized that the best thing she could do was tell people to stay away. She summed up the message she gave them: "'We are the warmest, most welcoming community in the country: please don't come. Please, please don't come.'" She was protecting two groups of people: the Orthodox Jews of Pittsburgh, who were already going to have their hands full guarding the bodies, cooking kosher meals, hosting relatives, and supporting one another in a time of communal grief, but more especially the families of the dead, who would not want strangers coming to the funerals and then their houses. And they especially would not want to receive Orthodox Jews whose strictly traditional mourning customs would seem alien.

The dead, after all, were not Orthodox. Butler had to tell those eager to visit "that not only have none of the shivas been announced yet, but when they are, these are not going to be shivas like what you are picturing"—shivas where the mourners have covered all the mirrors in the house, to ensure against vanity, and sit quietly on the traditional low stools, then pray with a quorum of ten. "Some of them, their shivas might look like a cocktail party. Some of them might not have shivas. I said, 'If these people have a bunch of men dressed in black suits with white shirts and big black hats come in, sit down, and just stare at them, that would be disastrous. They won't know where to hide. . . . They really don't want to meet new people.' "

For the most part, the potential visitors whom Butler reached got the hint and stayed away. But many didn't. The Jewish college student from a big state university who wanted to show his face just drove on up to Pittsburgh—that was a typical case. And some of the Jews whom Butler did reach did not take her advice kindly. She mentioned someone at "one very exclusive New York [City] day school" who "got very upset." " 'But you don't understand,' " the teacher said to her. " 'We have three buses of our best students that we want to send to you. How are you saying no, these are *our best, best students*!' I said, 'But this is not about you, and it isn't about your best students. It's about these mourners and what they need this week.' "

One Sephardi Jewish man from New York could not help himself. "I know that you don't really want us to come," he told Butler, "but I just, I have to be there. I can't be anywhere else, so don't be upset with me, but I'm coming anyway." He came, and the Butlers had him for a Shabbat meal.

———

THAT SEPHARDI VISITOR WAS APOLOGETIC, and he came alone. Months after the shooting, Butler spoke of him warmly. But she still had trouble tamping down her rage toward a whole passel of other New Yorkers—and they were, in the main, New Yorkers—who barged into Pittsburgh, uninvited, often after they had been warned off, to show the

Bronx rabbi Avi Weiss

yokels how things were done. Many in town were irked by Rabbi Avi Weiss, retired founder of a prominent synagogue in the Bronx, who came to town and twice in three days—once outside Tree of Life, again at Poale Zedeck synagogue—put his hands on police officers' heads and offered them the traditional three-line priestly blessing prescribed in the Torah.*

Some observers were moved, but others in the Pittsburgh Orthodox world considered it grandstanding. Shmuel Herzfeld, a disciple of Weiss's who leads a congregation in Washington, D.C., brought a large delegation of Jews to Pittsburgh. His people were adults who could fend for themselves, but what of the dozens of teenagers disgorged by school buses in front of the synagogue? About this kind of well-meaning class trip, one local rabbi told me, "Just the logistics of if you have, you know, forty-eight kids from a high school in New Jersey that sends them to Pittsburgh—you have to provide them with kosher food, right? That's yet another strain on a system that was kind of going bonkers in terms of figuring out what to do."

---

* The blessing is well known in Christian ceremony, too, and it comes from Numbers 6, where Moses instructs his brother, Aaron, and the priests to bless the Israelites with these words: "May the Lord bless and keep you. May the Lord look graciously upon you. And may he turn his countenance toward you and give you peace."

And then there were the New York City holy societies. As we've seen, Pittsburgh has two Jewish burial societies of its own, one Orthodox and one liberal, both highly experienced. In the whole country, there is probably no Jewish community the size of Pittsburgh's with more different kinds of Jews who feel called to the archaic tradition of washing Jewish corpses by hand and preparing them for burial. But the night after the shooting, an Orthodox holy society from New York City was organizing to go to Pittsburgh—and had alerted the media to its efforts.

"A Brooklyn group will try to recover every drop of blood belonging to the victims of the Pittsburgh synagogue shooting to satisfy Jewish burial requirements," the *New York Post* reported on October 28. "The Jewish faith necessitates that the dead are buried physically intact. So the non-profit group Misaskim has dispatched a team to comb through the Pennsylvania crime scene where 11 people were murdered Saturday to recover any of the victims' blood and possible body fragments left behind." The article went on to explain that the members of Misaskim planned to "work closely with crime-scene investigators." Rabbi Jack Meyer, Misaskim's cofounder, is quoted in full *Dragnet* mode: "'The perp is alive, and whatever charges are against him, you want them to stick, so we don't want to hamper the investigation one bit,' Meyer said."

Had Misaskim ("Attendants") gone to Pittsburgh with utmost humility, asking how they could help, they still, in all likelihood, would have been turned away with a polite thank-you. Had they not arrived at the same time as Chesed Shel Emes ("True Kindness"), another New York City holy society, they still would have been seen as interlopers, albeit well-meaning interlopers. But Misaskim did not just come uninvited, they came with the certainty of the city dweller educating the provincials—literally. "We're coming from the big city," Meyer told the *Post*. "We have the experience as a group to do it. There are people in Pittsburgh, but they definitely don't know how to deal with a tragedy of this magnitude."

As it turned out, the Pittsburghers knew how to guard the bodies, watch over them during transport, pray over them, and—when the victims' families asked—wash them before burial. Come Tuesday, the FBI would allow Wasserman and seven other members of the holy society inside Tree of Life, where they would begin collecting blood and bone (all of the body must be buried, and what organic matter can't be matched with a particular corpse is buried in a separate grave). The New Yorkers wanted to take charge of the effort, but Pittsburgh was having none of it. Monday night, Wasserman met with the two New York holy societies at his synagogue, on Murray Avenue.

"We sat down and informed the representatives of those other two groups of our discussions with the FBI, of our plans, of how we were going to approach it," Wasserman said. "They made some suggestions, and we said, 'Thank you, if that's advantageous, we will do it.'"

Then the New Yorkers insisted that they be allowed inside Tree of Life.

"We explained to them," Wasserman recounted, "that our local people have already volunteered, and we have more people ready to volunteer"—before it was over, members of both Pittsburgh holy societies would collaborate on the cleanup. "They began to argue with us and demand they be part of the group. I said, 'Look, you can stay outside, and if we need assistance, we'll absolutely come out and say, "Help us."' They continued to argue, said, 'Look, let us go in first, then you'll rotate in.'"

The New Yorkers were not taking the hint, and Wasserman, short on sleep, was growing short on patience.

"I was very definitive. I said, 'It's time for you to leave.'"

One of the New Yorkers took offense, saying to Wasserman, "Hey, we've been here for three days. Be a mensch!"*

Which further enraged Wasserman.

"I said to them, on the sidewalk on front of my shul, '*Get out of my city.* No one asked you to come, and in fact when you called we said not to come. And you dare say to me, "Be a mensch"? Get out of my city.'

"Then we went on to do the work, with our own people."

———

THE VISITORS KEPT COMING, all year long. Early on, Tom Hanks came for a memorial. In June, Jeremy Piven, star of HBO's *Entourage*, would come to town and attend Shabbat services at Tree of Life.

And in between, on the morning of Saturday, December 15, 2018,

---

* They had been in Pittsburgh "three days" only if they had left New York on Saturday night, after sundown, and arrived in Pittsburgh while it was still Saturday—a possibility. Otherwise, they had been in town two days. "I was already quite annoyed with them at that point, so perhaps I heard it wrong, but I don't think so," Wasserman told me.

Tom Hanks holding Joanne Rogers, Fred Rogers's widow,
at a unity rally at Point State Park on November 9, 2018

about two hundred people gathered at Rodef Shalom, the storied old
Reform temple on the western edge of Squirrel Hill, for the bar mitzvah
of thirteen-year-old Max Schachner, whose father, Sam, was the president of Tree of Life. "Rodef," as people call it—it means "seeker" or "pursuer," as in *rodef shalom,* "pursuer of peace"—is one of the largest Jewish
houses of worship in the country, and one of the most beautiful, and in
these days of falling attendance, it has more unused space than almost
any synagogue in the country. Its main sanctuary seats twelve hundred, and it has numerous smaller rooms, which the congregation uses
now and again; but the building was built (and rebuilt, and expanded)
for a congregation that had a membership of about twenty-three hundred families in the early 1960s, the peak era for religious attendance
in American history. Today it has a membership of about nine hundred
families, most of whom seldom attend, which is one reason that it was
able to offer space to two of the three congregations displaced by the
shooting: Dor Hadash and Tree of Life.

At Rodef, Tree of Life had office space, a room for all the mail and
gifts that it continued to receive, and Levy Hall, a chapel that seats 280
people. The morning of the bar mitzvah, Levy Hall was, for the first

time since those emotional weeks in the shooting's aftermath, nearly full. It had been almost two months since the shooting, it was coming up on the darkest week of the year, and the refugees of Tree of Life—victimized, displaced, traumatized—really needed a *simcha*, a joyous occasion.

Men wore coat and tie, ladies their Shabbat best. Children sat up straight. Rabbi Myers, always formal, on this day seemed cheerful, too. And the day rewarded everyone's attention. They got not only what they expected—a shyly triumphant bar mitzvah boy, who delivered a competent chanting of his Torah portion (that week it was the section of Genesis in which Jacob settles in the land of Egypt)—but also two surprises.

The first surprise was that the second member of the congregation called to the front of the room for an *aliyah*, the honor of reciting the blessing over the Torah, was Andrea Wedner, the Tree of Life member who had seen her mother, Rose Mallinger, shot and killed next to her, and who herself had been shot in the arm. When Myers called her to the *bimah*, she moved slowly, her arm still in a sling. She recited the several lines of the opening prayer, and then later she recited the closing blessing, as well. When she was finished, Myers stepped forward and addressed the room. "That was Andrea's first *aliyah*"—the first time she had said a blessing over the Torah—since the shooting, he said. Then the rabbi invited Wedner to pray the Gomel prayer, "which one recites after coming through a trial, or a trauma."

Wedner opened her prayer book and recited the prayer: "Blessed are You, Lord our God, ruler of the world, who rewards the undeserving with goodness, and who has rewarded me with goodness." And then everyone in the room said, together, "Amen." For many of Wedner's fellow congregants, this was the first time they had seen her since the shooting.

In the program, the seventh Torah reader was listed as Max, and the seventh *aliyah* was to go to his parents. But when the moment arrived, the rabbi said, "We have a special guest for the seventh *aliyah*." He paused, took an extra beat, and said: "I'd like to call to the Torah Robert Kraft." A short man with a mane of wavy white hair stood up in his seat, moved past the others in his row, and made his way to the head of the room. He was wearing a blue blazer, a white shirt, a solid pink tie, and black sneakers—the uniform mixed elegance with just a little insouci-

New England Patriots owner Robert Kraft wearing a Pittsburgh Steelers
yarmulke at a Tree of Life bar mitzvah, in their borrowed space
at Rodef Shalom

ance, the sweet plumage of a man richer than you, whoever you are. It
was Robert Kraft, the owner of the New England Patriots, and he was
wearing a Steelers yarmulke, emblazoned with Tim Hindes's STRONGER
THAN HATE/Steelers logo mashup. The Steelers were playing the Patriots the next day. Kraft recited the blessing, and after the Torah was read,
he said a few words to Max. Then he kissed the boy on the cheek, gave
him tickets to the next day's football game, and sat back down.

Afterward, at the luncheon in Max's honor, when Kraft was gone and
it was just family and invited guests, I met Max's aunt Molly. "I think
people have already moved on," she said to me. "We haven't. But the rest
of the world has."

_____

KRAFT'S VISIT WAS a very visible manifestation of the common urge
to do *something* (although he was in Pittsburgh anyway). Even after the
eyes of the world left Pittsburgh, and Tree of Life was no longer news,
the crime still exerted a pull. Giving money was one thing, but for many
Jews, and a surprising number of non-Jews, it was important to get to
Pittsburgh.

Rose McGee, founder of Sweet Potato Comfort Pie, claims to have baked over three thousand sweet potato pies to "strengthen existing—and nurture new—relationships through the creation and distribution of sweet potato pies," according to her organization's literature. She delivered her pies to Ferguson, Missouri, in the aftermath of the 2014 riots there, and she served pie at Mother Emanuel in Charleston, South Carolina, after the shooting there. McGee, who lives in Golden Valley, Minnesota, and was sixty-seven at the time of the Tree of Life shooting, borrowed the kitchen of a Jewish day school to ensure that her pies would be kosher, then shipped them to Pittsburgh for a Shabbat evening event, on February 8, with Tree of Life and Dor Hadash, at their new home at Rodef Shalom. McGee flew in to distribute them that night, then had a pie event the next morning for New Light, meeting at Beth Shalom. She felt ethnic cuisine was more meaningful than a check. "Why sweet potato pie?" she said. "Because I consider it to be the sacred dessert of Black culture. . . . When you can take that and carry it and take it into another culture—that's what relationship-building is about."

They kept coming: solo visitors, organizations bringing their conventions to Pittsburgh, people finding a reason and a way to get to town. A national association of holy societies announced that its 2020 meeting would be in Pittsburgh. (Because of COVID-19, it wasn't.) Most days scattered tourists walked past the fencing around Tree of Life, thwarted in their attempts to see inside. The summer after the shooting, over seventy Jewish motorcycle riders from across North America roared up to Tree of Life. They were hosted by the local Jewish bikers' group, the Mazel Tuffs.

"I am a member of YOWs (Yidden on Wheels) motorcycle club of Toronto since 2002," one of the riders wrote after the trip. "My club is a member of the Jewish Motorcycle Alliance (JMA), with over 45 clubs worldwide, including Israel and Australia. The signature event of the JMA is the annual Ride to Remember (R2R) which has the lessons of the Holocaust at its core, along with the theme of Never Again. Over the last 17 years I also participated in special rides, like the Paper Clip Ride to Whitwell, Tennessee, or the Pebble Ride to Trenton, Ontario . . . but this one in Pittsburgh on the weekend of August 23–25, 2019, was special."

13

The Money

BEFORE THE GOFUNDME PAGE set up by Iranian expatriate Shay Khatiri was closed down, on February 26, 2020, it had raised $1,265,200. Except for GoFundMe's small transaction fee, all that money was sent to Tree of Life. Khatiri had not realized, in the hours after the shooting, that three congregations met at Tree of Life; had he known, he would have set up his fund to support Dor Hadash and New Light as well. Other funds, too, were set up by well-meaning Jews and Gentiles from around the world, and nearly all of them benefited Tree of Life specifically. The Monday after the shooting, the University of Wisconsin chapter of Sigma Alpha Mu, the historically Jewish fraternity known to all as Sammy, created a page on GoFundMe, and it eventually raised almost $10,000 for Tree of Life. The Rose Mallinger Memorial Fund, created that Tuesday in honor of one of the victims who belonged to Tree of Life, raised almost $15,000. Nobody, it seemed, was raising money for New Light or Dor Hadash.

It was an understandable oversight, of course, and Khatiri and the Wisconsin frat boys were hardly to blame for focusing their efforts on Tree of Life. It quickly became clear, as people from around the world pledged money and asked where they could send checks, that the congregation called Tree of Life would be the one identified with the tragedy and would benefit financially from its name. It was hard to separate the building from the congregation that owned it; nobody thought, *What about the tenants?*

New Light and Dor Hadash members, who would need money, too, quickly realized what was happening. True, it was not their building that had been shot up: the cost of cleaning the building, of scrubbing blood from the carpets and filling bullet holes in the walls, and of its eventual renovation or rebuilding, would fall to Tree of Life. But the two smaller congregations were facing uncertain futures, too. Would they need to find new worship spaces, and would the new spaces come with higher rents? In this new, less safe world, would they have to hire security guards? And what about professional help, like counselors, or additional clergy?

Their fundraising window was closing, and as the dollars continued to pour in for Tree of Life, they began their own crowdfunding campaigns. Stephen Cohen, the co-president of New Light, started a GoFundMe page for his shul on Monday, two days after the shooting, and set the goal at $100,000. But a year and a half later, the page had raised just over $25,000, from about three hundred donors. (By comparison, Tree of Life had over eighteen thousand donors.) The websites of New Light and Dor Hadash quickly put up pleas for money, too. But they never got anything like the gush of contributions that came—and still come, in a trickle—to Tree of Life.

Eventually, Tree of Life agreed to share with New Light and Dor Hadash the money that Khatiri had raised, along with other donations that had come straight to Tree of Life but seemed intended for everyone affected—a total of $5.45 million. And over $6 million came to a catchall fund that was started, like Shay Khatiri's, within hours of the attack, by the Jewish Federation of Greater Pittsburgh.

And here it's worth taking a look at "the federation." In the United States, local Jewish communities tend to support philanthropic organizations known as federations. As of 2020, there were 146 local Jewish federations in North America—in cities with very large Jewish populations, like New York, Los Angeles, and Toronto, and those with tiny Jewish populations, like Cheyenne, Wyoming, and Biloxi, Mississippi. These local groups aren't all called "federations"; some of them have kept older names, like the Aurora (Illinois) Jewish Welfare Fund or the

Jewish Charity Fund of Aberdeen, South Dakota. For decades, many of
them went by the name of the United Jewish Appeal. These federations
are like Jewish versions of the United Way: umbrella organizations that
raise money from a large constituency, then distribute it to recipients big
and small. A typical federation cuts checks to the community's Jewish
elementary school, its Jewish nursing home, and its JCC, among other
groups.

In Jewish circles, the federations are a source of tremendous pride
and the target of great derision. On the one hand, they carry on a grand
tradition of Jewish self-sufficiency. It's the tradition of the Hebrew Immigrant Aid Society, now HIAS, the organization whose work with immigrants enraged the Tree of Life shooter. It's the tradition of settlement
houses, free night school, English classes for new arrivals, homes for the
aged, and Israel bonds. For digging deep into their pockets to support
their coreligionists, American Jews have almost no equals. (Their only
obvious betters would be the Latter-day Saints, or Mormons, who tithe
10 percent of their incomes back to the church.) Throughout history,
Jews have taken care of their own, and in the United States, the federations have become the primary vehicle for that largesse.

At the same time, the local federations have a reputation for being
cautious, risk-averse, milquetoast. The federation is very much your father's nonprofit, or maybe your uncle Myron's; it is the preferred charity
of the self-satisfied burgher, the cautious businessman, what used to be
called, in Yiddish American slang, the alrightnik. The federations strive
to be apolitical, but, of course, there really is no such thing. In the Jewish
world, avoiding politics can seem like an uncritical acceptance of Israel
and its government, or keeping quiet about an anti-immigrant president
in the White House. Left-wing Jews typically have no use for the federation, which has no use for them.

Right-wing Jews typically have no problem with the federation, and
may even be inclined to throw a few dollars its way, but they would
rather reserve their big checks for AIPAC, the Zionist Organization of
America, Aish HaTorah, or one of a hundred charities that work specifically to support Israel or do *kiruv*, religious outreach. The federation is
mainline, old guard, and stodgy, intentionally so. It's not bold enough
for donors who want a big, splashy impact. It's about consensus. Indeed,
for federation-minded Jews, the unity of *am Yisrael*, the Jewish people,

a unity that presumes that all Jews have a common good and can reach broad consensus about it, is more than a pragmatic fundraising mantra: it's a theological principle.

In a polarized America, the constituency for this kind of consensus philanthropy is shaky; many people want to give to conservative causes or liberal causes, gun rights or abortion rights. But it turns out that, when the storm comes, people need a big, sturdy tent, one that everyone can feel comfortable standing under. As of June 30, 2019, the Jewish Federation of Greater Pittsburgh had $289 million in assets and a staff of seventy-five, which included not just fundraising specialists, web designers, and accountants but also a security specialist (a twenty-eight-year veteran of the FBI), educators, staff rabbis, and liaisons to Israel. In normal times, one reason that some Jews do not give to the federation is that it doesn't "do anything": Why give to a pass-through philanthropy with (they assume) high overhead when one can just donate to a synagogue or a school? But in the hours and days after the shooting at Tree of Life, smaller institutions like shuls and schools were focused on what they needed: reassurance, comfort, and security—a feeling of security, plus actual security, the kind that comes from locked doors and armed guards. They were not about to organize a vigil, open to the public, in a hall that held 2,300 people, the day after the shooting—but the federation could and did. The federation lent its manpower to the JCC in the hours that it served as a gathering place for families waiting to hear about their loved ones. It organized security briefings for the terrified managers of Jewish organizations, from the rabbis to the directors of small Jewish preschools.

And the federation told people where to send money: to the federation.

In the aftermath of a mass shooting, thousands of people, all over the world, want to give money. After the Tree of Life attack, if you were in Shay Khatiri's social media sphere, or following Jake Tapper on Twitter, you might have sent money to Khatiri's fund. But absent a centralized, well-publicized effort to tell people where to direct their checks or online donations, money gets sent every which way. Five years after the shooting at Sandy Hook Elementary School, in Newtown, Connecticut, *Huff-Post* ran an article with the headline "Where to Donate to Honor Each of the 26 Sandy Hook Shooting Victims." Twenty children and six teach-

ers had been killed, and nearly every one of them had a nonprofit foundation or memorial fund started in their honor, usually by their family.*
After a shooter killed forty-nine at the Pulse nightclub, in Orlando, Florida, in 2016, those who wanted to send money could choose from the
OneOrlando Fund, the onePULSE Foundation, or the Orlando Victims
Fund (run by Equality Florida, a gay and lesbian activist organization),
among others.

In general, these funds are run ably and do good. But sometimes the
money falls into slippery hands. After nine clergy and worshippers were
killed during Wednesday-night Bible study on June 17, 2015, at Mother
Emanuel in Charleston, South Carolina, donations poured in. Two
months later, the church's secretary, Althea Latham, was let go because,
she said, she had misgivings about how the interim pastor and other
church leaders were stewarding the finances. She alleged that they were
mishandling cash donations that had been sent to the church, intended
for victims' families. Latham was not alone in alleging wrongdoing.
"Arthur Hurd, whose wife Cynthia died in the shooting, said he wit-
nessed women in the church's fellowship hall open envelopes addressed
to victims' families and remove cash and checks from them without
keeping a log of money received," according to a newspaper report published in 2019, after state authorities opened an investigation into the
church's finances. The investigation ended with a finding of no criminal
wrongdoing.

Within hours of the shooting, maybe minutes, the Jewish Federation
of Greater Pittsburgh was getting calls and emails from people around
the world, asking how they could donate. Some were savvy about Jewish
communal life, the kind of engaged Jews who knew that there would be
a local federation, with professional financial expertise, to entrust dollars to; others likely took to the Web and just did a Google search of
"Pittsburgh" and "Jewish" and found the federation.

On Sunday, the morning after the shooting, the federation "opened
a box" on its website, to use the fundraising lingo. Jewish federations
often put up rapid calls for money in response to a natural disaster, an
outbreak of hostilities in the Middle East, or anything that might moti-

---

* In honor of six-year-old Emilie Parker, one could donate to the Emilie Parker Art Connection.
The family of Daniel Barden, age seven, started an initiative called What Would Daniel Do, "with
the goal of inspiring others to share his kindness, compassion, selflessness, gratitude and appreciation for life"; a set of two "WWDD" bracelets costs four dollars, shipping included. And so on.

vate Jewish donors to give. This time the portal invited donors to "Give Now to the Fund for Our Victims of Terror" and to "Help Those Affected by the Attack at Tree of Life*Or L'Simcha, Dor Hadash and New Light." The federation's marketing director, Adam Hertzman, wrote the short pitch underneath, promising that "funds collected for Our Victims of Terror are earmarked for psychological services, support for families, general services, reconstruction, additional security throughout the community, medical bills as well as counseling and other services that may prove necessary for victims and first responders during their recovery. Our religious and day schools will also most likely require additional resources to help our youth process this tragic episode. This fund will help both the Jewish community members and the first responders affected."

The language of the appeal was written in the broadest possible terms, assuring every possible donor that her area of interest would be taken into account. But the federation neglected to require each donor to specify where her money should go. When the money came, then, it would bring questions with it.

———

THE MORNING OF THE SHOOTING, Chuck Perlow was with his wife in Tucson, on vacation. Born in 1954, he grew up first in the Stanton Heights neighborhood and then in Squirrel Hill, where his family moved when he was ten years old. Their house backed onto the Tree of Life property, and the synagogue's stained-glass windows spread late-afternoon light into their yard. "Our Friday-night dinners were the most beautiful you could imagine," Perlow said. As a young man, he left Pittsburgh for a time, practicing law in Detroit, before deciding to return to Pittsburgh to work for the family's hotel business.* Since relocating to Squirrel Hill in 1985, he had become one of the Jewish community's most generous philanthropists; he endowed a professorship in classical Judaism at the University of Pittsburgh, donated heavily to the Jewish day schools, and became a major donor to the Pittsburgh Kollel, an Orthodox house of study. Tree of Life had never been his synagogue—as a child, he had attended B'nai Israel, and now, in adulthood, he paid dues to both Beth

* In 1998 Perlow's father and his partner sold Interstate Hotels Corp. for $2.1 billion.

Shalom and Shaare Torah—but he was upset that he had been out of town when Tree of Life was hit. He flew home the next day.

Perlow knew he had a role to play. He got on the phone with Meryl Ainsman, the chair of the federation board and an old Squirrel Hill acquaintance; she'd been the class ahead of him at Allderdice. Ainsman told Perlow about the fund that had already been set up. Thinking about the huge task in front of them, he suggested they reach out to Kenneth Feinberg, the lawyer who had become the world's leading practitioner of a rather macabre new profession: disburser of victims' compensation money. After he made his name skillfully overseeing the September 11th Victim Compensation Fund (his official government title was "special master" of the fund), he was asked to perform the same role with the BP Deepwater Horizon Disaster Victim Compensation Fund and later with the victim-assistance fund established after the 2013 Boston Marathon bombings. The work has never let up, and more recently, in 2019, Boeing put Feinberg in charge of distributing $50 million to families of 737 MAX crash victims. Feinberg has many gifts, his supporters say, including a sharp legal mind, a patient manner, and the ability to take mountains of abuse while keeping his cool. It would have been proof of his skills if, after twenty years of deciding how much money to give, or not give, to bereft, grieving widows and children, he were no more widely loathed than necessary. Feinberg was actually *liked*.

By the end of the day on Sunday, the federation's fund had taken in over $100,000. On Monday, Perlow called Feinberg. On Tuesday, the fund grew to over half a million dollars. On Wednesday, the federation held its first conference call with Feinberg, who outlined for them the best practices, as he saw them, for how to deal with the money and all the problems it would bring. They needed legal counsel and an independent auditor. They would need a committee appointed to oversee the money. The committee should not comprise those who stood to receive money, which meant no victims' families, and no rabbis from the affected synagogues. And the committee, Feinberg said, should be independent of the federation.

This last edict was a bit tricky, since the money was coming to the federation, and the federation had a legal responsibility to decide what to do with it. And many of the Jews who would be natural fits to serve on such a committee had worked at the federation or served on its

Meryl Ainsman and David Shapira presenting the conclusions
of their committee's report

board. In the end, the federation's chief executive, Jeffrey Finkelstein, helped draft a charter that gave the committee final authority over how to disburse the money; having been charged by the federation with disbursing the fund, the committee would not have to return to the federation to approve its decision.

From mid-November to mid-January, the seven-member committee met nine times. Its chairman was David Shapira, whose family controls Giant Eagle, the supermarket chain with a branch in the heart of Squirrel Hill. Shapira is one of those figures whose admirers assure you that he has virtues besides his willingness to give away a lot of money—he gives time, too, sitting on numerous civic boards; he is a good listener and knows how to build consensus. He ran the committee swiftly and efficiently and created a sense of purpose that, to hear committee members describe it, felt truly spiritual.

"David Shapira was a fabulous leader for this effort," committee member Susan Brownlee, the former executive director of the Fine Foundation, a local philanthropy, said. "He listened to everybody, listened very respectfully, to all opinions. And he structured the conversations so we always arrived at something everyone agreed to. It was a different kind of leadership than I had seen before. And in this particular situation, it was perfect." She believed that the committee, too, was perfect, or something close. "It was a group of people," Brownlee said, "who cared desperately about the tragedy, and who wanted to do the right thing—particularly for the families, and for the police."

Ainsman—who as president of the board of the federation was, along with representatives of the three synagogues, invited to participate in the committee, although not to vote on its decisions—said that serving felt like "doing God's work."

In the end, the committee seemed to achieve the impossible: it made everybody happy. On March 5, 2019, the committee held a press conference to deliver its report, which included a synopsis of who would get what. Between October 27, 2018, and February 27, 2019, when the federation closed the Victims of Terror Fund, donors gave $6,302,803 in unrestricted donations. (Many checks listed specific intent, like a given victim's family, and those were sent along to the intended recipients.) Of that money, the majority, $4,367,523, would be given to "the families of those killed and to seriously wounded worshippers"—thirteen separate payments of $335,963.31 each, for the eleven murdered plus the two wounded survivors, Daniel Leger and Andrea Wedner. (For the dead, each family designated a family member to receive the check on behalf of the whole family.) The nine who had been "trapped in the building" but not killed or injured would get a total of $436,752, or $48,528 each. Then a total of $48,528 was given to "individuals on the premises during the attack," and half a million dollars for the six "physically injured police officers." Tree of Light got $450,000 as a congregation, and its two tenant congregations each got $100,000. Three hundred thousand dollars was set aside as "seed funds for memorialization, commemoration & education for community healing and safety."

In the aftermath of the announcement, there was no objection. Anything that could have gone wrong, didn't. There was, as far as the committee could tell, no infighting within the families about who would accept the money for the family (and then distribute it as the family saw fit). The portion of the money set aside for "individuals on the premises" could have resulted in a free-for-all of people who claimed to be on the synagogue's grounds but weren't; the only evidence the committee asked for was a signed copy of a statement that read, "I attest that I was physically present on the Tree of Life Synagogue property at

5898 Wilkins Ave., Pittsburgh, PA 15217, but not inside the building, on the morning of October 27, 2018 between approximately 9:45 am when the shooting began and approximately 10:15 am when police took control of the site." The form was disseminated by all three congregations, and a notice was placed in the *Jewish Chronicle*. The committee never disclosed how many people applied for this money, but Ainsman, the federation president, said that everyone who asked, got. There was no quarrel, no controversy. "They had to self-identify," Ainsman said, "and basically we figured if somebody is going to lie about it, they are going to lie about it. You say you were there, you were there." As for the two cases in which two members of a family died—the Rosenthal brothers, and the couple Sylvan and Bernice Simon—the families got a double portion. That seemed fair to everyone.

The committee took some chances in how they distributed the money, principally in allocating funds for those who were not killed or injured. According to Ainsman, the advice Feinberg gave them—after an initial conference call, he communicated with Shapira, the committee chairman, who relayed notes of their conversations—was that they should "not get involved past the people killed and injured." In other words, no money for bystanders, no matter how close by. "He said [there could be] infighting in the community, you could open up a can of worms." But the committee decided that the money for those on the premises was crucial. After all, in no sense was this tragedy limited to those actually shot and their families; federal dollars were coming, for improved security at houses of worship and other Jewish buildings, and for mental health services over the next several years. Besides, one elderly Tree of Life member had become famous for having been on the premises: Judah Samet, the eighty-year-old survivor of Bergen-Belsen who was President Trump's guest at the State of the Union address.

The committee concluded that "this was absolutely a community tragedy," Ainsman said. The money had to be spread beyond just the victims' families and the survivors of the shooting. The people of Squirrel Hill seemed to agree. "There was not one word—and these are Jews!—not one word that we did something wrong," Ainsman said. "And believe me, if there was, we would know."

14

_∞

The Scene of the Crime

O N TUESDAY, the day that President Trump visited Tree of Life, Daniel Leger was in the hospital for the fourth day in a row. He was lying in bed, a breathing tube down his throat. He was with his wife, Ellen; his two grown sons, Noah, who was forty-five, and Jake, forty-two, as well as Noah's wife, Chris. His ex-wife, Jo, had been in and out and may have been there this day—he couldn't remember for sure. His congregation, Dor Hadash, was praying for him. He had been through multiple surgeries and was in stable condition. It was time, his doctors thought, to remove the tube. After the slow process of extubation was completed, Leger immediately tried to speak. "His voice is all craggly and scraggly," said Ellen, "and I hear him say *argh argh argh*. And I can't understand. And *then* I understand—he's saying the Sh'ma"— the central prayer of Judaism, attesting to the singularity of God. Leger gasped for more air and then, looking at his family around him, said, "I love you all so much." And then he said something that showed that he knew exactly what had happened to him. He said, "May God forgive him." "Then I knew," Ellen said, "that he was completely intact, because that is completely his thinking. That is who he is."

Leger was released from the hospital on November 26, 2018, almost a month to the day after he had been shot in the abdomen and pelvis and nearly bled to death, sprawled on a staircase at Tree of Life. Leger felt ready to get back to his reading, his cello, his dogs and cats, and, in good time, his job as a nurse and hospital chaplain. His doctors agreed that he was ready to resume life at home.

The weeks ahead were not easy. Before the shooting, Leger had been a seventy-year-old who didn't feel seventy, but now, for the first time in his life, he really felt his age, and his fund of energy, always limitless, was now frustratingly finite. He was napping all the time. It would be a while, he realized, before he could return to work. In his first couple of months at home, it was all he could do to walk the dogs or get to the supermarket.

And when he went to the supermarket, he faced an unexpected challenge: his newfound celebrity. Squirrel Hill, already a small village where an old-timer couldn't take a promenade or shop for provisions without getting waylaid for gossip or a hug, was now a fishbowl, with eyes widening at the sight of someone whose ability to walk upright again seemed like proof of God himself. "For those people who are seeing you for the first time, it's like they want to relive it all over again, and it's like a miracle to see you and to hug you," Ellen said to Dan five months after the shooting, when I was sitting with both of them at their home. "And you can't squelch that, because that's a person's real feelings. They're really genuinely so touched."

Leger got it—as a chaplain by profession, he was used to standing by quietly, listening, absorbing other people's pain, hearing things he had heard many times before. But just the same, he got tired. "The attention I would get needed to be managed, and that took a whole other measure of energy that was in short supply," he said. Walking around Squirrel Hill, knowing that every attempt to buy a loaf of bread could end in watching an old friend dissolve into tears, "has been both a really wonderfully comforting phenomenon, and at times a very deenergizing phenomenon."

Overall, of course, the outpouring of love made things better, not worse. In his work, Leger had nursed or comforted thousands of his fellow Pittsburghers, and many of them were eager to return the favor: his box of get-well cards was overflowing. Old friends wrote from out of state, strangers wrote from abroad. Members of Dor Hadash checked in constantly, and they left meals and fresh-baked challahs at his and Ellen's door. But even with a community of hundreds or more rooting for him, Leger was suffering, and not just physically. For all his faith, for all his capacity for forgiveness, he had been shot, and badly wounded, in an attack that had killed eleven people, including one of his best friends. He knew that even after the challahs stopped coming, he would not be all better; his recovery would not be a straight path. But very early on, almost immediately after he got out of the hospital, he had an idea for something he could do to help himself along. He had to go back to the scene of the crime.

After being shot, Leger had fallen onto a flight of stairs and was left facing a wall. He felt fortunate that his hearing aids had not fallen out, else he would have been unable to hear what was going on around him. As it was, he could hear the awful racket, although he could see none of it. His memories had a nightmarish quality but were vague. He needed to see the place, touch it—"verify that reality," he said. It had to become real for him, so that he could move on. He called the FBI, and the agent who had interviewed him in the hospital agreed to take him back inside the building. So on January 22, 2019, "a snowy day in January," Leger and Ellen met up with the FBI agent at Tree of Life.

"The first place I needed to go was the stairs where I had been lying, and show Ellen, and see what it looked like," Leger said. He looked up and down the stairwell, then at the stairwell on the other side of the wall he had been facing, a parallel set of stairs that leads down to the area where the New Light congregation prayed. As he looked at the walls above the stairs, he thought, "My God, the place was basically destroyed from gunfire—the walls had holes in them, the ceiling had holes in it. There were places cleaned with a bleaching agent, where there must have been blood on the floors. It was clear the building itself was so damaged, so desanctified, so desecrated." From the stairwells, he headed toward the Tree of Life congregation's chapel but stopped near the door. "I went up to the entrance to the chapel and looked in, but I didn't want to walk around in there a lot. My ability to get around was limited. I had a cane." But he had seen more than enough. "The sanctuary itself had been desecrated that way, too." Some pews had been removed and were stacked in the hall behind him, so that the blood could be washed off them. "There were gaps in the chapel where people had been killed." The holy society had cleaned the floors where the pews had been.

Leger went back to the stairs and descended, carefully, using his cane. He wanted to see where the New Light members had been killed.

He walked into the kitchen, where the shooter had found Dan Stein and Richard Gottfried. "I could see so easily that there was nowhere to hide in that kitchen, nowhere for Richard and Dan to conceal themselves," he said. "If somebody walked in there with a rifle, they were just sitting ducks." He saw spots where the floor had been bleached, and he understood what that meant. He walked out of the kitchen and into the small New Light chapel. He walked past the *bimah* and into the closet where Barry Werber, Carol Black, and Melvin Wax had hidden. He thought, in particular, of Mel, who like him was hard of hearing. In his deafness, Wax had thought the shooting was over and had opened the storeroom door, which is how the shooter found him. "Remembering Mel and his pretty profound hearing loss, and imagining him trying to figure out what was going on, and opening the door to try to figure out what was happening . . ." Leger trailed off.

He walked back upstairs and sat down on a bench in the lobby. He looked up at one of the doors to the outside and saw that it had bullet damage. The FBI agent walked over and handed Leger his overcoat and prayer shawl; he'd had them with him the morning of the shooting and had never gotten them back. They had both been cleaned. He was especially glad to see his prayer shawl again. He and Ellen had been married underneath it; it had been strung between poles to make the top of his wedding canopy. The FBI agent handed him a box and said, "Your shoes are in here." Leger was repulsed. "I said, 'Don't open that, I don't want them. You can do whatever you want with them.' I had this awareness that my feet were on the stairs below me, my head was at the top, and it seemed extremely likely to me that those shoes had been full of blood. I didn't want to look at them, I didn't want to have anything to do with them. In retrospect, it was a bizarre reaction."

He handed the box back to the FBI agent and sat on the bench with Ellen. The agent asked him if there was anything else she could do. Leger told her that she had done enough, that she had helped him do what he had come to do. "I remember getting up and walking out the door with Ellen, and this incredible sense of—I don't know the right word—*liberation* is a word that comes to me. A sense that a burden had been lifted from me, that my shoulders felt lighter, and I could walk out of that place and not have this sense that it had power over me. And feeling confident that in future days, when I would pass it in the car, or walking in the neighborhood, as much as the memories were always going to be powerful, I wouldn't have the questions of *Gee, what's it really like in there now?* . . . It was emotional. I remember crying, I remember Ellen supporting me. We were both pretty teary. We went home, had some lunch. I remember taking a nap."

———

TEN WEEKS LATER, on April 7, 2019, Leger walked from his house to the Jewish Community Center, where he had agreed to take part in "Parkland to Pittsburgh," a town hall meeting featuring survivors of both the Parkland and the Tree of Life massacres. It was cosponsored by WTAE, the local ABC television station, two of whose reporters served as the evening's moderators. Leger sat onstage with eight other guests, including a teacher and a student from Parkland and Pittsburgh's mayor, Bill Peduto. The room was packed.

The first question of the night went to Leger, who looked a little shrunken and not entirely happy to be there. He wore a corduroy blazer and, on his head, a teal blue yarmulke with a colorful border. He clasped his hands as he spoke. Some of the survivors of that day refrained from speaking to the public, but others decided it was their duty. Leger was among the dutiful.

"Since this is your first time talking about what happened on October 27, can you tell us what you're comfortable in discussing about what happened to you that day?" WTAE's Mike Clark asked Leger.

"I remember many things from that day," Leger replied, going on to talk about his love for Shabbat, its "juxtaposition with the awfulness of what ensued." He talked about preparing for services with Jerry Rabinowitz and another Dor Hadash congregant, Martin Gaynor, then hearing the gunshots. He spoke of his and Jerry's instinct, as a doctor and a nurse, to rush to help others. "We probably went in exactly the wrong direction," he said. "Jerry's gone. I'm here."

Leger's raw, affecting story was the highlight of the evening, which was edited and packaged as a one-hour special, aired two nights later on WTAE. Most of the hour was not particularly illuminating. The narration over the video montage that opened the hour was sickly sweet, in the way of local TV news when it decides to serve its community: "Countless elements of life can divide us and do . . . but if we pause . . .

and listen . . . we'll remember the one thing that supersedes all our differences—we're all human. . . . On Pittsburgh's darkest day last October, we saw the bonds of community grow stronger—and the power of love win."

During the panel discussion, Clark, the moderator, kept reaching for uplifting lessons; it seemed very important to him, for example, that the Pittsburgh survivors and Parkland survivors be seen as having bonded closely, although they had spent only a couple hours together. He asked Leger to "talk about how important it was for you and Andrea [Wedner, another survivor] to meet with our new friends from Parkland," a question Leger sidestepped, speaking instead about how good it had been to get closer to Andrea and her husband, Ron.

Near the end of the event, WTAE's Shannon Perrine, walking through the audience with a microphone, announced that there was time for "one more question," and she introduced Barry Werber. Many in the room knew that Werber was one of the eleven Tree of Life survivors. He was standing next to Perrine wearing a STRONGER THAN HATE/Steelers T-shirt and his Air Force veteran's cap. As he began to speak into her mic, it was as if the evening had at last found its purpose.

"My question is specifically for Daniel, [and] for Ivy," he said—Ivy being Parkland teacher Ivy Schamis, sitting onstage next to Leger. "How do you get by being reminded day in and day out—newspapers, television, radio, sleep—of the horror you went through? I've had professional treatment, I've had friends commiserate with me. But no one knows the feeling unless you have gone through it." Werber's voice cracked, and he bit his lower lip, which was trembling. "How do you do that? That's my question." He was speaking louder now, as if he were demanding answers. "How do you do that? How do you feel comfortable in a crowd? How do you feel comfortable going into your house of worship, Daniel? How do you feel comfortable going into a movie theater? How do you stop looking for the first exit? How do you stop looking for security? How do you go through that? I've tried. I've talked to people. I've talked to professionals, as I said before. But I can't find out from a fellow survivor how they do it. The people that I know that have survived, or relatives of those that have died, don't really want to talk about it. How do you get through it?"

When Werber began, Leger was not sure who this man in the audience was, speaking through such obvious pain. Since October 27, both men had been invited to attend a victims' grief group, organized by the Center for Victims—the same local nonprofit that provided the "canine advocates" for comfort in the days after the shooting—but while both attended sporadically, they had never crossed paths there. It seems likely that they had nodded at each other at some point, maybe exchanged pleasantries at Tree of Life on a Shabbat morning, but if so, Leger had no recollection. "I didn't know Barry at all," Leger later said. But Werber knew who Leger was, and as he spoke, it dawned on Leger who he was, and what the two men had in common. He wanted to give Werber a good answer, one that would help him get past his pain, to the place where Leger felt that he had arrived. And as he began to formulate what he would say, how he would answer Werber's desperate questions, he realized for the first time just how much the visit back to Tree of Life, three months earlier, had mattered.

"I am blessed with a wonderful wife," Leger said. "She is my rock. And one of the things that we did together was to go back into the building with the FBI. And it was really important to do that, and to be able to not be carried out this time, but to walk out. And to see the place where I was, to verify that reality. To see the place where eleven of my friends were murdered. To be able to have someone stand by me during that, and to be able to walk out and together know that this place no longer has power over me."

———

"WHEN HE SAID going back into the building had helped him, I thought to myself, *I don't want this shooter to have any strings on me. I'm not his puppet,*" Barry Werber said sometime later. "So I made arrangements." When he got home, he sent an email to Janet Cohen, the wife "and right-hand person," as Werber put it, of New Light's co-president, asking if she could help get him inside the Tree of Life building.

On April 10 she wrote back saying that she was working to get him access, but in the meantime he should think about whom he might want to accompany him back inside. "Barry, tomorrow I'll be in a meeting with people who can work to arrange your visit to the building," she wrote. "Do you want to see if a therapist can come with you? Is there someone you want me to ask, or do you want to talk to a therapist about this?"

Barry replied that he would ask his psychologist, Tim Murphy, but he was worried that Murphy would be unable to attend, as his granddaughter was being treated for cancer in New York City. He looped Murphy into the email thread, and that night, at 11:55 p.m., his doctor wrote back. "I will go with you."

On Wednesday, April 17, Werber and his wife, Brenda, met up with Murphy at Jewish Family and Community Services, and from there they drove the short distance to Tree of Life. Outside the building, they were met by Alan Hausman, the Tree of Life board member who took the lead on security matters. He had a key.

Werber is a lively little man. He has a little brush moustache, wears little hearing aids, and lives in a little house in a little East End neighborhood that most of the Jews left long ago. Inside his home, hanging on the glass doors of his china cabinet, there is a dog-bone-shaped trinket on which is written A SPOILED ROTTEN DACHSHUND LIVES HERE. The décor is a mix of dog humor—elsewhere in the house, a cartoon is captioned: THE MORE PEOPLE I MEET, THE MORE I LIKE MY DOG—and Pittsburgh sports memorabilia. Werber is the kind of man who fights adversity with humor: his wife, Brenda, was battling cancer, so he wore on his polo shirt a green pin that said, in white letters, I HATE CANCER.

But he reverted to a different tone—reflective, somber, tremulous—when he described that visit.

"Going into the building was surreal, with the bullet holes and some broken glass in the lobby," Werber said. "I walked around there for a little while, and they said, 'Do you want to go down to your sanctuary?'" The sanctuary was where he had fled to the storage closet at the front of the room. "And I said okay. They didn't want to rush me." They asked if he wanted to take the elevator instead of the stairs, but Werber recoiled at the idea. "If I could not walk down those steps, then part of the reason for being there was pointless," he said. It was at those steps that he'd had "the first inkling" of what was happening that morning, "as that is where we saw the body of Cecil Rosenthal, of blessed memory, and realized the danger we were in."

Werber sat down, gathered his resolve, then got up and went to the

Barry Werber (right) with Pittsburgh police officer Mike Smidga,
who was hit by gunfire at Tree of Life, photographed on February 27, 2019

top of the stairwell. "It was tough, but I walked down the steps," he said.
Hausman, from Tree of Life, and Murphy, Werber's psychologist, walked
with him, but Brenda, who has trouble with stairs, stayed behind. And
from the bottom of the steps, he walked into New Light's small chapel,
and he placed on the *bimah* a photograph that he had taken in 2017, of
Richard Gottfried carrying one of New Light's Torah scrolls into the
Tree of Life building, during the ceremonial parade when the congregation first moved in. "I said a blessing. And I looked around the room.
The room, of course, was in total disarray. The chairs were nowhere like
they had been."

From the *bimah,* he walked with Hausman and Murphy toward the
storage closet where he had hidden. "I looked around a little bit, and
then I guess I said, 'Can I go into the storeroom?'" Hausman told him
that he could. He walked into the room, and Hausman turned the light
on—it was the first time Werber had seen the room in the light. He was
stunned at how small it was. He had in mind a depth of about twenty
or thirty feet. Instead, he realized that, crouching in the dark closet, he
could not have been more than ten feet from the shooter, and probably
less. "That shook me up."

After leaving the storage room, the three men walked into the kitchen, where Stein and Gottfried had been killed. "That room also was a mess," Werber said. "After that, we went back upstairs, rejoined my wife, and left the building."

———

IT HAD BEEN IMPORTANT for Dan Leger and Barry Werber to go back into the Tree of Life building, but neither had any interest in praying there again. "That section of the building should not be used, as far as I'm concerned, for worship," Werber said. He felt that the structure could stand, and the huge old sanctuary, which his congregation never used, might as well stay. But the part that he and his fellow New Light congregants used—its days were probably over. "I wouldn't mind if they either repaired it or totally gutted it and tore it down and rebuilt it as some sort of a museum or as some sort of memorial. But as far as a house of worship? That particular part of the building, a house of worship? I say no. So New Light needs a new home." Several other New Light members told me they agreed. One told me that Sharyn Stein, the widow of the slain Dan Stein, "would never go back into that building." New Light had taken over a small chapel on the ground floor of the Beth Shalom building, and its members were happy there. Their Tree of Life days were behind them.

Dan Leger felt the same way. Speaking for himself and some other survivors, he said, "I think we pretty unanimously feel that it would be impossible to go back to feeling like it would be a place that we could be celebrating *simchas*"—joyous occasions—"without leveling the place and starting again. And that's not gonna happen." His congregation, Dor Hadash, was renting space from Rodef Shalom, an arrangement that was working out well enough. It was far from ideal—the old Reform temple's grand Moorish building on Fifth Avenue was precisely the kind of imposing, institutional edifice that the countercultural vibe of Dor Hadash set itself against. But Dor Hadash, which had never owned property, had always prided itself on being more than whatever space it happened to be renting. It had merely traded one old, establishmentarian landlord, Tree of Life, for another, nearly as old and many times as wealthy. Dor Hadash liked being the itinerant tenant.

Not everyone felt that the building had to go. Some members of the three congregations—including members who were inside the building that morning—did not have the vexed relationship with the physical space that Leger and Werber had, and they did not see a need for the building to be torn down or even renovated. Joe Charny, for example. He was the oldest survivor, ninety years old on the morning when the shooter had looked at him and then decided, for whatever reason, not to pull the trigger. Charny had grown up in a large family in Philadelphia, in the Jewish neighborhood of West Oak Lane. He graduated from Central, the city's elite public boys' high school, served in the army during World War II, then attended Swarthmore College. At the University of Pennsylvania's medical school, he encountered a problem: "I was a Jewish doctor who can't stand the sight of blood!" So he and his wife, whom he had met at Swarthmore, went to Pittsburgh, where he had been accepted into a residency program in psychiatry. He ended up on staff at the state psychiatric hospital in Woodville, fifteen miles from his house in Squirrel Hill.

One day, when he was in his sixties—he could not remember the exact year—his career ended. "I always started my day at seven o'clock by sitting down with the superintendent [of the hospital] and running through things for the first hour," he said, recalling his last day at work. "And I showed up, and lo and behold my boss was not there. I asked

Joe Charny

for her, and I was told, 'She's been terminated, and you're gonna be terminated today.'" A friendly woman in human resources, as angry at
the hospital as Charny was, helped get him a pension that Charny said
he "didn't really deserve."

A few days afterward, as his wife was about to leave for work, she
looked at him and said, "Don't sit around feeling sorry for yourself." It
was seven-fifteen in the morning, and he had nothing to do all day. So
he decided to go to synagogue. "I figured, *Oh, well, all right, I'll go over
to Tree of Life and go to services.* And that's how it started!" He never
held a steady, paying job again, but for the next twenty-five years or so,
he would help make the morning minyan at Tree of Life.

Charny had no patience with the idea that he was some sort of victim. He had refused to attend any of the victims' support groups, and he
said that when his children visited after the attack, he convinced them
that they could go back home, back to their lives. A widower since 2013,
when his wife of sixty-two years died, Charny said he was fine by himself. And he said he was not traumatized.

"I don't think that I had what you would call fear," he said. "I knew
it was happening, but I never felt that I was in trouble." He heard loud
noises, and then, when he looked up, "there were all these dead bodies. . . . I wasn't in the mood to stay there. . . . I mean, when he pointed
the gun at me and had a chance to shoot me and he didn't, I figured, *All
right, get the eff out of here!*" And after he successfully got the eff out,
he chalked his escape up to chance, contingency—the stuff that we all
know life is made of. "I didn't feel this sense of, *Oh, boy, I'm really lucky!*
I mean, shit happens, and it just so happens that it didn't happen to me."

Charny's sanguinity may have been the height of mindfulness,
the fruit of years of psychoanalytic training and practice, or simply
pure acceptance, but when I asked him why some people bounce back
so quickly, while others are never the same, he said that he had been
through a lot in his time, seen a lot, had successes and failures. He had
prepared for this. He had been to war ("I could write a book about my
few months in Trieste"). He had seen men get very, very sick, not just
emotionally but physically ("VD was a big thing with military per-
sonnel"). And he had, he felt, washed out as a doctor ("You know, I've
been through difficulties throughout my psychiatric career. It was not a
success").

Charny evinced no sense of shame that after being laid off he had never found another job, which seemed significant. Bright Jewish boy, Swarthmore, Penn Med—big things had been expected of him. It could be that he was simply very evolved, knew that personal relationships matter more than worldly success, and that he took great pleasure in his long, enduring marriage and successful children. He spoke of them with great pride: his daughter and his son. And then there was his son who had died.

"With David . . . it was a tragedy," he said. "David was absolutely brilliant." Charny's younger son had attended Yale and then started medical school at Penn, "with the idea that he would follow his father's footsteps." But medical school was not for him. "He really was not a natural as a doctor. He was more intellectual, very much mindful. And so we got a nice little note from him telling us that he was leaving medical school, but that he had gotten a full scholarship to Harvard Law School, and that's where he was going. And he went to Harvard, and as things happened, he ended up as a full professor, the youngest full professor they had ever had at Harvard Law School. I mean, it was really great. But he was gay, and he got AIDS, and he died about a week before his forty-fifth birthday."[*]

So maybe when you've lost a son to AIDS, being the guy in the room who's not murdered is not the worst thing that can happen to you. He summed it up this way: "You know, it's different being ninety-one than it is being some other age."

Charny said that he wanted the Tree of Life congregation to return to its building. He did think some remodeling was in order, but not because there was anything haunted about the old space. Rather, he had always been perturbed that the sanctuary faced south, when it's the tradition in the diaspora to orient a synagogue toward Jerusalem, hence facing east. He figured a rebuild was a chance to correct this mistake. But he did not cotton to the idea that the synagogue was now too despoiled to pray in. "I feel the other way!" he said. "To show them that there is some shit I will not eat, I'm gonna go back there!"

---

[*] Later I found David's *New York Times* obituary, which said that he had died on August 31, 2000, "after a short illness," and that he was "survived by his partner, Ahmad H. Tabari."

15

The Building

Tree of life now had a big name and more fundraising potential than ever before, but it had been housed in a decrepit old building even before it was a crime scene; now it was a decrepit old building with some very bad juju. Attendance was low, but Squirrel Hill real estate prices were high. Chatham University, crowded onto a small campus just across the street, was rumored to have been making overtures for years about acquiring the building. There would be other offers, too. So why keep it?

This was the kind of opinion that might get murmured over the salad bar at the Eat 'n Park on Murray Avenue—but only quietly. You might hear it tentatively broached in the gym at the JCC—but only after heads were swiveled to see who was on the next exercise bike. To suggest that the crime at Tree of Life was an occasion for the synagogue to unburden itself of the building was considered by many a sacrilege. But it had become a very common sort of sacrilege, like eating bacon or gossiping, so common that one wondered if it really counted as sacrilege at all.

The irony here was that, before October 27, 2018, wondering how long Tree of Life could hold on was not even a minor sin; it was more like a casual pastime. Its membership figures had collapsed in the past quarter century, which was not unusual for a Conservative synagogue, but its troubles had been dramatically public. Alvin Berkun said that when he retired as Tree of Life's rabbi in 2005, the membership "was about a thousand families"—it wasn't, but it had been earlier in his rabbinate. Fourteen years later, board member Irwin Harris told me that Tree of Life had "two hundred twenty to two hundred fifty [member families], but a lot of those are 'soft memberships'"—including people who had stopped paying dues. And the attack might have made some people *less* likely to pay up. "Some people say to me, 'Why do I have to pay for tickets, when you have that pot of money?'"

After Berkun left in 2005, he had been succeeded by Avi Friedman, who after one year left for a synagogue in Summit, New Jersey; the website of his New Jersey synagogue, Ohr Shalom, says that he had come from Tree of Life, a "550-member Conservative congregation in Pittsburgh, Pennsylvania." Another rabbi, Stephen Listfield, was hired in 2006. But he didn't last long. The way Listfield remembered it, about a year after he arrived at Tree of Life to begin a five-year contract, the synagogue president came to him and admitted that the congregation did not have 550 families, as Listfield had been told when he had applied for the job, but more like 350. Finances were so bad that the board needed to rent space to another congregation—and they had reached terms with Or L'Simcha, a small synagogue recently founded by Rabbi Chuck Diamond. What's more, Tree of Life was expecting that the congregations would soon merge and Diamond would become the rabbi of both.

In other words, Listfield had to go. He got paid through 2009, then was out. "I was at the business end of that AR-15," Listfield told me, pushed aside for a man who, as far as he could tell, was "the most reviled person in all of Jewry since at least Ethel and Julius Rosenberg."

The controversial "Rabbi Chuck," as he likes to be known, is peripheral to the Jewish life of Squirrel Hill today—and yet people can't stop talking about him and how peripheral he is. Diamond was born in 1955 and grew up in Squirrel Hill, on Aylesboro Avenue—now Tammy Hepps's street—next door to my dad and his family. The Diamonds attended a small Orthodox synagogue. After college, Diamond started law school but soon took a leave of absence and, while living at home, began working part-time at Beth Shalom, in Squirrel Hill. Working in the Jewish community proved leagues more interesting, more rewarding, than black-letter legal textbooks. He had always loved his summers at Camp Ramah, the Canadian branch in Utterson, Ontario, two hours north of Toronto. He talked with a favorite camp rabbi, Israel Silverman, and his wife, Gloria, and they urged Diamond to think about the rabbinate. He liked the idea. He had never been "overly impressed" with the rabbinical students he had known at Camp Ramah, and he felt he could do better. "I thought I had something to offer," he would later say, with a bit of understatement. He matriculated at Jewish Theological Seminary, in New York City, in 1980. He didn't exactly take to his studies, but he had a good time. "I was tired of school in a way," he said. "I was known for my juggling. I would emcee all the parties. They used to kid I was at rabbinical school on a basketball scholarship." After graduation, he took a job on Long Island, in Great Neck, where he worked until 1989. Then he and his wife and children moved to a synagogue in Detroit, briefly, before returning two years later to Pittsburgh, where he was hired as an assistant rabbi at Beth Shalom.

Diamond was at Beth Shalom for fourteen years, serving under Rabbi Berkun. During that entire time, he was known—as he had been known in Great Neck and Detroit, and as he was known at Camp Ramah, where he returned every summer on staff—as the children's rabbi. Kids were his specialty. He loved them, and he was good with them. It wasn't just his juggling skills, his love of hoops, his shameless silliness on the dance floor, or his corny jokes. It was also his infectious love of Judaism. He loved Bible stories, and he wanted to get children and teenagers to love them, too. In the woods, around the campfire, in discussions about Jewish ethics, he talked to Jewish teens without talking down to them.

Staci Bush, a Squirrel Hill native, born in 1975, knew Chuck Diamond from her summers at Camp Ramah, where she said he was a powerful presence. "I think he honestly taught a lot of kids their Jewish morality," she said. "I think camp was really where he shined, and that was his home. . . . I know that every camper, at least every kid that went to Ramah, felt that way about him, that he was the greatest camp rabbi. Because he knew how to tell a good story. He liked to teach."

Bush remembered after-dinner activities in which Diamond split the kids into groups and assigned them different countries, then told them to make world peace. "It was *How do you figure out the world's problems?* If you had to figure out Israel, they'd make somebody Jordan, and somebody Syria. . . . Diamond would facilitate frank discussions about big questions. You'd have to debate: one person would be for intermarriage,

Chuck Diamond on the lake at Camp Ramah, in Ontario, in 2013 or 2014

one person would be against it. And you'd go far beyond—it made you think about all the things you didn't have to think about yet."

In Squirrel Hill, however, Diamond was divisive. Some of the adults loved his shtick and loved how he engaged their children. But others had trouble taking him seriously. When a more somber or formal tone was called for, he often fell flat. He was not the man they wanted to preside over their weddings, bury their loved ones, or offer pastoral counseling. They could not imagine taking their confidential worries to the funny, juggling rabbi. "I always felt, in terms of funerals or weddings, the ones I did were successful, and for the very most part, they enjoyed it," he said. "Others who didn't use me didn't feel I was serious enough or formal enough. You're gonna run into that wherever." Eventually, Beth Shalom began to feel like a poor fit, and after one particular negotiation of a new contract—"the contract negotiations from hell," which took away "a part of [his] soul"—he asked to be let out of his contract so he could leave the synagogue.

And then Diamond promptly did the unthinkable: he started a rival congregation, Or L'Simcha. Starting a new congregation nearby—when it began, Or L'Simcha met in a rented space two miles from Beth Shalom—was a huge breach of Squirrel Hill etiquette, a violation of the

Conservative rabbinic association's rules of conduct, and above all, a middle finger to his former employer. Diamond was brought before the ethics committee of the Rabbinical Assembly, where he faced a two-year suspension, one that would not allow him to work for any Conservative synagogue; Diamond says he resigned from the organization before it could take any action against him.

Diamond was popular enough with a minority of Beth Shalom members, in particular the parents of bar and bat mitzvah students who had adored him, that his departure caused a major schism: about 125 families left Beth Shalom to follow him to Or L'Simcha. In 2008, three years after starting it, Diamond moved his new congregation into rented space at Tree of Life. Two years later Tree of Life, still hemorrhaging members, entered into an agreement with Or L'Simcha, merging the two congregations and inviting Diamond, the rabbi who had only five years earlier split a nearby shul in two, to be the senior rabbi of the newly created Tree of Life*Or L'Simcha (which is still the official name of what everyone calls Tree of Life; the asterisk between the two congregations' names has puzzled typesetters ever since). In absorbing Or L'Simcha, Tree of Life grew by about a hundred member families, and the board of the merged congregation, ecstatic about the new families, the new revenue, and the rosy prospects for the future, signed Diamond to a ten-year contract. It seemed that Tree of Life was back.

It wasn't to be. Membership at Tree of Life*Or L'Simcha peaked the next year, in 2011, and declined every year thereafter. The young families with children that Diamond was so famous for attracting just weren't coming anymore. He was by now in his mid-fifties, and his cool factor was beginning to dim. And families shopping for a shul to join were likely to hear about Diamond's past, the bridges he had burned.

Then there was the botched circumcision. In April 2013, Diamond presided over the bris of a baby boy, born to a woman he had known from Camp Ramah who now attended his congregation. While Diamond was emceeing, offering prayers and bantering with the gathered friends and relatives, Mordechai Rosenberg, the *mohel*, or ritual circumciser, made the cut—and severed the boy's penis. Diamond heard the *mohel* say, "We have to get him to the hospital!" and when Diamond looked down, "there was blood everywhere." As Diamond described it, he sprang into action, potentially saving the boy's penis. "I have this emergency mode I can go into," he said. He made sure all the other children present were rushed out of the room, and he yelled for somebody to call 911. "The parents ended up driving the baby themselves to the hospital. Children's Hospital reattached the penis. The kid is five years old. He is fine." Diamond had done nothing wrong, but he was traumatized. He was filled with rage at the *mohel,* who was soon performing brises again.

Unsurprisingly, Diamond said he suffered some post-traumatic stress after the circumcision, but it was nothing that he felt affected his rabbinate. Whatever the case, Tree of Life*Or L'Simcha was losing members. The board, saddled with Diamond's lucrative ten-year contract, wanted him to take a reduction in salary. He refused, both sides lawyered up, and finally in September 2016, it was announced that the following June he would be leaving Tree of Life*Or L'Simcha.

Diamond left, but he never went away. He still lived in the old family house on Aylesboro. He was unemployed, which just gave him more time to promenade around Squirrel Hill. He kept up a lively presence on Facebook, and he continued to lead a small, informal monthly gathering called Kehillah La La, a play on *kehillah,* or community. And when the shooting occurred at Tree of Life, which just a year and a half earlier had been his congregation, he ran over to the building and began granting media interviews; in the days to come, he was one of the most ubiquitous faces on television news. One could see him the day of the shooting on KDKA, the local CBS-TV channel, outside Tree of Life, wearing a fleece-lined jacket and a Pirates baseball cap, offering incorrect guesses about who was inside—"maybe forty people"—and reflecting on his state of mind when he was the rabbi. When asked by a reporter if he had worried about antisemitic attacks in synagogue, he said, "When I was there, in the back of my mind, I always had the thought of something like this happening, and what I would do." The same day he was on Canada's Global News; the next morning, ABC's *Good Morning America;* the next day, he was quoted in *Time* and gave a long interview to MSNBC's Chris Hayes.

Over the course of the week, there was muttering about Diamond's being one of the faces of the tragedy. On the one hand, the media were seeking out any and all Pittsburgh clergy that week; other rabbis, like Rodef Shalom's long-retired Walter Jacob, were pulled out of retirement to go before the cameras. And Diamond always made it clear that he was the *former* rabbi of Tree of Life. And yet he "was just roaming the streets, looking for cameras," in the words of one local Jewish leader, somebody who had worked closely with him over the years.

One week after the shooting, the next Shabbat morning, Diamond invited followers to a "healing service" that he led in front of Tree of Life. Television cameras were there, and the Associated Press sent a reporter, whose dispatch ran in newspapers around the country. "Parents clutched their children, couples leaned on each other and bystanders wept as about 100 people gathered in a steady drizzle outside the desecrated Tree of Life synagogue for what a former rabbi called a healing service one week after the worst attack targeting Jews in U.S. history," the AP's Ramesh Santanam wrote. Wearing a rainbow-striped prayer shawl, "Rabbi Chuck Diamond led a service of prayers, songs and poetry and reminisced about some of the worshippers killed. . . . Diamond called the victims 'angels given to us, full of love and life.'"

He was still sharing his thoughts six months later, in one of his prolific Facebook posts. "Little did I know at that time," he wrote on May 14, 2019, "that our decision for a mutual separation"—that is, his leaving the synagogue—"would save my life. Otherwise on the morning of Oct. 27, 2018, I would still have been the Rabbi at Tree of Life*Or L'Simcha. . . . It is very sobering to think that under a different scenario I would have been there. My friends all agree that I would have most likely run towards that first loud noise which sounded like a coat rack falling. Upon hearing the shots they say I would have confronted the shooter and tried to talk to him. I have been a leader in some capacity for most of my life. In emergencies I have always clicked into 'an emergency mode.'"

As this post made the rounds, it struck many as a masterpiece of narcissism, exalting the author while diminishing the rabbis inside the building who had nearly been killed. Whatever one already thought of Chuck Diamond was confirmed, to a tee. Some were aghast, but his admirers on Facebook left fulsome comments: "You're a beautiful person. We are blessed that you were spared. Keep doing good things," one woman wrote. "So glad you weren't there that day, so you could help lead us through the aftermath," wrote another.

But if Diamond acted as if he were now a major national figure, he wasn't wrong—the shooting had elevated all the rabbis in town, making them important players. And now that they, and their congregations, were forever part of the American Jewish story, the question of what to do with the Tree of Life building became rather more complicated. After October 27, 2018, it was all of a sudden impolite to say out loud that Tree of Life might want to sell its building. The only ones who could talk that way were those who bore the scars, physical and emotional, of having been inside the building: Daniel Leger and Barry Werber had the authority to come right out and say what they thought, delicacy be damned. Otherwise, I met only one person who would entertain the idea, out loud, that maybe the Tree of Life congregation should just leave the Tree of Life building: Daniel Schiff, a Reform rabbi from Australia, who was employed by the Jewish Federation of Greater Pittsburgh as their "foundation scholar," a role that allowed him to be an itinerant lecturer and teacher, and sometimes gadfly, around Greater Pittsburgh.

"I have said for a long time," Schiff said, "in this community, given that Reform and Conservative and Reconstructionist congregations are not going to have a long-term future—and let's be real, those three congregations were under the same roof . . . because they didn't have the strength of numbers to be independent—I've always believed that we should rationalize our real estate in Pittsburgh. And the more that

Daniel Schiff

we could share real estate, the better off we were. So I'm simply cautious about the idea of putting more money into a piece of real estate that, while it certainly would serve a purpose for the next several years, may not serve a purpose for the next ten to twenty years."

―――――

BUT IT WASN'T UP TO Daniel Schiff to decide. Or to Dan Leger, Barry Werber, or the gossips in the locker room at the JCC. It was up to the board of directors of Tree of Life, which owned the building and had been landlord to two other congregations, who were facing an unusual new situation: for the first time in anyone's memory, there would be money.

There's a tawdry line about the endless market for all things Holocaust: *There's no business like Shoah business.* The Shoah—that's the Holocaust, in Hebrew—business includes concentration camp tourism, books and movies about the Holocaust, and so on. The Shoah-business principle applied to Tree of Life: where there has been cataclysmic human suffering, money will be spent. Now that Tree of Life was the site of an instantly legendary antisemitic crime, its building and grounds meant something new. The millions already donated would not be enough for the major renovation that some had in mind, but it seemed impossible that American, and world, Jewry would not pony up the rest. This was hallowed ground.

Some had trouble looking at the building and changed routes to avoid it; others could not wait to get back inside. Still others preferred a compromise position, according to which the main husk of the building would be kept, along with the large old sanctuary (which had not been in use on October 27), while rooms where people had been shot would be reconfigured to look totally different. At the same time, the entire building, which was somewhat dilapidated, could be cleaned, updated, and brought up to code. Tree of Life would thus salvage from this horror a spiffier, more functional building, one that would greet the expected tourists and pilgrims with a welcoming restored façade and would serve its congregants and the local Jewish community with an improved, more functional space inside.

No synagogue would have felt confident making a decision like this, but Tree of Life was especially ill equipped. Like all synagogues, Tree of Life was led by a board of unpaid laypeople; many of them seldom attended services. Tree of Life had no professional staff besides the rabbi, and all of a sudden, this board of directors had what seemed like a million new stakeholders: Squirrel Hill, which would forever be receiving disaster tourists; the Jewish community of Pittsburgh, which included thousands who felt that the attacker had come for them, too; American Jewry; and worldwide Jewry. Whatever the board decided to do, everybody would have an opinion.

As they began to look around for answers, it quickly became clear that there was no obvious precedent. After the Columbine High School shooting in 1999, Jefferson County, Colorado, had reopened the school—and in the years since, it had become a magnet for gawkers, trespassers, conspiracy theorists, and assorted other obsessives. In fact, at the time of the Tree of Life shooting, the Jefferson County school district was formulating a plan to raze the school building and rebuild it nearby—"to reduce Columbine's morbid allure," as *The New York Times* put it. When the district presented the plan for public comment in June 2019, it provoked an angry controversy, with some residents arguing that "tearing down Columbine—even twenty years later—would be a capitulation to school shooters." The plan was shelved, the high school stands, and the school district switched gears, opting to landscape the grounds to give the school more privacy. Newtown, Connecticut, went ahead with a demolition of Sandy Hook Elementary School and constructed a new building on the same property. At Marjory Stoneman Douglas High School, in Parkland, Florida, the freshman building, site of the 2018 mass shooting, is still standing, because prosecutors want to preserve it as evidence (for the time being); but the school has constructed a new building on the property and plans never to use the old one again. Meanwhile, the state has given the school district one million dollars for a memorial to the victims, although the district seems unlikely to put the memorial on the school grounds, since a steady stream of visitors would be disruptive.

There are abundant examples of crime scenes that never returned to everyday use, but in other places the locals' sense of dignity demanded a quick rebound. Members of Mother Emanuel, in Charleston, were back inside, praying, days after the murders there. In Israel, the national mythology holds that if there's a café bombing during breakfast, the debris is swept up and the café is open by dinner—keeping on keeping on is a matter of patriotism.

So what would Tree of Life do? In the twenty-first century, an organization facing a tough decision hires a consultant. As it turned out, Tree of Life didn't have to hire one, because Dan Rothschild volunteered. Over the past thirty years, Rothschild had become the go-to architect for renovations in Jewish Squirrel Hill. He had done jobs for numerous local synagogues and Jewish agencies, and his history with the Tree of Life building stretched back to 1995, when he designed the renovation for its social hall, or pavilion, as it is known.

Rothschild took a special interest in architecture in the aftermath of "10/27"—as it was beginning to be called—and not just because of its Jewish dimension. He and his partners had developed a specialty in trauma-informed design, thinking about how to use architecture and design to help people heal. The firm had led a design project in Haiti after the 2010 earthquake, and Rothschild had been on-site at a public housing project that he was doing in Puerto Rico when the Drug Enforcement Administration rolled in to make a drug bust.

"Often the communities and neighborhoods we work with have undergone some kind of trauma," Rothschild said, "whether it's violence or abject poverty, something that has disconnected them from other neighborhoods. . . . We have experience going into these neighborhoods, embedding ourselves, and designing processes to extract information, communicate, and build up positivity. That is not an architecture thing, it's an urban design and planning thing. It has been part of our process for thirty years."

Rothschild conducts an extensive series of interviews, not just with whoever is footing the bill—the developer, the synagogue, the government agency—but with all who will be affected, including potential residents. He gets their stories, then figures out how the stories could infuse his design. In 2005, when he was asked to design a new apartment building in the Hill District, he first gathered longtime residents for three months of occasional evening gab sessions. In one of their meetings, they got to talking about music and about the neighborhood's past as a hub for jazz.

"There was a small jazz club across the street from our site that hadn't been occupied for decades but back in the day was one of the central jazz venues in Pittsburgh," Rothschild said. "Pittsburgh was the halfway point for jazz musicians driving from New York to Chicago, so they would stop off and play at this venue, the Crawford Grill. People would talk about what they experienced at the Crawford Grill. Many were musicians themselves." Rothschild realized that music, for this neighborhood, "was like renewable energy." On one side of the building that he designed, running along Wylie Avenue, he created a jazz wall of fame, featuring the names of twelve local musicians, chosen through a survey that was distributed throughout the neighborhood. The names are written on limestone panels, right above the first floor glazing, creating a monument to jazz hundreds of feet long.

"So with those tools in our toolkit," Rothschild said, "knowing we have dealt with nonarchitectural processes to help people and neighborhoods recover from trauma, and couple that with our thirty-year history working with Jewish institutions, and you see the largest trauma in Jewish history in the United States happen at Tree of Life—we get a call: 'Can you help us?'"

The call was from Michael Eisenberg, a past president of the congregation, and he wasn't sure why he was calling. He knew that they needed an architect, but he did not yet know what for. Rothschild promised to help them figure it out. Beginning in November, Rothschild held regular private meetings, more than one a month, with different groups, including members of each of the three congregations, families of the victims, and people who had been inside and survived. His job—at least for the time being—was not to come up with a set of architectural drawings but rather to produce a memo synthesizing the wishes, hopes, and fears of hundreds of people who would have feelings about whatever became of the building. The inventory would not be exhaustive, as it would inevitably omit the concerns of thousands of Pittsburghers who would have strong opinions; but if he did his job well, it would be a fair survey. He collated everything he had heard into a report for the Tree of Life board.

The board never let the public see Rothschild's memo. All most people knew was that, a year after the shooting, the Tree of Life building was still closed for business—dark, inaccessible, and locked, its doors bolted. There was an ugly wire-mesh fence around it, decorated with

The fencing around Tree of Life decorated with children's artwork

children's artwork printed on windscreens, a vain, failed attempt to put a cheery face on a broken body.

We all know how dispiriting it is to live or work next to a building perpetually under construction, how we yearn for the scaffolding to come down, for the grass to be replanted, for new shrubs to be set into the ground, and for the doors to open and welcome people once more. Now imagine that the building has been shut not for renovation but by murder. That was what people saw at the corner of Shady and Wilkins, and nobody was entirely sure when they would see something new.

The truth is that, more than anything else, the synagogue's board was simply paralyzed. It could do anything. It could go big with a major renovation, or it could sell its damaged building, get seven figures in the robust Squirrel Hill real estate market, and relocate to a smaller structure, while establishing a healthy endowment.

But to make any decision at all seemed presumptuous. After all, this was Squirrel Hill, where every synagogue belonged, in its way, to the whole community. Danny Schiff, the rabbi who was skeptical about any Tree of Life renovation, had an immigrant's perspective on the Squirrel Hill way. When his family came to Pittsburgh, they expected to leave after three years, to make a home in a more cosmopolitan city, like Tel Aviv or Jerusalem or Melbourne. But they stayed,* won over by "this geographic closeness, which also leads to the sense that we have to deal with each other reasonably," as he put it. "We're going to live next door to each other. We really can't be fighting with each other. We can't be rude to each other. And there really is no point to that. So it's not as if we've forgotten that there are differences in Jewish life. Of course, there are differences in Jewish life; they're acknowledged and they're real. But we try to cope with them decently. . . . You know, when I think about other places, either the levels of vitriol make being together unpleasant, or the geography simply means that there are multiple different centers of Jewish life, but no one center of Jewish life. Or the reality is that the people have just become entirely disconnected from one another. And I think that that's not true here." This closeness, this connection, bred a democratic ethos that made Squirrel Hill a uniquely pleasant place to live. It also meant that some tough decisions might not get made.†

* Schiff now spends about half the year in Israel.
† In early May 2021, Tree of Life announced that noted architect Daniel Libeskind, designer of the Jewish Museum Berlin and the Dutch Holocaust Memorial of Names, had been hired to work on the redevelopment of the Tree of Life site.

16

The Springtime

O N THE MORNING OF APRIL 27, 2019, six months after the attack on Tree of Life, a nineteen-year-old with an AR-15 semi-automatic rifle entered Chabad of Poway, a small Orthodox synagogue twenty-five miles north of San Diego, and shot four of the people present for morning services. It was Saturday morning, the Sabbath, and also the last day of Passover. Three were injured and survived, including the rabbi, Yisroel Goldstein, who lost his right index finger. Lori Gilbert-Kaye, sixty years old, was killed.

Jews all over the country, but especially in Squirrel Hill, got a sinking feeling, as the question of the past six months now had an answer: No, this was not a one-off. Yes, it was going to happen again. But to the next question—*So what now?*—Jews had a range of answers, depending on what kind of Jews they were.

For secular Jews, or those without strong ties to synagogues or other Jewish organizations, the Poway attack did not heighten any sense of personal danger; those who seldom entered Jewish spaces had little cause to worry for their lives. This was just another antisemitic tragedy in the era of mass shootings.

The most observant Jews in Pittsburgh, the Orthodox, were a resilient group. Antisemitism, of course, did not feel new to them. Because their clothing made them visible as Jews, many had experienced harassment on the streets, something that almost nobody in the non-Orthodox community could say. And the Orthodox often had close emotional ties to Israel, not to mention relatives there. The episodic violence and terrorism in the Middle East were their experience, too. For the Orthodox, the Tree of Life attack, as horrible as it had been, was part of the river of Jewish history, which is periodically fed by Jewish blood.

"Within the Orthodox community, this was experienced somewhat differently, due to the way that terror incidents in Israel are observed and internalized on a communal kind of basis," said Daniel Yolkut, the rabbi of Poale Zedeck, who on the night of the attack had given Nina Butler the task of keeping well-meaning Orthodox from flooding the neighborhood. For more secular Jews, he explained, "part of the trauma of Tree of Life was that this does not fit into any kind of preexisting narrative." For most Americans, Jews and Gentiles, the story of Jews in America is one of high incomes, higher learning, and liberation from oppression. For them, "the American Jewish narrative is not about Jews being killed." But for the Orthodox—whether the Modern Orthodox, who tend to be theologically Zionist, or the more stringent Orthodox, the Haredi Jews, some of whom are anti-Zionist in theology but still have strong family

Daniel Yolkut, the rabbi of Poale Zedeck, with his son Chaskie
at MetLife Stadium on January 1, 2020

ties to Israel—the Jewish narrative is, in no small part, about Jews being imperiled.

He gave as an example the kidnapping, on June 12, 2014, of three Israeli teenagers hitchhiking home in the West Bank. For three weeks, all Israel was fixated on the fates of Naftali Fraenkel, sixteen, Gilad Shaer, sixteen, and Eyal Yifrah, nineteen. In Orthodox communities in the diaspora, the kidnapping was daily news as well. One weekend in the middle of the three-week crisis, which ended when the boys' bodies were found on June 30—the Israeli government blamed Hamas, one of whose members was sent to prison for his role—Yolkut visited his brother in Teaneck, New Jersey. In the Orthodox neighborhood in Teaneck, "every third lawn had lawn signs with pictures of those three boys, with the hashtag #bringbackourboys on top of it," Yolkut said. For the Orthodox community, Jews being kidnapped, attacked, or blown up was not shocking. And the rituals that came afterward—the names of victims being read aloud in synagogue, the reports back from somebody who might have traveled for the funeral or shiva—were expected. What happened at Tree of Life produced, then, "a very familiar sense of adrenaline," Yolkut said. "Let's call it unpleasantly familiar."

Ironically, it was the Jews in the middle who continued, in the winter and into the spring, to feel the most strain. Let's call them the affiliated non-Orthodox. These Jews belonged to a Reform, Conservative, or Reconstructionist congregation; maybe they never attended, maybe they went once or twice a year, for High Holy Days, or maybe they were regulars. They might have little interest in shul but some interest in occasional meetings of political organizations like Bend the Arc. They were the oldsters whose bridge games and book clubs were filled with friends they had known since the days of fancy soirees at the Concordia Club, the now-defunct Jewish social club of the old Squirrel Hill elite. They were the regulars for water aerobics at the JCC's swimming pool, and the Jewish Allderdice alumni who were proud that their Allderdice grandchildren were keeping up tradition. They were the widowers whose primary religious observance was Sunday in front of the TV, cheering on the Steelers, but who would never think of *not* cutting an annual check to the federation. These were the people who, having lived an idyllic Jewish life in a modern urban shtetl, had been forced, by the events of October 27, 2018, to think about security for the first time.

And now Poway.

For some Jews, before Poway and especially after, talking about anti-semitism, educating people about it, and girding the community against it became a daily occupation. Every synagogue board was having discussions about security. Nobody wanted synagogues to be fortified bunkers, as in Europe, but was it enough to lock the doors and have a friendly greeter open them? Did there have to be an armed guard? What about cameras? For observant Jews, was it okay to carry a mobile phone, since saving a life outweighs observing the Sabbath?

A lot depended on how bad things seemed to be. Nobody was attacking Orthodox Jews on the streets of Pittsburgh, as they were in Brooklyn. At the same time, if you subscribed to the daily email blast from the Security Community Network (SCN), an office that coordinates security efforts for Jewish schools, synagogues, and camps, not a day went by when you didn't receive a digest of bad news. An SCN email the week before the Poway shooting included links to stories with the headlines "New Jersey School District Hit with 6th Swastika Incident in 5 Months" and "New Mexico Café Owner Closes Shop Following Backlash to Anti-Semitic Facebook Post." A week before you would have gotten links to "Video Depicts Rapper Performing Anti-Semitic Song as Part of Gaza Conference at University of North Carolina," "Second Instance of Anti-Semitism Reported Within the Same Week (California)," "White Nationalist Signs Posted Across Miami University (Ohio)," and "Swastika Spotted on Goldwin Smith Hall Exterior; Drawing Concerns About Campus Climate [at Cornell] (New York)."

And while occasionally the antisemitic acts seemed trivial or only plausibly antisemitic (not all anti-Israel activism should be categorized as antisemitism), the truth was that a lot of people seemed to be spray-painting swastikas. A lot of people loved to heap blame on Jews. And not only on far-right websites. Michael Palombo, a member of the left-wing Occupy movement, took to Facebook to blame Jewish landlords for rising rents. "Why is it so often a Jew is behind the suffering of others?" Palombo wrote on Facebook. After the ensuing outrage, he closed his vegan café in Albuquerque, New Mexico, and returned to Facebook to say he was sorry. "This has been one of the most painful and embarrassing moments of my life," he wrote. "Again, my deepest apologies and hope someday that I'm forgiven and most of all I forgive myself."

These stories, which described increasingly precarious Jewish life in America, were also reported by national Jewish publications like the *Forward* and *Tablet* and recapitulated in the back pages of local Jewish publications like the *Jewish Chronicle*. If you were getting these emails or skimming these websites, the attack on Chabad of Poway was sad, scary, and not entirely surprising.

Rather, the Poway attack was, in a very peculiar way . . . *energizing*. For those waiting for the next synagogue attack, the next shoe to drop, well, here it was—proof of everyone's worst fears, proof that the synagogues were right to install new cameras and bar the doors. Here was confirmation that Jews really did have a place in the American conversation about hate crimes.

There is a reason soldiers re-up for another tour of duty. Life away from the theater of war lacks its intensity and purpose. Eric Lidji, the archivist responsible for keeping the public record of what happened at Tree of Life, said in July 2019 that the Poway attack in April had returned people to the peak feeling of those moments back in October, a feeling that had subsided in the winter. The memories of the sirens and ambulances had receded, and the visual reminders were now part of the landscape. Tim Hindes's Steelers-inspired poster was still visible everywhere, from shop windows to the yarmulkes on men's heads, and hundreds of the Stars of David made of paper or yarn had survived the winter and were still swinging from the branches of trees. But they no longer made people pause in their day, much less made them cry. The trauma tourists were largely gone, the emissaries from around the world had disappeared. If people heard a siren now, they no longer thought that somebody was shooting up a synagogue.

"There's a period where normal daily life feels really dull, because we were used to such emotional intensity for so long," Lidji said. He pointed out that the Poway shooting, falling on the last day of Passover, coincided with one of the four annual recitations of Yizkor, the public memorial service for the dead, and this would be the first Yizkor since the eleven deaths at Tree of Life. Moreover, Yom HaShoah, Holocaust Remembrance Day, was to begin four days later, at sunset on May 1. For those attuned to the Jewish calendar, the arid emotional winter was abruptly over. "Yizkor, the six-month anniversary, Poway, then Yom HaShoah—and all of a sudden you're back in that emotional intensity again," Lidji said. "So you're back in that rush. But it's not a good rush."

————

FOR THOSE IN SQUIRREL HILL who had been getting better, who at last were able to pass hours, sometimes even entire days, without thinking about 10/27, the Poway shooting was a setback. They were "back in that rush," as Lidji put it; the mood was once again agitated, dangerous, adrenaline-charged. For the next few weeks, the rabbis were again giving sermons on the theme of violence against Jews. The guards at synagogues, who had been assuming a more relaxed posture, were paying more attention, their hands a little bit closer to their holsters. People looked around, checked in all directions.

Then, toward the middle of May, the mood lightened again. The Jewish calendar helped things along, moving as it did from Holocaust remembrance and liturgies for the dead to one of the happiest days in Judaism. The night of June 8, a Saturday, was the beginning of Shavuot, which commemorates the giving of the Torah on Mount Sinai. Shavuot is one of the truly underappreciated Jewish holidays.* For one thing, it celebrates something that all Jews, regardless of their political ideology or religious practice, can endorse: the birth of ethical monotheism, the idea that there are certain rules, like not killing and stealing, that all human beings should abide by. Plus, on Shavuot, one is supposed is to eat yummy dairy treats such as cheese blintzes, cheesecake, or ice cream. That night in June, Squirrel Hill's Jews were being publicly happy.

And this year on Shavuot, Kesher Pittsburgh, whose founder calls it a "post-denominational, Priestess-led space" that is "multi-generational, everyone-friendly, encouraging of curiosity, and joyfully Jewniversal," and doing work "at the intersection of spirituality and social justice," was having a party. Kesher is the creation of Keshira haLev Fife, Pittsburgh's local *kohenet,* or Jewish priestess, and one of its most colorful, and well-connected, characters. Fife was born Sarah Gross in 1978 to a Filipina mother and a white, Ashkenazi father whose family had been among the founders of Torath Chaim, a now-defunct synagogue north of Squirrel Hill. Tree of Life became Sarah's childhood shul: it's where

* The other is Sukkot, when you are commanded to build a hut and eat and sleep in it for a week. Which is loads of fun.

her future husband, Tim Fife, studied for his conversion—since he had no faith to leave, he likes to say he "joined" Judaism, not converted to it—and where they were married.

Sarah and Tim Fife moved to Australia, where in 2011 she fell ill with a rare condition that required many rounds of chemotherapy. "When you have a lot of time to lie in bed, there are a lot of things to think about," she said. "I can remember some nights lying there and just saying, 'Okay, if I wake up tomorrow, could you please give me some direction, or some sense of what it is that I'm here to do?'" She remembered the calling she had felt as a child, when she once informed a room of her fellow kindergarteners that she hoped to grow up to be a rabbi. And so in 2012, when her health had returned, she flew back to the United States for a conference of the Jewish Renewal movement, where she met the women who told her about the Kohenet Hebrew Priestess Institute.

To most traditional Jews, this program, which trains priestesses in earth-based Jewish ritual, would be unrecognizable as Judaism. It uses language that owes more to paganism than to Judaism, language that would strike many Jews as heretical. ("The first four retreats," its literature reads, "train students in ritual skills based on thirteen archetypes of the ancient Hebrew priestesses: the Weaver, the Maiden, the Midwife, the Prophetess, the Mother, the Wise Woman, the Shrinekeeper, the Queen, the Mourning Woman, the Shamaness, the Seeker, the Lover, and the Fool.") While it's not your typical Judaism, this is the Judaism that spoke to Fife, who along the way took two new names, Keshira haLev, "like the song of the heart." When she and Tim returned to Pittsburgh, she started Kesher Pittsburgh (Connection Pittsburgh), to realize her vision of a progressive group that would meet for monthly Friday-night services and infuse their lives with that "joyfully Jewniversal" spirit.

Most Jewish communities have nobody like Fife, and in those that do, that person is very much on the fringes. In Squirrel Hill, most clergy accept her as one of them. What she lacks in traditional *yichus*—lineage—she more than makes up for in charisma. She is a Jew of color, she can sing, she calls herself a priestess, she's smart, she holds a crowd. You meet her, and you know immediately why people follow her. A minority of local rabbis, especially among the Orthodox, are grudging about her role in the community. But her events get turnout; she plays a public role. As it happens, she is visible in one of the iconic photo-graphs from the week of the shooting: she can be seen in the widely circulated photograph of a Black man standing in front of Sixth Presby-terian Church at the conclusion of the anti-Trump rally, holding a sign that reads JEWISH LIVES MATTER. She is standing on the church steps, behind the man who has never been identified.

The day of the Tree of Life shooting, Fife held an eight o'clock gather-ing for Kesher Pittsburgh at their usual meeting space, a borrowed room at a private school in the Shadyside neighborhood. But over the next few days she felt adrift, a spiritual leader who was not entirely sure what her role was; she was called to do *something*, but what? Later that week, a colleague reached out to her and said that some local Jews needed "heal-ing support"—the kind of support that Fife could help them find. In the days after the shooting, numerous healers and alternative practitio-ners—of yoga, reiki, therapeutic touch, bodywork, and much more—had begun offering their services, at a discount or, often, for free. Most were local and reputable, but some were sketchy interlopers. Fife, work-ing with a local acupuncturist, helped "create a walk-in space where

An unidentified man holding a sign the day of the anti-Trump rally, with Keshira haLev Fife behind him

people could go for complimentary treatment." They set up at a family's house in Squirrel Hill, where healers could receive patients. "So then it was like my personal caseload," Fife said.

And she kept gathering her community of Kesher Pittsburgh, along with its loose affiliates and fellow travelers, for regular Friday-night prayers, holiday celebrations, and ceremonies to honor the New Month. (Jewish months follow a lunar cycle, and there are women's groups that meet to herald the new month with prayer and song.) For Shavuot, she invited everyone to the backyard of her friend Maggie Feinstein, a third-generation Squirrel Hill resident who, with her husband, owned just about the coolest property in Squirrel Hill. From the front, the house abutting Frick Park looked like a modest three-bedroom, but if you took the path around back, you found yourself at the bottom of a hill, like the stage of an amphitheater. The hill was planted all over with flowers and shrubs, its wildness intact. Stairs wended up the hill to a plateau, where there was a brick patio and a fire pit. Beyond the patio was the park, its hiking trails just yards away from the spot where Fife and her friend, the cantor Julie Newman, set up their instruments.

It was eight o'clock, still daytime in early June. Ice cream was being served at the bottom of the hill, and s'mores at the fire pit were promised for when the evening's program was over. Fife's work didn't replace houses of worship, but for this crowd of thirty or forty, it felt essential. There were brief speeches—Sara Stock Mayo, the song leader who helped the Squirrel Hill teens with their program the night of the shooting, spoke about the neighborhood as *mishpochah*, family—and then Newman began playing her guitar. She and Fife led everyone in the call-and-response chorus of Australian rocker Ben Lee's "Song of the Divine Mother of the Universe": "Tell me mother, can you hear me sing / Your love is everything / Heart and soul / Breath and skin / Your love is everything." Then everyone present was invited to share their "truth," whatever they were feeling right then. Newman, the cantor and guitarist, spoke about how, in her desire to love Torah stories, she often "hit walls" and "hit speedbumps," when she got to stories that portrayed God as angry and ruthless. (Then another round: "Tell me mother, can you hear me sing / Your love is everything.") Another woman stepped forward to talk about environmental justice. ("Tell me mother, can you hear me sing / Your love is everything.") A young child said in a quiet voice,

"I am willing to fight for people who don't have very much." Another child said, "I am willing to fight for animals who don't have homes or shelters."

It was not only Shavuot but Saturday night, and so it was time to end Shabbat, leave sacred time, and return to the profane. Newman got her guitar going again, and she and Fife sang the prayers, others joining in, as the Jews around them performed the Havdalah ritual: make the traditional blessing over the wine; pass around a spice box, or a loose clove or a cinnamon jar grabbed from a spice rack, and take a whiff; and inspect one's fingernails in the light of a blazing candle, their reflection confirming that there is enough light to merit a blessing. Everyone wished each other *shavua tov,* a good week, and it was on to the s'mores. And nobody had talked about murder.

———

AS SPRING TURNED INTO SUMMER, the pageantry of grief really was receding. At times, things could feel almost normal.

Two nights before the Shavuot s'mores party, the Allderdice High

Evan DeWitt with his
principal, James McCoy,
at the Allderdice graduation

School graduation was held in a huge, sweltering indoor sports arena on the Pitt campus. The program was largely given over to short speeches by the twelve valedictorians.* Proud families were decked out in their graduation best, waving banners and preparing to hoot and woot for their graduates. One of the valedictorians, Evan DeWitt, leaned into the theme of antisemitism.

"Today, June 6, marks the seventy-fifth anniversary of D-Day," said DeWitt, a regional leader of the B'nai Brith Youth Organization, an international Jewish youth group. "For Jews, D-Day was the hope for liberation in 1944, the lowest point my people had ever faced. I speak as if these events were long-forgotten memories, yet we are facing a new low point in our modern day. The same hatred that led to mass genocide three-quarters of a century ago is again rising in our home country. I would like to tell you that I am not afraid, but this year has been more difficult than I could have ever imagined."

Of the other eleven student speakers, a few alluded to Tree of Life. "Together we pushed back: against gun violence, against hatred, and against the forces trying to subdue us," one said. But more of them just went all in with sturdy, time-tested senior-year clichés: "Wherever we go and whatever we do, may we always be friends when we meet again," and "What I learned in my time at Allderdice is that the most important thing is to be true to yourself." And in this reversion to cliché, there was normalcy. Another public event that was not about death.

———

TISHA B'AV IS THE BLEAKEST HOLIDAY on the Jewish calendar. The ninth of Av, Tisha B'Av in Hebrew, falls between mid-July and mid-August; in 2019 it fell on August 10. It is an ill-timed holiday for Jews (in the northern hemisphere, anyway), coming in the midst of trips to the seashore, long-planned family reunions, summer camp by the lake. Tisha B'Av is the day when, according to legend, numerous calamities took place, including the destruction by Nebuchadnezzar of King Solo-

---

* Allderdice now follows the increasingly common practice of naming multiple valedictorians. I had never heard of this, but apparently it's a thing. In 2015 one of the seventy-two valedictorians from the 2014 senior class at Dublin Jerome High School, in Ohio, wrote in *The Washington Post:* "Traditionalists argue that this system degrades the distinction. Maybe so, but the merits of this approach are far greater. Creating a system that promotes personal achievement over unhealthy competition and that rewards hard-working students without hindering anyone's ability to succeed should be applauded."

mon's Temple, in Jerusalem, in the year 586 B.C.E., driving the Jews into the Babylonian exile, and the razing of the rebuilt Second Temple, in 70 C.E., by the Romans, leaving only a retaining wall of the building, known today as the Western Wall. To commemorate these losses, Jews fast for the day, refrain from wearing leather, and abstain from sex.

The liturgy of Tisha B'Av is the Bible's book of Lamentations, known in Hebrew as Eicha. Lamentations is as sad as Judaism gets. Jews sit on the floor in a darkened room, lit with candles, as Lamentations is chanted in a minor key *trop,* or cantillation system, reserved for this day. Lamentations, attributed to the prophet Jeremiah, consists of five poems about the destruction of Jerusalem.* It begins *"Eicha!"*—Alas!—"lonely sits the city once great with people! She that was great among nations is become like a widow," and it continues with every thinkable metaphor for abjection. Jerusalem is a widow; a fallen woman; a parent whose children have been enslaved. Children beg their mothers for food, but there is none; rather, mothers "eat their own fruit, their new-born babes." This is lonely suffering, suffering without hugs or fellow-feeling: "When they heard how I was sighing, there was none to comfort me." It is bleak stuff.

But the first Tisha B'Av since the murders, as it was observed in the downstairs ballroom at Beth Shalom, down the street from Tree of Life, was strangely cheering. It was a community event, for all the non-Orthodox congregations, and about 150 people came, a good turnout for what is treated as a minor holiday. Those in attendance were greeted by the "canine advocate" dogs from the Center for Victims, the dogs that had been in residence at the JCC the week after the shooting and had been seen around Squirrel Hill in the months since. The dogs were flopped out, ready to be petted in the lounge just to the right of the ball-room where services were held. Cindy Snyder, the clinical director of the Center for Victims, explained that, in talking with members of the therapy group she was conducting for families of those killed at Tree of Life, she had learned that Tisha B'Av was a "potentially triggering" event. She said that the "long-range planning committee" had requested that both the dog team—the three dogs and their handlers—and two therapists be on-site, so they were all at Beth Shalom.

---

* While scholarship tells us that Lamentations was written after the destruction of the city and King Solomon's Temple, it is treated as if it were written beforehand, foretelling the destruction to come.

ABOUT THAT "long-range planning committee" that invited the dogs: in the ten months since the attack, there seemed to be as many organizations and committees helping Squirrel Hill process, grieve, and cope with the deaths as there were actual deaths. There were old outfits like the federation and Jewish Family and Community Services (JFCS); newer efforts like the Center for Loving Kindness, which was housed at the JCC, which was also soon to house a new "resiliency center," paid for with Department of Justice dollars, to be called the 10.27 Healing Partnership; a weekly group that met to focus on "resiliency," including planning the 10.27 Healing Partnership; private therapy groups for survivors of the attack and family members of those killed, both run by the Center for Victims; the focus-grouping of architect Dan Rosenthal, helping Tree of Life decide what to do with its building; various interfaith dialogues; and more.

It was never entirely clear how many of those closest to the attack, how many of the survivors and the victims' relatives, needed this alphabet soup of well-meaning associations. Many emphatically did not. Joe Charny said he had no need, and Miri Rabinowitz, Jerry's widow, wanted no part of them. Dan Leger attended some of them, sometimes, and had mixed feelings.

"Some people have not dealt with their own shit for a long time, or ever," Dan Leger said. "And so when something as horrendous as this happens, you bring all that with you. And if you haven't dealt with it enough to be able to get it out of the way, and be sensitive to what other people need, and what you need yourself, then your expression of anger, frustration, misreading, projecting—it all just bubbles over and prevents other people from getting what they need."

Whatever their contributions, these groups collectively made a statement: Squirrel Hill, unlike other communities hit by mass shootings, would lose none of the survivors to suicide; there would be no lawsuits and no squabbles over money; there would be no feuds.* Squirrel Hill,

---

* Two survivors of the Parkland massacre have killed themselves, as has a parent of a Newtown victim. And there have been more suicides: "The death by suicide of someone connected to a school shooting is, unfortunately, a familiar story line," writes Ashley Fetters in "Lasting Grief After a Mass Shooting," *Atlantic*, March 28, 2019. "Carla Hochhalter, the mother of a student injured in the 1999 shooting at Columbine High School in Colorado, took her own life six months

progressive and forward-looking, would build on the latest trends in trauma-informed, victim-centered counseling. It would, in the contemporary jargon, "hold space" so that others' voices could be heard. Squirrel Hill would thank its Gentile allies, would engage in interfaith partnerships, would open its hearts and its doors.

One could, though, hear it muttered (including by survivors themselves) that some of this supporting, scaffolding, and witnessing involved expenses of time and money that might have been better spent elsewhere. But how does one put a price tag on displays of goodwill, solidarity, and neighborhood pride?

———

BEFORE THE LAMENTATIONS SERVICE, Jeremy Markiz, the junior rabbi of Beth Shalom, addressed the crowd. He was young, only thirty, when the attack happened, and he loved talking about the internet's potential to help spread Judaism. In his short talk, he said that he was prepared for some of those present to become overwhelmed. "If you need it," he said, "we have therapy dogs. We have counselors on-site. Take a break if you need it."

The lights were dimmed, people got on the floor. Trays of lit tea candles were passed around. To complete the reading of Lamentations, there was a lineup of ten chanters. Two of the chanters, rabbis Jonathan Perlman and Jeffrey Myers, had been inside Tree of Life that October morning. On 10/27, both men had been relatively unknown outside the Jewish community; Myers, of course, was new to Pittsburgh. In the months since, they'd had very different fortunes.

Myers, as we saw, had become a celebrity. Perlman, meanwhile, had been depressed and anxious. His congregants adored him, but they also had to protect him. At times, he seemed vigorous, as when he and his wife took five New Light congregants on a joint trip, with a local Baptist church, to Charleston to meet with survivors of the Mother Emanuel shooting. But in the months after the attack, he had often found it dif-

---

afterward; family members later stated that the tragedy had exacerbated her preexisting clinical depression. Greg Barnes, a Columbine student whose best friend died in the massacre, committed suicide a few weeks after its first anniversary. And in 2008, eight months after the shooting at Virginia Tech, a 21-year-old student named Daniel Kim took his own life in an act that his parents said was linked to the shooting."

Jeremy Markiz

ficult to lead services at his own small congregation. "I tended to really suffer and be depressed about the other three that lost their lives downstairs and in the building," he said in August. "I really had no control over anything else. I felt very helpless in terms of other people in the building." After the shooting, he suffered from insomnia, which lasted into the following summer. He could seem discombobulated, and several congregants had reported seeing him forget where he was in the service, or forget to put on his prayer shawl until his wife, Beth, reminded him. On a Shabbat morning in June, he became disoriented while leading services, and he was taken away in an ambulance; his wife told me that he had accidentally taken the wrong dosage of a prescribed sleeping medication.

In the first few months after the shooting, a crew of Conservative rabbis from around the country, from as nearby as central Pennsylvania and as far away as Whitefish, Montana, had passed through Pittsburgh, one Shabbat at a time, to lend Perlman a hand. They would come to town, attend the New Light service in the borrowed chapel downstairs at Beth Shalom—fifteen people, sometimes twenty—and help however they could. They would read Torah, sit up front, sing loudly, and schmooze before and after the service, lending a confident rabbinic presence while Perlman sat with his family and marshaled his strength.

Perlman and Myers had a "friendly relationship," as Perlman put it, but it was not my sense that they were close. In my interviews with both, I seldom heard one mention the other. Although during the shooting they had been yards apart, a stairwell away, from each other, few people in Squirrel Hill would have seen them together since, except when they shared the stage at Soldiers & Sailors hall the next night. Just to see them together chanting Lamentations made the night less sad.

And Tammy Hepps was there. She chanted the second half of chapter three, picking up at Lamentations 3:34, a few lines after the message begins to turn from one of total despair to one of budding hope. As recently as 3:13, Jeremiah is still wailing—lamenting—over what the Lord has done, and it's nothing good: "He has shot into my vitals the shafts of His quiver." But then, at verse 22, something new: "The kindness of the Lord has not ended, his mercies are not spent. They are renewed every morning." Hepps took over, chanting in the Hebrew a portion in which Jeremiah decides that the Lord is compassionate enough to hear his petitions. Rather than just lament, he will ask, even demand, that the Lord take his side once more against his foes: "I have called Your name, O Lord, from the depths of the Pit. Hear my plea; do not shut Your ear to my groan, my cry!"

Lamentations goes on like that, about half an hour in all. The readers took their turns; the mourners shifted on the floor. At the end of Lamentations, hope crowds out despair, enough that Jeremiah can conclude with this plea: "Take us back, O Lord, to Yourself, and let us come back; renew our days as of old!"

As people stood up after the service, they did not bid each other farewell. There are no warm embraces on Tisha B'Av. But when night comes and the holiday ends, Jews enter their period of consolation. The following Sabbath is known as Shabbat Nachamu, the Sabbath of Comfort. The next holiday, a month and a half away, is Rosh Hashanah, the Jewish new year, the birthday of the universe.

—⊱∞⊰—

17

The High Holy Days

R OSH HASHANAH AND Yom Kippur are the worst time of year
to get the usual feel of a congregation; they are the days when
twice-a-year-Jews swell the ranks of the regulars, when rabbis
give their stemwinder sermons, when the rugs are vacuumed and the
flowers are fresh. Rosh Hashanah began at sundown on September 29,
2019. Attending services the week before, on Saturday morning, September 21, would give a more accurate picture of the state of things.

That morning Tree of Life was still meeting at Rodef Shalom, in the
main sanctuary, a cavernous space with an organ. The room had last
been filled to capacity in the early 1960s, at about the time my teenage
father last attended services there, when American church and synagogue attendance was at its peak. The Rodef Shalom congregation
now used the main sanctuary on High Holy Days, and this morning
they were meeting in a small room down the hall, which was inhabited
by Rabbi Aaron Bisno, a harpsichordist, a guitarist, and about twenty
members, most of them old. Rodef Shalom is a temple, like so many others, to join but not attend.

Tree of Life was faring no better. By ten-fifteen, an hour after services
began, there were fourteen people in its room, including the rabbi and
me. By the end, around noon, there were twenty-nine in total, including
two out-of-town guests, which was not unusual. People passing through
Pittsburgh would now make a pilgrimage stop at Tree of Life, say hello

to the rabbi after services, and grab a bagel with the members. This morning it was Scott and Marla Berger, married jewelry designers from Scottsdale, Arizona. They were fit and tan and New Age–earnest, and they were eager to talk about "the intention stick," a small amulet they sold through their website and on their travels across the globe, which would channel your intentions and send them into the universe. Since the Bergers had created the intention stick in 2016, it had cured wearers of marital woes, health problems, and more, they said. Intention sticks cost from $59.99 (stainless steel) to $3,199.99 (white gold).*

This was a typical Shabbat crowd for Tree of Life. The rabbi was there, along with his wife, some regulars from before 10/27, like Audrey Glickman and Joe Charny, and a couple board members, including Sam Schachner and Michael Eisenberg, the president and former president. In July the *Jewish Chronicle* had run a hopeful story about millennials coming together to support the congregation. "'I grew up at Tree of Life, and I knew I wanted to get more involved than just showing up for the High Holidays,' said Andrew Exler, 29, a tax and accounting specialist. . . . His family are longtime members of the congregation, and his parents were married there. 'We want to keep things going,' he said." But the group never met, and he had failed to get other people his age to synagogue. He had spoken with the rabbi, whom he revered—"I can confidently say he might be the best person I have ever met"—about doing a very short service once a month, under an hour. "I have told him that if he could do that, I could get thirty people there," Exler said in July 2019. But that had not yet happened.†

Low attendance was, of course, typical for Conservative Jewish institutions, but there had been reason to hope that Pittsburgh would rally for Tree of Life. But hardly anyone new had joined, and most longtime members continued to pay their dues but never attend. "Tree of Life's members will do everything for the eleven dead," one local rabbi told me, "except show up in their place."

* They gave me my intention stick for free.
† "There are nine founders," Exler told me. "We've been meeting, trying to figure out what we are: Are we young adults, are we thirty-to-forty-year-olds, do we happen to be single? [We want] to look thirty years down the road, in whatever building we have, and see a lot of kids." He wanted to draw young Jews for whom religious observance was not important. "You don't have to be there for Friday-night services. We are trying to do cultural stuff, interfaith stuff. We have people who want to be sporty, have alcohol, people who don't want anything to do with alcohol, people who want to go to Shabbat services, but maybe have some food first."

Outside Heinz Field in
Pittsburgh, where a group of
longtime friends—
including Andrew Exler,
second from right—
raised around $30,000
for Tree of Life

THE HIGH HOLY DAYS, Rosh Hashanah followed by Yom Kippur nine days later, are the two days a year when a rabbi gets a great turnout from his or her congregation. Nobody who goes to synagogue at all skips the Jewish New Year or the Day of Atonement. A shul that may get 25 people on a regular Shabbat could balloon to 250, and the synagogue that gets 250 finds itself with 1,000. With crowds like these, High Holy Days are the best services of the year on which to do business, spiritual or pecuniary. At many synagogues, Kol Nidre, the evening service that begins Yom Kippur, is interrupted by the Kol Nidre Appeal, a big fundraising ask. And the sermon on the first day of Rosh Hashanah is when the rabbi makes his Big Point, whether about Israel or immigrants' rights or gun control. Or about commitment to Judaism. It's his chance to urge, or guilt, people back into the pews.

For High Holy Days, Tree of Life had to relocate again, temporarily. Calvary Episcopal Church, which in its glory days had been to the city's Protestant gentry what Rodef Shalom had been to the Jewish establishment, had offered its beautiful old Gothic structure in the Shadyside neighborhood. Tree of Life needed a big space, in case it got a big

Calvary Episcopal Church volunteer William Stevens covering a crucifix
in preparation for Tree of Life's High Holy Day services there

turnout. When the morning came, September 30, members of Calvary
Episcopal were on hand as guest ushers, welcoming their Jewish friends.
Crosses had, out of consideration, been covered up. Security was tight.
But the crowd was normal for Rosh Hashanah. The bump in enthusiasm
for Tree of Life, manifested in dollars, letters, attention, and affection,
had not affected attendance.

Still, it was a good enough crowd. When Jeffrey Myers took the pulpit
to deliver his sermon, people leaned in, wondering how he would use this
moment. They knew he would talk about 10/27, but what would he say?

When Myers finally spoke, after the prayers and Torah reading, he
at first avoided the topic on people's minds. Instead, he spoke about how
much Jews hated going to synagogue. He reassured them that he sympa-
thized. After all, he said, "the Hebrew's difficult, especially since ninety-
nine and forty-four one hundredths of you don't speak or understand
it. . . . You wonder why you subject yourself to this year after year after
year." This year, he said, it would be better, with new music and dra-
matic readings by actors. If people would stick around after his sermon,
and give the rest of the service a chance, they just might come away with
warmer feelings about synagogue.

Then he turned to the shooting. "That just leaves one big question that no doubt most of you came here wondering: *Will he talk about it?* And we all know what I mean by *it*. October 27, the enormous elephant in the room. Well, sorry to disappoint you, but after untold sleepless nights I decided not to talk about it today. Today is a day to celebrate the fact that we're all here. We are here, and no anti-Semite is ever going to stop me from doing Jewish, not now and not ever." If people wanted to hear him give a sermon about *it*, they would have to come the next day! People laughed as he made this challenge. Rosh Hashanah has a second day of services, but it's one that very few non-Orthodox Jews observe.

The smaller group that did return to Calvary Episcopal the next morning heard a sermon that would stay with them: a brutally candid assessment of the state of the synagogue, a plea for help, a challenge. It was a confrontation, really. Despite all that Myers and his congregation had gone through together, and despite all his congregants' professed love for him, they weren't doing what he most needed them to do: show up. He was calling them on it.

"As promised yesterday, today I'm going to talk about *it*," Myers began. He was high above the congregation, in the pulpit, looking out at the Jews scattered in the church's nave. "What a year it has been." He spoke of the ongoing mass shootings, of the need to oppose hate—or, as he called it, "the h-word." The effects of the h-word could be seen in "the violent use of guns, the spray-painting of swastikas, the assault and battery of someone because of their sexual orientation," and more. He had spent many days on the road, giving a stump speech about the corrosive effects of hatred, urging people never to use that "four-letter word." He wanted his own community to join him. "I encourage all of you to take on my H speech oath. Don't use it!"

And then, turning away from the events of the past year, Myers took his flock back to the day before the shooting. "Despite all that happened to us," Myers said, "the challenges that we faced on October 26, 2018, have not gone away." And those challenges were, literally, existential. "The Tree is an aging congregation. If we do not reverse that trend, we will cease to exist in thirty years. We will not reach our bicentennial." He spoke of an old friend of his, Daniel Hurley, a Catholic priest in Massapequa, Long Island. "During his tenure," Myers said, Hurley's church had had a membership of "sixty-five hundred families. . . .

Their Christmas services were literally every hour on the hour. Well, he used to lament to me about what he called 'submariner Catholics.' They would surface twice a year, Christmas and Easter. What I did learn from the monsignor was that low attendance at regular worship services was not a Jewish problem but an American problem." And that American problem was staring Tree of Life in the face: "Well, my dear congregants, when seven of your Shabbat and weekday regulars are murdered, and seven people don't step forward, what is a synagogue to do?"

Myers hinted at emerging plans for the building, saying that Tree of Life was "poised to become the most incredible center for Jewish life that the United States has ever seen." There was talk in the air about reconfiguring the damaged areas to provide offices for new tenants, including the local Holocaust education center. In fact, the following week, at the evening service beginning Yom Kippur, president Sam Schachner would at last give a glimpse of Tree of Life's plan for the building, promising a "cooperative, collaborative space located at the current Tree of Life*Or L'Simcha site," newly configured for "exhibit spaces, classrooms and training spaces, and . . . worship." People were talking about a complex that was part synagogue, part Holocaust museum, part 10/27 memorial. It could draw everyone from local worshippers to international tourists.

"Imagine that we do undertake a massive rebuilding," Myers said. "Of what value is this task—the endless meetings, the costs associated, the commitment from communal partners—if so many of our members find no value entering the Tree other than as submariner Jews?" Raising his voice, he called out, "Is there not one adult education class that might interest you? Is there a cultural event that would beckon you, or a social event?" If not—if nothing could get people through the new building's doors more than twice a year—the future was plain to see. Would Tree of Life "become a mausoleum to our horrific recent history?"

Myers had never sounded frustrated in public before; it went against his nature. He surely knew that the very sight of him, seemingly okay, would help others be okay. In private, he talked to his wife, talked to his therapist. When he was angry, he pursed his lips, smiled, and moved along, to shake the next hand. He was usually so *cool.*

"At this very moment," Myers said, "let's play poker. I call your hand. Either you are all in or you fold. And permit me to remind you that if you fold, the thirty-year clock starts ticking. I invite all of you to be all in. We are poised for this amazing journey. When we reopen, and we most certainly will, I want the entire world to say, *Wow. Look at what they have done.*

"To do anything less disrespects the memory of our eleven martyrs and gives a victory to the perpetrator of this horror. Do we want an epitaph to appear that says: 'Poor little Tree, cut down by H'? I said these words at the Soldiers & Sailors vigil nearly one year ago: 'It ain't happening on my watch.' Not now. Not nohow. Not never!"

He was getting loud—not evangelical loud, but for a rabbi plenty loud, the loudest anyone had ever heard Jeffrey Myers.

"Are you in with me?" He paused, looked out at the room. It was an old room. There were no babies crying. But people were sitting up, paying attention.

"Are you?

"If you are in with me, get up out of your seats, wake up, and say so. You don't have to be a Southern Baptist! You don't have to sing 'We Shall Overcome.' You just have to be in with me. Are you in? Let me hear you!"

A few voices called out—"Yes" or "We're with you"—but mostly they nodded. They would keep paying their annual dues, that much they could promise. But as to coming around the building more—they just didn't know.

"Thank you," Myers said. *"L'shana tova tikatevu v'techatemu.* May each of you be inscribed and sealed for a good year."

———— ❦ ————

18

The Anniversary

I T WAS A QUARTER TO FIVE in the afternoon on October 27, 2019. There were long lines in front of Soldiers & Sailors, as hundreds waited to get funneled through the doors. It was almost time for the memorial service marking the first anniversary of the shooting. The Hebrew-calendar anniversary would not be until November 16, but there was a general acknowledgment that 10/27 was the day the community should come together.

But how to come together? This had been the subject of much discussion since the previous November. A long-term planning committee, which comprised family members of the victims, survivors of the attack, a representative from the U.S. attorney's office, a rabbi from the federation, and more, had wrestled numerous questions to the ground. They had decided on a daylong series of events, culminating in a big memorial in the evening. The federation branded the day: there was a logo, two hands enclosing a Star of David and a heart, all encircled by the words REMEMBER. REPAIR. TOGETHER—the day's theme, which had been announced in mid-August. There was a website where people could sign up for a community-service event in the morning and Torah-study sessions in the afternoon.

When the day came, hundreds participated. There were blood drives, special events for teens and for old people, a tree planting, and a chance to "help out your librarian by identifying missing books" at the Squirrel

Hill branch library. Study sessions, held at Rodef Shalom, included "We Can't Do It Alone: Joining Together Against Hate" and "Algorithms of Loving Kindness." They concluded at three-forty-five, giving people an hour to get to Soldiers & Sailors, a quick walk away on the Pitt campus.

In the plaza right in front of Soldiers & Sailors, a police dog wandered around. Athletes from the University of Pittsburgh were marshaling into some sort of formation, for a ceremonial purpose as yet undisclosed, in their finest warm-up gear, the student version of an officer's dress blues. A woman wearing a Red Cross CRISIS RESPONSE reflective vest was offering American Red Cross tissues (two-ply, fifteen to a pack). A group of men in yarmulkes—mostly of the all-black variety, one with the Steelers logo and the words STRONGER THAN HATE—prayed the afternoon service. It felt like the end of *Ghostbusters,* when the Haredi Jews, Hare Krishnas, and various end-time millenarians line the streets of New York to herald, and ward off, the world-destroying Stay Puft Marshmallow Man.

Inside, the stage was lit in deep cerulean, and a sign-language interpreter stood at the ready, two large video screens behind her. The crowd was neither boisterous nor somber. The event started ahead of time.

On the first anniversary of the shooting, Jeffrey Myers addressing a capacity crowd inside Soldiers & Sailors

Jonathan Perlman making his plea for gun control

There was a flag procession, involving men and women in uniform—
from a distance it was hard to tell if they were police, National Guard,
or ROTC. Then the Pitt athletes marched down the center aisle and laid
flowers on the stage. A crisply produced movie featured a montage of
relatives of the deceased. A Christian minister and Muslim lay leader
spoke movingly. Doris Dyen, a Reconstructionist rabbi and member of
Dor Hadash, offered the prayer for those who have come through danger. Jeffrey Myers continued his campaign against "H-speech."

When Myers finished, the ceremony had gone on fifty-five minutes.
It was supposed to last only an hour, but there were still four speakers
left, including the mayor and the governor. When Jonathan Perlman,
the New Light rabbi, went to the lectern, some in the audience were
concerned. Over the High Holy Days, he had still seemed anxious and
uncomfortable, as if he'd rather be anywhere but in the public eye, and
his sermons meandered. This was no time to go long.

And he did go long, speaking for twelve and half minutes. Most of
his talk was ho-hum. He spoke of Cain's famous line from Torah, "Am I
my brother's keeper?" He segued to the story of Noah and the flood. He
chastised the media. "I would like to chide the members of our press . . .
not to retraumatize the victims and survivors of this event, and to know

when a hot story—maybe it needs to be told next week, and to just leave us alone, so that we can mourn." He was meandering. Then he said this: "And I would like the government, this year, federal and state government, to finally take action on gun control."

Now this was something. At first, there was a murmur, and within seconds, applause. The crowd got up on its feet—about three-quarters or more. Others crossed their arms, glowering.

"We must not delay, for the sake of the victims of this crime," he continued. "And we must begin to eliminate some of these weapons, and to figure out a way to keep weapons out of the hands of killers."

Then it was on to the politicians to read poems and offer soothing words to close out the night.

———

INJECTING A POLITICAL NOTE into the proceedings had taken a good deal of courage. The planning committee, led by Amy Bardack, a rabbi who worked for the federation, had decided that the whole day was to be completely apolitical. The day had to be "victim-centered," to use the term I kept hearing, and the victims' relatives wanted to keep politics out.

The rhetoric of victim-centeredness could, at times, take on an Orwellian tone. Six weeks before the anniversary, on September 11, 2019, an unusual meeting was convened at the offices of WQED, Pittsburgh's public television station. About fifteen journalists met with about fifteen members of the city's Jewish community to discuss how to cover the upcoming anniversary. Those in attendance included the news director from the local NPR affiliate, TV and newspaper reporters, employees of the federation and the Jewish social work agency, Jeffrey Myers and other rabbis (including Bardack), and relatives of the victims.

The purpose of the meeting, as described later in an article by two journalists who helped convene it, was "to overcome misconception and mistrust" between the media and those they covered. According to Andrew Conte, a former journalist now teaching at local Point Park University, and Darryl Ford Williams of WQED, the meeting generated rules for the media to follow. Some of the suggestions were useful. For example, they asked reporters to respect people's observance of the multiple Jewish holidays in October and reminded them that members of three congregations, not just Tree of Life, were murdered that day.

But then the document instructed the media to "tell the right stories." It should "amplify the stories the Jewish community wants to tell." Furthermore: "The community would like Oct. 27 to be free from politics." The document also insisted that the "primary focus should be that the attack was an act of anti-Semitism." And even more emphatically: "If you don't tell the story of anti-Semitism, you're not telling the story." And finally, it urged reporters to "focus on how the community has grown, emotionally and spiritually over the past year."

The document even gave reporters approved language. "It's OK to use the word 'victims,'" it reads, "but give thought about how it's used so that people closest to the attack are not stripped of their status." Reports should "avoid use of 'anniversary,' a word typically associated with something positive," and should also avoid "tragedy," because it's "typically associated with accidents and not acts of terror." Finally, "victims and their advocates strongly prefer that media outlets not name the shooter or show his image."

It's true that it was Conte and Ford Williams who first asked for this meeting—it's not as if local Jews set about to instruct the media on how to cover the anniversary. But the fact that the local media and the local Jewish establishment were on the same page only illustrates what Perlman was up against: a broad consensus, at least among those willing to speak up, that the anniversary should have no sharp edges. It should be ecumenical, interfaith, apolitical. The message should be one of strength through unity. For a day, at least, nothing could be seen to divide Pittsburgh.

If the event at Soldiers & Sailors were really about the victims, and this was what their families wanted, then this might have been a reasonable framework. But the day was not really about the victims, notwithstanding all the rhetoric and the video tribute to them. The victims had already been buried and mourned, and they would be remembered again on the Hebrew date of their remembrance. How many of the dead could the mayor, the governor, and the Pitt basketball players even name? They, like most of the twenty-three hundred who filled the auditorium, were there to mark a civic holiday, a new sacred day in the Pittsburgh calendar. They were there to show that they were "stronger than hate."

But with all enforced shows of civic unity—like giving thanks on

Thanksgiving, or showing love of country on the Fourth of July—not everyone is feeling it. Some object to the politics, or the erasure of politics. Others are uncomfortable with the sentimentality. Shows of "unity" are always fictional, in that they require the elision or suppression of differences, if only for a day. While some derive pleasure or comfort from these performances, others find them troubling. If you don't subscribe to the tenets of the community, then the performances seem dishonest, even coercive.

A month after the anniversary, in an email, Danielle Kranjec, the Hillel educator at Pitt and Carnegie Mellon who had delivered student-baked challahs all over Squirrel Hill the Friday after the shooting, said she felt that the narrative of strength and unity had obscured how much people were still hurting. "For me," Kranjec wrote, "the number one thing that is not reported is just how messed up so many of us still are. I had an anxiety attack in shul recently when my youngest child was not literally within arm's reach." Her son now refused to wear his yarmulke outside, and he got nervous when non-Jews could see her "Jew bling," like her Star of David necklace. "I love all of the positive messages about community and resiliency, and I don't deny their truth," she said, "but what is also true is the deep pain of what happened that many of us are still living with. White supremacy, Jew-hatred, and gun violence are all still threats. No amount of 'stronger than hate' can actually change that. I am so fucking sick of 'stronger than hate.'" She hadn't gone to the Soldiers & Sailors event. "We left town that weekend."

Dan Leger was at the event. As a religious man and a professional chaplain, he knew that people needed ceremonies to mark milestones; he understood that the one-year mark was a big deal and could not go unnoted. But he was allergic to the kind of rah-rah pomp that characterized events like this one.

"'Hated' was too strong a word," he said, when asked how he had reacted to the event. But it wasn't far off. "First of all, I don't like those kinds of big gatherings that are formalized," he said. And his worst fears were confirmed when the evening began, in a show of utterly tone-deaf irony, with a military procession. "Especially when the honor guard walked in with rifles in their hands—that just was so completely inappropriate."

As somebody who had been shot and survived, Leger had been

treated all year with a reverence that entailed his inclusion in all decision making. He was not, technically, the family member of anybody who had been killed, but he was consulted whenever the victims' families were. (The other worshipper who had been shot and survived, Andrea Wedner, was the daughter of one of the murdered, Rose Mallinger, so she, too, was included in such meetings.) Invited to various therapy groups and planning groups, he nevertheless always felt like a bit of an outsider. Erstwhile conscientious objector, amateur cellist, voracious reader, yarmulke-wearing spiritual seeker who was going to be a priest but found a home in Judaism, Leger was both more intellectual and more religiously observant than most of the eleven killed. Also more liberal.

Leger's beloved congregation, Dor Hadash, was powerfully identified with social action—it was their pro-immigrant Shabbat that had, after all, led the shooter to them. Over the past year, members of Dor Hadash had thrown themselves into gun-control advocacy, meeting with congresspeople and state legislators, and helping persuade the Pittsburgh City Council to ban assault-style weapons. (The Pittsburgh ban was struck down by a state judge on October 30, 2019.) All of which meant that, when asked to help enforce the rule that the anniversary events be apolitical, he didn't like it one bit.

As the day approached, Leger was conflicted. In the morning, he skipped the breakfast at the JCC for the survivors and the victims' families; he went to morning prayers at New Light instead. But when it came to the evening event, he decided that his place was with the victims' families. "I figured, you know, we belong together," he said. "We need someplace to be together. And this was one of those places and times."

Being in solidarity with the victims' families, he knew, meant sitting through an event with no talk of gun control, or white nationalism, or Trump. He didn't like it, but he had made his peace with it, and had even persuaded others to abide by it. So when Jonathan Perlman said what he did about guns, Leger was torn in half.

"I felt very, very, very conflicted," Leger said. "I feel like Jon really found his voice at that moment, which was beautiful to witness in a way—had it not been for the fact that it was precisely what those families told everybody not to do! And there were some people who actually . . . got up and left, they were so distressed by it." At least four relatives of the victims had walked out when Perlman made his pitch for gun control. Leger joined the standing ovation, briefly. "I got up reluctantly, but I did stand for a moment. And then I sat back down. . . . I felt, *Finally, Jon is healed enough to have found his voice about this stuff.* But I was absolutely horrified that he found it in that moment. It was just the wrong place."

———

"I WILL BE perfectly fine," Howard Fienberg said, when asked about to Jonathan Perlman, "if I never have to talk to him again."

Fienberg is the son of Joyce Fienberg, one of the Tree of Life members murdered on 10/27. He is in his forties, a lobbyist living in the Virginia suburbs of Washington, D.C. He is a quiet man; his voice doesn't go up, but when he speaks about Perlman, his rage comes through.

"The families had been part of an extensive negotiation. . . . One of the only things that all of us agreed on was not bringing politics into the discussion of our loved ones, and at this event in particular we weren't going to be a part of it if it was a political event. . . . That was crapping on . . . all of us." Fienberg wanted to walk out but didn't. "I dug my fingernails into my legs and didn't want to add to his spectacle. You wouldn't have seen it, but the staff and people running the event flashed lights at him, trying to get his attention, trying to get him to stop. . . .

"It wasn't a memorial for *him*."

———

"I DIDN'T THINK THAT I was saying anything objectionable at the time," Jonathan Perlman said in late January, three months after the Soldiers & Sailors memorial. "I don't remember getting any cues from anybody beforehand that I couldn't mention gun control."

Some in Pittsburgh would obviously find this hard to believe. But there was no written document laying out the expectations for the evening, nothing that Perlman, Myers, or any of the others had had to sign. Amy Bardack said, "We had regular meetings, maybe three of them, with the large group of everyone involved. So Jonathan was in the room." People had agreed that politics wouldn't come up, she said, so no document was necessary. She also said that the speakers had been asked to submit their comments in advance, which Myers did but Perl-man did not.

The minutes of the June 27, 2019, meeting of the Long Term Resil-iency Planning Committee describe, under the heading "Input from Victims' Families," the "wish of the families for [the] commemoration not to have feel of a rally," with "nothing that would elicit applause" and "no political statements [or] issue-driven remarks/events." According to the copy of the minutes that I obtained, Perlman was at the meeting (and according to the minutes he spoke there, too). Of course, the fact that one committee member—Cindy Snyder, of the Center for Victims—presented this wish list, on behalf of a group of victims' relatives who had been participating in a support group, did not mean that Perlman, or anyone, agreed to abide by it.

Yet according to Bardack, she and Perlman had discussed the mat-ter of politics explicitly. "When I sat down with him"—in August, she thought it was—"one on one, to ask him if he would feel comfortable giving a talk, understanding that these were the parameters, that politi-cal issues such as gun control and the death penalty would not be men-tioned, he said yes."

Certainly the fact that Daniel Leger got the message, and prevailed on the pro-gun-control membership of Dor Hadash to go along with this restriction, suggests that it was not left vague. But it's possible that Perlman heard "no politics" or "no anti-Trump discussion" and figured that so long as he avoided naming the president, or attacking Republi-cans, or advocating for any specific piece of legislation, he was on safe ground. It's also possible that he went to the meetings but had entirely forgotten their content. There were certainly moments in the year after the shooting when he was in the room but his mind was not.

When victims' relatives approached him and said that he had broken an agreement, he was, he said, surprised. "I said, 'I don't remember that,' which was true," he recalled. "Maybe they had a meeting and I didn't attend it. Sincerely, I didn't know we were restricted in any way. . . . I wanted to say what was in my heart."

Shortly after the anniversary, the long-range planning committee held its next meeting, to talk about the event. Many of the usual mem-bers came, including Bardack; Michele Rosenthal, Cecil and David's sister; and Rose Mallinger's daughter, Andrea Wedner, who came with her husband, Ron. Perlman did not attend, but New Light's co-presidents, Stephen Cohen and Barbara Caplan, were there to absorb all the anger directed at their rabbi. It was not an easy meeting. According to several people I spoke with, various demands were floated. One person wanted Perlman to give a public speech apologizing for his words, while another asked that he be reprimanded by his congregation (whatever that would mean—there is no formal process for congregational reprimand in Judaism). None of this would make anything better, but there was a strong sense that Perlman had to try.

Cohen and Caplan knew something had to be done. They had to keep the peace in their home, Jewish Pittsburgh. So they met with their rabbi and told him how unhappy people were, and they made it clear that he had to apologize. "If he hadn't," Cohen said, "he might have been fired."

And so Perlman went on a short apology tour. The way he remembered it, there were a few conversations, some by phone, at least one over coffee. He sent an apology letter to some of those who were angry. He explained to people that he'd misunderstood the rules: "I said I didn't understand, said I was sorry. I think people accepted that." He didn't reach everyone who was angry. Howard Fienberg never heard from him, and that suited Fienberg just fine. But Perlman made amends well enough, smoothed things over.

Looking back on the evening's events from a distance, Perlman sounded mindful of the hurt he had caused, to others and to himself. He'd made new wounds before the old ones were healed. But most of the audience members he'd heard from didn't see it that way, he said. Mostly, what he heard was *Good job*.

———

FOR TAMMY HEPPS, the entire year had been a parade of good intentions and bad ideas. The Jewish Federation, the community of therapists, most of the local rabbis—they had collectively decided to focus on healing, soothing, caring. And this was fine. But something was missing. Hepps noted that the anti-Trump march the Tuesday after the shooting had pulled together in one place thousands of local Jews, far more than most synagogues, Jewish schools, or the JCC could ever gather. (In fact, it was more Jews than are in all the synagogues throughout the Pittsburgh area, in total, on a given Saturday.) But this astonishing success had not been heralded as the triumph it was, and she believed that it had been undercovered by the press, including the *Jewish Chronicle*.

Hepps recognized that "plenty of beautiful things" had happened. She was not insensate to all the acts of *hesed*, lovingkindness, with which Squirrel Hill had enveloped the survivors and the victims' families. But it had done so by excluding activism and politics, and that was how "this community fell short."

She wondered if this shortcoming was inevitable. Was it possible that a community could have lovingkindness or activism but not both? "Parkland was the opposite," she said, comprising "people who didn't know each other, whereas we all know each other. They had no institutions for dealing with this, whereas we have institutions." But in the absence of institutions—in the absence of schools and shuls and a federation and a Jewish social work agency and a Giant Eagle supermarket where you bumped into friends—"they went the activist route." They took to Twitter and the airwaves, hit the road for rallies across the country, and gave the gun-control movement a national youth wing. "If you look at what the Parkland kids and parents did—nothing like that came out of our community. I hold myself to blame for that. I am part of one of the groups that should have been doing that."

Squirrel Hill had been remarkably resilient, and that was something to be proud of. But peace had been purchased at a price. "Maybe time will tell," Hepps said, "whether the right thing to do was focus on the community healing each other, and maybe what we have done in terms of helping victims will be the model. But I am a realist—this happened because of political things, and it will be fixed if other political things happen."

She couldn't say that she was surprised. This apolitical muddle struck her as entirely predictable, this turning inward very Jewish. As much as Jews are known for their involvement in politics, Jewish radicals have always been the outliers. More typically, Jewish communities have taken care of their own business and prayed to be left alone, ever since being conquered in Jerusalem in the year 70. "Our community has been designed and perfected over two thousand years to be completely impotent in a moment like this," she said. "If the thing we are best at in Pittsburgh is keeping the community together and looking out for each other, then that is the best of what we accomplished in that first year. But as Jews, that's not the best we're called to be."

Epilogue

I AM USUALLY UNMARKED," Robert Zacharias said late one afternoon in December 2018. "Zach" had been mentioned in the press for
attending a rally put on by IfNotNow, the left-wing Jewish group,
and we were talking about Pittsburgh's radical Jewish scene. As it
turned out, Zach was not deeply involved politically—he was more of a
curious seeker, in his politics and in his religion. "I'm usually just, like,
some boring person—there's really not much to comment on if I walk by
or bike by or something. I'm just some dude. But if I'm wearing a yarmulke, I'm part of an identified special weird class. There's something
unique and unusual about me that makes me not merely some dude:
potentially a person to commit violence against or be angry at, potentially somebody to be appreciative toward . . . somehow separated from
the masses."

Zach teaches at Carnegie Mellon—physical computing, the art and
science of building novel interactive objects, "everything from a motion-
activated cat toy to an automated yarn-ball winding machine to a device
that helps people experience a dance performance through touch." There
is an astonishing normalcy to him, a true absence of danger, but it would
be unfair to accept his self-description of "boring." Rather, he is exceptionally likable. He is tall and lanky, blue-eyed, reddish-bearded, and
soft-spoken. He is the summer camp counselor with a guitar who could
really sell "Kumbaya."

Zach was born in 1985 and grew up in Maplewood, New Jersey. His family belonged to a large Reform temple that they seldom attended. After college, he moved to "so-cool Greenpoint," in Brooklyn. He worked at an education nonprofit, and he was in "a cool apartment, living the ostensible dream." But it didn't feel like a good fit. "It didn't seem like I was actually enjoying it as much as I was supposed to be enjoying it on paper."

As he tried to figure out who he was and where he wanted to be, he wandered into a semblance of Jewish community. In 2013 he went on a date with a Jewish woman who told him about some email lists that served unaffiliated, progressive Jews. He and the woman never went out again, but he got on those email lists, and he learned about some offbeat Jewish worship groups. He started occasionally attending services with Shir HaMaalot, which followed Friday-night Shabbat prayers with potluck dinners. (The dinners had three tables: one for vegan food, one for vegetarian, one for kosher.) At an event at Romemu, the Upper West Side community known for its spirited musical services, he met Amichai Lau-Lavie, the founder of yet a third community that intrigued him, Lab/Shul, which calls itself "an artist-driven, everybody-friendly, God-optional, pop-up, experimental community for sacred Jewish gatherings."

Zach never became a regular with any of these groups, but they kindled an interest in Jewish religious life. When he left Brooklyn for Pittsburgh, he found overlapping Jewish communities including IfNotNow (whose politics he considered a bit too strident), a small, home-based branch of the Chabad movement (whose Orthodoxy was far from what he believes in), and Moishe House, a Jewish communal-living house for recent college graduates (whose typical hanger-on was, he admitted, much closer to college age than he is).

The morning of the shooting, Zach had been hanging with an IfNotNow friend at her apartment in Bloomfield, northwest of Squirrel Hill. After getting the news, Zach went home. He checked in with his family and friends, and a couple hours later, in midafternoon, he went to the Giant Eagle supermarket to buy soup and yahrzeit candles, small candles one lights to honor the dead. Before he left, he dug into his closet for one of his yarmulkes. He put it on and left for the market. That was

Robert Zacharias,
in Mellon Park,
August 2020

the first time he had ever worn a yarmulke when it wasn't Shabbat, a
Jewish holiday, or some other special occasion.

Zach kept the yarmulke on his head at the Havdalah planned by the
Allderdice students. He has been wearing one ever since.

"It is a new experience for me to be wearing a yarmulke out in the
world on a regular basis," Zach said. "It has these interesting implica-
tions." He mentioned a night when he and his girlfriend had been trying
to decide where to go out to eat. "I was like 'Well, Gooski's is open'—
and then I was like, 'But . . . I heard they have some Nazis.'" Zach was
referring to the rumor that, at some point, some sort of neo-Nazi punk
band had played a gig at Gooski's, a small dive bar in the Polish Hill
neighborhood. Zach figured the rumor was probably false, but his head
was spinning with possibility. He'd thought about the overlap between
punks, many of whom lived in Polish Hill, and various strains of white
nationalist ideology.

And then he realized that if there *were* neo-Nazis hanging out at
Gooski's, he now looked like a target. "But I didn't want to take my yarmulke off to go to Gooski's and have dinner. *That* doesn't feel right.

That's some kind of bizarre paying-of-obeisance to the ghost- or not-ghost-Nazis, and I don't want to do that. But I also don't want to *not* go to Gooski's if I want to go to some neighborhood bar that has vegan kielbasa!"

The yarmulke complicated *everything.* If he took off the yarmulke, the neo-Nazis, real or imagined, would win. If he kept the yarmulke on but skipped Gooski's, the neo-Nazis, real or imagined, would still win, by depriving him of tasty vegan kielbasa. But if he said yes to the yarmulke and to Gooski's, he put his visibly Jewish self in sight of the real or imaginary neo-Nazis. (To be clear, there is no evidence that neo-Nazis hang out at Gooski's.)

Zach weighed his options, screwed up his courage, and took himself and his girlfriend to Gooski's. When he stepped inside, he took a look around, and his first thought was, *These are not people who want to hurt me. They're not antisemitic people here.* He saw a coworker at the bar, reading *The New York Times* app on his iPhone as he drank a beer and smoked a cigarette. It was all copacetic.

But the yarmulke was not finished with him yet. He and his girl-friend sat at the bar and placed their orders. "I made a very expensive order by mistake . . . and I was like, 'Oh, I shouldn't get all that.'" He turned away from the bar to look at his menu, to figure out what to order instead. And as he turned away, he noticed the bartender noticing his yarmulke. And then he was immediately concerned that she would see his changing his order as a manifestation of his Jewishness. "I was like *Oh God*damn*it. Now I'm a money-grubbing Jew!* Like, I'm complaining about the expensive order and adjusting my order to be less expensive! So I felt bad about that, because now I'm a symbol of 'all the Jews.' I am the standard-bearer for all these people for whom I don't bear a standard!"

Zach was still feeling like the guy in a yarmulke who had flagged a problem with his restaurant tab when something compounded his misery. He lifted his bottle of Yuengling to his mouth to have a sip, and a bit sloshed out and landed on a man sitting next to him at the bar. It was just a tiny bit of beer, and it seemed that the man didn't notice. So Zach elected not to say anything. "I thought, *Oh, he doesn't notice, doesn't matter.*" But no sooner had Zach elected to let the matter drop than the man turned around—he *had* noticed. Zach quickly apologized, hoping to make everything right. But it was too late. "I was like, 'I'm sorry, I spilled some beer,' but I hadn't said it when I spilled it. So yet *again* I think, like, *Now I'm a jerk, a selfish, unapologetic Jew person.* So it's even worse! Everything is bad!" He threw his hands up in despair. A public Jew can never win.

Those moments of discomfort were not enough to get Zach to doff his yarmulke. It became part of his regular getup, and the times when he felt self-conscious or worried about his appearance became fewer. Still, there were occasions when it seemed prudent to cover up. One time he went for a walk in the woods outside Pittsburgh. "*I am out in deer-hunting country,*" he remembered thinking to himself. "*I don't know who the hell is here, but if I'm going to run into some backward, racist jerk in Pittsburgh, it's going to be out in the woods where there's deer-hunting permitted. . . .* So I wore a hat over my yarmulke in case I ran into somebody."

The only time he took his yarmulke off was when he went home to New Jersey for Thanksgiving, the month after the shooting. His parents had "always been leery" of Zach's surging interest in Judaism—his month on a kibbutz in Israel, his frequenting various alternative Jewish spaces in Brooklyn and Manhattan. So somewhere along the Garden State Parkway, he took his yarmulke off. "I thought I'd get a lot of comments, and confusion. . . . I thought all my cousins would give me weird grief about it. I thought my parents would be confused by it. I thought they would all think I was signaling some virtue that I didn't mean to be signaling, or that I was garnering pity, which I didn't mean to be garnering"—pity as a Pittsburgh Jew, one month after Tree of Life. "Of all the things I could have been afraid of, like what random strangers were thinking in Pittsburgh, I was actually afraid of my family. And so I didn't give them the opportunity to even worry along those lines. I took it off."

———

IN THE AFTERMATH of a mass shooting, there is the collective response, and there is the individual response.

The collective response included the fundraisers, the marches, the memorials, the funerals, and the large worship services; they were the work of organizations and federations, synagogues, social work agencies, and sometimes impromptu bands of teenagers or concerned citizens. There is no question but that in the first days and weeks after the attack, these visible group efforts were a comfort to those who felt victimized, whether those whose parents were murdered or anyone in the neighborhood who just felt sad, which was most everyone.

Being in a neighborhood that immediately marshaled mourners, raised dollars, and put up memorial art, in shop windows and in tree branches, was simply better for the soul than not being in such a neighborhood. It was good to have an obvious crossroads, Forbes and Murray. It was good to have a neighborhood firehouse, the kind of place where a disabled adult could make friends for life, friends who would come to the shiva at his family's house. It was good to have a neighborhood high school like Allderdice, and to have a supermarket like Giant Eagle. Just walking around—because this neighborhood was walkable—people got hugs. The Jewish community had worked assiduously to hold Squirrel Hill together as a safe, happy place for Jews. This had not been left to chance; bureaucrats and nonprofit executives had planned for it. They had raised money and made it happen. Their labors had ensured that when Jews needed a Jewish neighborhood most, they would have one.

At the same time, there were limits to what large chunks of money, overseen by decent bureaucrats and honest nonprofit boards, could do. The Tree of Life congregation had stagnated, in a number of ways; people were not coming, and the building's future was uncertain. The federation had raised money, but it was pretty easy to see the limits of that money: it would not be enough to renovate Tree of Life, not in the manner that the board seemed to be hoping for, and money was not going to bring new members to Tree of Life or young people to New Light. What members of Dor Hadash wanted, more than anything, were some new gun-control laws in Pennsylvania, and they were no closer on that front. As for the individual payouts to victims' relatives and to those caught inside, recipients said that it didn't matter much. You take the money, but you never forget where it came from.

Then there were the individual responses to 10/27, which reflected a sense of place just as much as the collective responses did. Take Rob Zacharias. On the day of the crime, being in, or even near, Squirrel Hill gave everyone a Jewish stake. A year after the attack, Lynn Hyde, who had been spurred to conversion after 10/27, was still studying with her rabbi, excitedly nearing the date when she could become a Jew. The following March, quarantined because of the COVID-19 pandemic, she went before her three-rabbi tribunal on a Zoom call and answered their questions. Satisfied with her answers, they pronounced her a Jew.

In January 2020, Dan Leger, feeling stronger all the time, and his friend Martin Gaynor, another one of the eleven to get out of the building alive, decided to embark on a years-long project to study a page a day of Talmud, in honor of their slain friend Jerry Rabinowitz.* At first, they met in person, and then, with the quarantine, over the internet. As they conversed daily about the ancient sages' arguments—when and how to pray, how to wash one's hands, what kind of jewelry and body ornamentation is permitted—they thought often of their old friend. Gaynor liked to imagine Jerry laughing with them over the crazy minutiae, like the rabbis' disputations over where one may urinate. *You guys have spent an hour going back and forth over pishing!* Gaynor imagined Jerry thinking.

————

MORE THAN A YEAR AFTER the shooting, Leger was talking about some of the beautiful things he had seen since being shot. "I think that one of the great things that came out of this whole experience was the falling away of walls between the Orthodox community and the more progressive community, between the Jewish community and the Christian community and the Muslim community, between communities of faith and law enforcement," he said. "All those walls just went away for a while." The walls were coming back, he said, but it had been nice to see.

When they talked about those early days after the shooting, people in Squirrel Hill could sound paradoxically nostalgic, even cheerful. Love! Neighborliness! Acts of kindness! The sense of mission, the chance to do one's thing on a big and important stage. One rabbi, from a Pittsburgh-area synagogue not involved in the attack, literally seemed about to burst with pride talking about that first week. "God bless those eleven souls," he began, before pivoting to the real heart of the matter: "It was the best professional week of my life. I got an opportunity to do

---

* They were participating in Daf Yomi (Daily Page), a tradition in which Jews around the world study one page of Talmud a day, in sync with each other, so that they all finish the whole Talmud in seven and a half years. A new cycle of reading started in January 2020.

what we're trained to do. And from every indication, I acquitted myself well. And I'm proud of it, right?"

That enlivening feeling of fullness was always there, alongside the piercing sense of loss, each in its place. A regular at one of the three congregations at Tree of Life had been out of town the day of the shooting. He had played a crucial role in the community during the year afterward, but he couldn't forgive himself for being away that morning. "I wasn't here for my people," he told an FBI agent whom he encountered after speeding back to town. He was sure that if he had been present, he would be dead. "I would have charged him," he said, meaning the shooter. "I think that's more than likely what I would have done. I would've given everyone time to get out."

Compared with those who were inside Tree of Life and survived the attack, and with other members of the three congregations, the victims' surviving spouses and grown children were less likely to talk with reporters and more reluctant to appear at public events. They were suffering more, which was not surprising. They had no role to play, except the mundane, predictable role of the bereaved. If, as Winston Churchill said, nothing in life is so exhilarating as to be shot at without result— the predicament, more or less, of survivors like Joe Charny and Audrey Glickman—then perhaps nothing in life is so painful as to love someone who has been shot at successfully. The victims' relatives were the most fragile and the most easily angered: when Jonathan Perlman gave his speech in favor of gun control at Soldiers & Sailors, it was not those within earshot of the bullets who were enraged, but those who had had to bury their parents or brothers.

———

ON SATURDAYS OVER the past year, attendance at New Light had been up. One of the new participants was Eric Lidji, the archivist. A graduate of an Orthodox high school, he had long since drifted away, becoming basically a High Holy Day Jew. But the day after the shooting, he put on tefillin, the small boxes containing bits of Scripture that Orthodox men affix to their head and one arm during morning prayer. It was something he had not done in years. "It was probably the first time since 2005," Lidji said. "Thirteen years." He started going back to synagogue, and he ended up a morning regular at Shaare Torah. Then he heard that New Light had lost three of its members who chanted *haftarah*, the weekly portion from the prophetic writings, something he had not done since his bar mitzvah.

As it happened, he was looking for a way to help. His professional work had thrust him into the spotlight—he would be the subject of a long profile in *The Atlantic*—but he felt the need to do something for Squirrel Hill that was entirely personal, out of the public eye. "I needed," he said, "a private, quiet thing that was actually helpful, and that had nothing to do with my job." Chanting *haftarah* could be that thing.

The *haftarah* melody came back to him. "It's surprisingly intuitive," he said. "The first one took me a long time, and then once I figured out what it was like, I was able to get through them pretty quickly."

New Light was not Lidji's regular, weekday shul, but here he was—one Saturday when I stopped by, I saw Lidji get up, clear his throat, and launch into the reading from the prophets. He couldn't believe, he told me later, the tiny congregation's resiliency. "They have no margin for error," he said. It was clear to Lidji that he belonged. These were his neighbors, they needed help, and he could help them. "I had heard through the grapevine that they needed people to fill that role. And I thought, *I bet I could do it.*"

Acknowledgments

To all who talked with me about the Tree of Life shooting: *Thank you*. You make me want to recycle John Allison's spiel from a footnote in the Prologue: "Yes, Pittsburghers have a certain decency. But it's not the midwestern variety, which in my (limited) experience is about being nice and not talking about unpleasant things. Pittsburghers, to overgeneralize, have more of the decency of empathy—they will get nebby, they will try to do a nice thing for someone."

Although my family now lives mostly in the diaspora, a few remain in Squirrel Hill. Thank you cousins Stefi Kirschner and Gil Schneider and, for your open-door (and open-bar) policy, Aunt Alece and Uncle Dave Schreiber.

Between interviews, I passed many hours at Amazing Books & Records, in the heart of Squirrel Hill. Proprietor Eric Ackland is an educated man and a deep soul, and every time I dropped by his store, he said something that I knew would improve my book. I count him as a friend.

A dedicated group of journalists worked this story in the first days, before I arrived. I would like to single out Emma Green of *The Atlantic*, Peter Smith of the *Pittsburgh Post-Gazette* (where the whole Pulitzer-winning team did remarkable work), and publisher Jim Busis and reporters Adam Reinherz and Toby Tabachnick of the *Pittsburgh Jewish Chronicle*. Other professionals I am honored to work with: agents David

Kuhn, Nate Muscato, and Allison Warren; research assistants and fact-checkers Annie Rosenthal, Elliot Lewis, Eve Sneider, Karys Rhea, Maggie MacFarland Phillips, Marie-Rose Sheinerman, and Ani Wilcenski; and fellow writers Gavriel Savit, Ben Cohen, Rand Richards Cooper, and Michael Scott Alexander, who read early drafts. At Knopf, editor Jonathan Segal shaped this book, paring away anything that took the focus off Squirrel Hill. I am also grateful to his assistants, Samuel Aber and then Erin Sellers. Janet Biehl expertly copyedited the manuscript, and Ellen Feldman, who has Squirrel Hill ancestry herself, was the ideal production editor. Text designer Cassandra Pappas, jacket designer Jennifer Carrow, and mapmaker Ariana Killoran made this book into an object even more evocative of the neighborhood it's about. Attorney Celeste Phillips offered wise suggestions that went beyond legal matters.

I got financial support from the Covenant Foundation, the Pulitzer Center, and the Yale Program for the Study of Antisemitism. I am fortunate to have a group of old friends who keep me thinking about topics like community, faith, friendship, and resilience—and so in their way have contributed to this book. In order of how long I've known them: Adam Ondricek, Derek Slap, Seth Lobis, Doug McKay, Jerry Vildostegui, Jed Shugerman, Willard Spiegelman, Jonathan Pitt, Tim Holahan, Andy Boone, Matt Higbee, Jeff Sudmyer, Tom Bontly, Matt Polly, Liam Brennan, and Mike Hurwitz. Dave Cullen and Patrick Radden Keefe offered encouraging words, drawing on their own reporting experience, bucking me up at key moments. *Todah* to the members of Beth El–Keser Israel, in New Haven, Connecticut—especially Tamara Schechter.

I wish to single out for thanks one Yale colleague in particular, the recently retired Fred Strebeigh. His concern for others, and for avoiding clichés in one's prose, is unsurpassed.

This book began as a special episode of *Unorthodox,* the podcast I host for *Tablet* magazine. This project belongs to all my *Tablet* colleagues, but especially to those who work with me on *Unorthodox:* Stephanie Butnick, Liel Leibovitz, Josh Kross, Sara Fredman Aeder, and Robert Scaramuccia. Paul Ruest engineered the show for years and will forever be part of it. To the J-Crew, our enthusiastic chorus of podcast listeners, who help us wrestle with questions timely ("Do Jews prefer Saran wrap or aluminum foil?") and timeless: thanks for Thursdays.

I began life as an Oppenheimer and then joined up with the

Fremmers—some serious good luck. I thank them all, wherever they are, from Springfield to St. Paul, from Austin to Chicago, from the Lower East Side to the Upper West Side. The home I kept leaving for Pittsburgh is the one I share with Cyd Oppenheimer and our children, Rebekah, Elisabeth, Klara, Anna, and David. The family consensus is that "real writers" write fiction, but the other consensus is *looove.* So they forgave my absences and even inquired after the people I was writing about. Guys, thanks for walking the dogs when I couldn't, and for letting me win at Scrabble sometimes. For you, I'll try writing a novel.

Notes on the Reporting

Between November 2018 and March 2020, I traveled to Pittsburgh thirty-two times and interviewed about 250 people. I say "about" because while 175 interviews were prearranged, with me taking notes or making a recording or both, I also had numerous casual conversations that verged into interview territory. (Often I took out my notebook, but sometimes I scribbled my recollections later; if I quote from such conversations, it's only after double-checking the wording with my sources.) Nearly everyone I spoke with was willing to be quoted by name, but some were not; I used these latter interviews for context, and only in three cases have I quoted anonymously. The majority of my interviews were in person, although I would often follow a personal meeting with a phone call, email, or text message; the rest were by telephone.

I tried not to accept hospitality from the people I was writing about—I always picked up the tab for coffee—but in two cases I got a home-cooked meal from somebody who appears in this book: Sam Schachner and his family had me for Rosh Hashanah dinner, and Jonathan Perlman and Beth Kissileff and one of their daughters hosted me for dinner one Friday night. I was also treated to one dinner out, as I mention in the notes below. (I wasn't fast enough to pick up my share of the tab and chose not to make a fuss.) I like to think that the warmth my hosts showed did not affect my good judgment as a reporter; it probably did, but then so did the generosity of all the Squirrel Hill residents who gave me their time, knowledge, and gossip.

Below, in place of endnotes, I offer discussions of how I gathered the material for each chapter. I also delve into certain choices I made, such as my decision to name the alleged shooter. I am sure that I have made some errors of fact and judgment, and I will be grateful to anybody who writes to point them out; my email address is mark.e.oppenheimer@gmail.com.

PROLOGUE

Tammy Hepps was exceedingly generous with her time. We met in Pittsburgh on July 17, 2019, for our first interview, and spoke again in person as she was supervising the cleanup of a Jewish graveyard on the first anniversary of the shooting, October 27, 2019. In between, we had numerous email and text exchanges and telephone calls, and she continued to help me fill in gaps and check facts well into the following year.

Photographs of Tammy Hepps and the Rothsteins were snapped by numerous photographers. Jeff Swensen's photograph for Getty Images seems to have been the version picked up by the most publications around the world, and it's the one I reproduce in the book; Agence France-Presse syndicated a photograph as well, as did the *Pittsburgh Post-Gazette,* whose photograph was shot by Alexandra Wimley.

Not very much has been written about the shooter, Robert Bowers. The most comprehensive article is Rich Lord et al., "How Robert Bowers Went from Conservative to White Nationalist," *Pittsburgh Post-Gazette,* November 10, 2018. As of this writing, Bowers has not yet been tried. I expect that if he comes to trial, there will be more attention to his life leading up to the attack. That may be a big *if*—Bowers is being charged under a federal statute that carries the death penalty, and he has pleaded not guilty. I think it is likely that he will change his plea to guilty in exchange for a sentence of life in prison.

There is a lively debate about whether to name the (alleged) perpetrators of acts of terrorism or mass violence. I sympathize with those who would rather I did not; I understand that naming a perpetrator rewards him with the fame he may be seeking, may help create a persona that inspires copycats, and makes survivors and victims' relatives uncomfortable. Nevertheless, in a work of journalism or history, I am not at liberty to erase an important fact—who the perpetrator was—from the record. This is a truism when it comes to the murderers of millions—we need to know the names Hitler and Stalin—and it is no less true for the murderer of eleven.

I interviewed Anne Rosenberg by telephone on September 17, 2019, and she continued to answer my questions, often by text.

Greg Zanis, of Crosses for Losses, died on May 4, 2020, and he was well eulogized by the national media. I had a lengthy telephone interview with him on August 7, 2019, during which he talked about his trip to Pittsburgh; I followed up with several shorter telephone calls in the months afterward. In describing his life, I drew on Hal Dardick, "Crosses Help Bear Heavy Burden of Violence," *Chicago Tribune*, October 28, 1997, and Emily S. Rueb, "He's Made Thousands of Crosses for Victims. These 5 Were for His Neighbors," *New York Times*, February 17, 2019, as well as many retrospectives written after his death.

Everyone remembered the scene at the Jewish Community Center in the hours after the shooting differently—for example, in some versions, it was chaotic, in others eerie and calm. A lot probably depended on what hour the person arrived. In describing that afternoon, I relied on interviews with many people who were there, including Tammy Hepps, Miri Rabinowitz, Jeff Finkelstein, Carolyn Ban, and Ron Symons.

Tammy Hepps told me the story of her sleepover at Yael Silk's house and the morning after, and my interview with Yael Silk helped firm up some of the details, especially about the anti-Trump letter.

For those curious about the history of Jews in the Pittsburgh area, there is Jacob S. Feldman, *The Jewish Experience in Western Pennsylvania: A History, 1755–1945* (Pittsburgh: Historical Society of Western Pennsylvania, 1986). But I learned more from conversations with archivist Eric Lidji and historian Barbara Burstin than I could have learned from all the books written on the subject.

David Shribman's op-ed "Anti-Semitism Comes to a City of Tolerance" ran in *The New York Times* on October 28, 2018.

1. THE ATTACK

I interviewed Carolyn Ban three times by telephone, the first on July 17, 2019. For the information about Robert Bowers's father, see Jack Healy and Julie Turkewitz, "Man Said to Be Pittsburgh Suspect's Father Killed Himself amid 1979 Rape Case," *New York Times*, November 2, 2018.

Of the eleven who were inside Tree of Life and survived, I interviewed nine, most of them multiple times: Joe Charny, Martin Gaynor, Audrey Glickman, Daniel Leger, Jeffrey Myers, Jonathan Perlman, Stephen Weiss, Andrea Wedner, and Barry Werber. Unsurprisingly, all had different memories of that morning; I did my best to reconstruct the events from what they told me and from numerous newspaper, radio, and television reports.

The *Post-Gazette* archives offer two summaries of that morning that, based on my independent interviews, strike me as reliable. Shelly Bradbury, "Timeline of Terror: A Moment-by-Moment Account of Squirrel Hill Mass Shooting," ran the day after the shooting. Even better is Bradbury's online interactive feature, "Unbroken," which first posted on November 4, 2018. "Unbroken" is terribly moving—the video shows floor plans of the synagogue, photographs of the victims, a screenshot of Robert Bowers's final social media post, aerial images of Squirrel Hill, and more. The audio portion, which for months I did not know existed (the button to turn on the audio is hidden in the upper right of the screen), includes the police radio transmissions ("There is an active shooter in the building . . .") and the sounds of shots fired from the SWAT team's radios. Watch "Unbroken"—it will make everything in this book more vivid to you.

Both of Cecil and David Rosenthal's sisters told me, in emails, that nobody in the family wanted to speak to me, so I based my descriptions of "the boys" on publicly available sources. The *Post-Gazette*'s interactive feature "Remembering the Victims," which ran on October 28, was helpful. Of the many profiles of victims and survivors, a particularly charming one was by Isaac Stanley-Becker, "In Pittsburgh, a Holocaust Survivor Was Four Minutes Late to Synagogue, Escaping Death a Second Time," *Washington Post,* October 29, 2018, from which I took Judah Samet's quotations in this chapter. (I did interview him once, at the luncheon after services at Tree of Life on September 21, 2019.)

Augie Siriano, the Tree of Life custodian and the one non-Jew in the building that morning, did not respond to an interview request I made through Tree of Life. His quotation comes from an interview he did with local television, now online as Lynne Hayes-Freeland, " 'They Were Like Brothers to Me': Custodian Who Escaped Deadly Pittsburgh Synagogue Shooting Mourns Lost Friends," KDKA-TV, October 29, 2018, pittsburgh.cbslocal.com/2018/10/29 /pittsburgh-synagogue-shooting-survivor-custodian/.

Jeffrey Myers's statement "I heard him execute my congregants" was made on NBC's *Today* show on Monday, October 29, 2018.

2. THOSE INSIDE

I interviewed Jeffrey Myers three times, in January and July 2019 and in March 2020; each interview was about an hour. He was generous with his time but also emphatic about his boundaries; interviews had to be arranged long in advance, and he was not the type to respond to a quick email query or to hop on the phone. There is never an unguarded moment. Given what he had suffered, and his ongoing responsibilities to his congregation, I was grateful for whatever time he could give. My sense of the man, and his rabbinate, was fleshed out by interviews with congregants including Joe Charny, Michael Eisenberg, Laurie Zittrain Eisenberg, Audrey Glickman, Irwin Harris, Alan Hausman, Sam Schachner, and others. Myers's friend and former congregant Neil Brandt shared warm memories of Myers's years in New Jersey.

On the history, and contraction, of Conservative Judaism, a good place to start is Daniel Gordis, "Conservative Judaism: A Requiem for a Movement," *Jewish Review of Books,* Winter 2014. Gordis has a point of view—he is a Cassandra—but he sums up the data, much of it drawn from the Pew Research

Center, clearly. For more about online ordination and Mesifta Adath Wolko-wisk specifically, see Josh Nathan-Kazis, "Online-Ordained Rabbis Grab Pul-pits," *Forward,* December 3, 2012.

It is very difficult to get accurate figures on the declining membership of Tree of Life. One reason is that nobody is sure what "membership" means in American Judaism. There are Jews who come to a given synagogue every week but never fill out the paperwork to become members; others fill out the paper-work but are too poor to pay any dues. Still others pay dues and attend regularly but then move away, or stop coming, without ever resigning their member-ship—at what point are they considered inactive or nonmembers? According to Kerry M. Olitzky and Marc Lee Raphael, *The American Synagogue: A His-torical Dictionary and Sourcebook* (Westport, Conn.: Greenwood Press, 1996), p. 318, "In 1995, membership at Tree of Life stood at 850 family units." Numer-ous sources told me that by the time Myers was hired in 2017, the membership stood between 200 and 250. Barb Feige, Tree of Life's executive director, wrote to me on October 20, 2020, "We can confirm 200–250."

Jonathan Perlman spoke with me many times, in person and by telephone. I interviewed his daughter Tova, too. At the time of the shooting, I had known his wife, Beth Kissileff, for about five years through my work as a part-time edi-tor for *Tablet,* an online Jewish magazine, for which Beth does freelance writ-ing. I have never been directly responsible for assigning her work, editing her work, or paying her, but I have given her informal advice, and I continued to during the year after the shooting. (We talked about some essay ideas she had and what publications they might be a good fit for.) I cannot see any conflict of interest here, but I feel it is worth disclosing this connection. With that said, Beth, like her husband, also spoke with me at length and answered numerous queries by email. And I have quoted from her essay "The Man I Married," *Tab-let,* May 31, 2013. Their daughter Ada Perlman's memories from that day can be found in her essay, "After Parkland, I Said, 'It Could've Been Me.' Now It Is," *Times of Israel,* November 27, 2018.

The *Post-Gazette* article, posted the evening of the shooting, that identified Daniel Leger as a survivor, and quoted Randall Bush on Leger, was "UPMC Chaplain, in Critical Condition, Identified Among Squirrel Hill Shooting Sur-vivors," by Adam Smeltz.

3. THE GENTILES

For this chapter, I am indebted to Tim Hindes, Lynn Hyde, and Shay Khatiri for granting me interviews. To hear Lynn Hyde tell her story in her own voice, listen to the May 28, 2020, episode of my podcast, *Unorthodox,* and to hear Shay Khatiri, listen to the November 15, 2018, episode. Khatiri's story was catnip for the national press, and there is a plethora of feature articles on him; one of the best is by Josefin Dolsten, "How an Iranian Asylum Seeker Raised over $1 Million for the Pittsburgh Synagogue," *Jewish Telegraphic Agency*, November 9, 2018.

There is a rich literature on the Steelers football team and what it has meant to Pittsburgh. The classic is Roy Blount, Jr., *About Three Bricks Shy of a Load: A Highly Irregular Lowdown on the Year the Pittsburgh Steelers Were Super but Missed the Bowl* (Boston: Little, Brown, 1974). More recent works on the Steelers include Gary M. Pomerantz, *Their Life's Work: The Brotherhood of the 1970s Pittsburgh Steelers* (New York: Simon & Schuster, 2013), and Ed Gruver and Jim Campbell, *Hell with the Lid Off: Inside the Fierce Rivalry Between the 1970s Oakland Raiders and Pittsburgh Steelers* (Lincoln: University of Nebraska Press, 2019).

4. THE YOUNG

I interviewed Emily Pressman at "the big table" in Starbucks—the very same one where she and her friends had met to plan the Havdalah service that Saturday night. Sara Stock Mayo first sat down with me at 61C, a rival, independently owned coffee shop. Keshira haLev Fife was the first person I interviewed for this book, and we met at Dobrá Tea.

5. THE ARCHIVIST

Eric Lidji sat for three lengthy interviews at the Rauh archive and also answered numerous questions by email. Emma Green of *The Atlantic*, one of the first reporters from outside Pittsburgh to arrive after the shooting, produced consistently good articles that enriched my own understanding of the events. One of the last pieces she wrote was about Lidji: "Will Anyone Remember 11 Dead Jews?"—it ran on October 25, 2019. The piece he wrote for *The Believer*, "The Tale of Backwater Spiritualism: Eight Years of Folk in the Age of Psychedelic Rock," ran in the January 1, 2004, issue—it's brilliant, one of the best pieces of music criticism I have read, well worth looking up. (It's available online.)

I write: "Quick: name somebody from Pittsburgh aside from Mister Rogers." And I realize that there is a dearth of Fred Rogers in this book, considering how central he is to Squirrel Hill's *amour propre*. Everyone in Squirrel Hill old enough to remember *Mister Rogers' Neighborhood* can tell you that until his death in 2003 he lived in Squirrel Hill, so it literally *is* Mister Rogers's neighborhood. His widow, Joanne, remained a revered Squirrel Hill figure until her death in 2021. The Friday night after the shooting, Aaron Bisno, the rabbi of Rodef Shalom, invited Joanne to join him onstage at his temple—for no reason other than that she is a soothing figure in Squirrel Hill. See Mahita Gajanan, "Mr. Rogers' Widow Offered a Message of 'Love' After Anti-Semitic Murders in Her Late Husband's Neighborhood," *Time,* November 3, 2018.

6. THE BODY GUARDS

Daniel Wasserman told me about his life and work during a long interview at his synagogue, and he answered follow-up questions by text and telephone. The story of his fight with the state over control of the burial process deserves a book of its own. Stephen Pincus, one of the lawyers who represented Wasserman, spent a good hour on the phone with me explaining the twists of the case, then sent me hundreds of pages of documents. A contemporaneous account of the case was Jamie Moss, "Pittsburgh Rabbi Wasserman Favorably Settles 'Funeral Director' Interpretation Case," *Pittsburgh Jewish Chronicle,* December 17, 2012. Emma Green wrote about Wasserman, his holy society, and their work as body guards in "The Jews of Pittsburgh Bury Their Dead," *Atlantic,* October 30, 2018. Jason Small talked with me about building caskets.

I learned about the New Community Chevra Kadisha in interviews with Malke Frank, Dan Leger, Ron Symons, Michelle Wirth, and Dave and Jan Zimmer. "Washing the Dead in Pittsburgh," Jordana Rosenfeld's essay on *tahara,* appeared in *Jewish Currents* on October 24, 2019.

7. THE FUNERALS

For the funerals, I relied on eyewitness accounts, some of them by people who did not wish to be named, and on *Post-Gazette* reporting, in particular Bill Schackner and Peter Smith, "Community Gathers at Funerals for Tree of Life Synagogue Shooting Victims," October 30, 2018. Peter Smith is one of the country's great daily religion reporters, and his work the week of the shooting—which helped win the newspaper a Pulitzer Prize for breaking news reporting—and in the months afterward leaves its fingerprints all over this book.

I wish there were more Jerry Rabinowitz in this book. I had several long conversations with his widow, Miri, and his name came up in conversations with dozens of other Squirrel Hill residents. He was, by all accounts, a great healer and a true mensch. I first read Michael Kerr's recollections of his former doctor in Nick Keppler, "Pittsburgh Shooting Victim Jerry Rabinowitz Treated Gay Men with AIDS Before It Even Had a Name," *Daily Beast,* October 29, 2018, and was sufficiently moved to track down Kerr and speak with him myself by telephone.

On June 6, 2019, looking for the firefighters who had been close with David

Rosenthal, I stopped by 18 Engine on Northumberland Street. Inside, I found four firefighters eating lunch, the French Open on the TV in the background. Three of them, it turned out, had been to the Rosenthal shiva; one of them was Debo, who had been David's best friend at the station. Those guys invited me to sit down and spent an emotional hour telling me everything they remembered. It was a tough but very rewarding day to be a reporter.

A friend of mine, a fellow reporter, surreptitiously turned on his iPhone's recording app at the Rosenthals' funeral. My quotations from that event are direct transcriptions from the audio file he gave me. Both Berkun rabbis, father and son, spoke with me and shared reminiscences of "the boys."

8. THE TRUMP VISIT

The overview of our nationally polarized politics was influenced by *Why We're Polarized* (New York: Avid Reader/Simon & Schuster, 2020), Ezra Klein's fascinating, disturbing book, published while I was working on this book. David Wasserman's Whole Foods/Cracker Barrel factoid can be found in his piece "Senate Control Could Come Down to Whole Foods vs. Cracker Barrel," FiveThirtyEight.com, October 8, 2014. The Pittsburgh voting results can be found online at https://results.enr.clarityelections.com/PA/Allegheny/. The statistics about age by state were compiled by the Population Reference Bureau, in Washington, D.C. On western Pennsylvania's support for Trump, see Andrew Small, "The Pittsburgh Area Really Did Vote for Trump," *CityLab*, June 2, 2017. (It helps to know that "metropolitan statistical area" refers to a contiguous region integrated by transit and economy. Pittsburgh's includes parts of Ohio and West Virginia.)

There is great debate about the severity of antisemitism in the United Kingdom and mainland Europe. The debate is often polarized along left-right political lines: conservatives and Zionists tend to be more fearful (some would say alarmist), while liberals and non-Zionists are more sanguine. I am of the school that while it is still possible for a Jew to live a happy, secure life in most of Europe, matters are much worse than they were five or ten years ago. For some preliminary reading, see Eylon Aslan-Levy, "A Deep Look at the 'Sickness' of the British Left," *Tablet*, September 1, 2016; Marc Weitzmann, *Hate: The Rising Tide of Anti-Semitism in France (and What It Means for Us)* (New York: Houghton Mifflin Harcourt, 2019); Adam Nossiter, " 'They Spit When I Walked in the Street': The 'New Anti-Semitism' in France," *New York Times*, July 27, 2018; Sam Knight, "Jeremy Corbyn's Anti-Semitism Crisis," *New Yorker*, August 12, 2018; and Helen Lewis, "Why British Jews Are Worried by Jeremy Corbyn," *Atlantic*, December 10, 2019. On Corbyn and British irony, I especially liked Rebecca Mead, "Jeremy Corbyn and the English Fetishization of Irony," *New Yorker,* August 27, 2018. It should be noted that in December 2019 Labour lost the general election and Corbyn agreed to step down as the party leader.

The night of the shooting, *The Washington Post* reported that Trump had said in Illinois that he would travel to Pittsburgh: "Upon arriving in Murphysboro, Ill., Trump said he would travel to Pittsburgh, though he did not offer specifics on timing. He also defended his campaign schedule, saying, 'We cannot let our schedule or our lives change.'" See Seung Min Kim, Katie Zezima, and Amy B Wang, "Trump Says He Will Travel to Pittsburgh After Deadly Synagogue Shooting," *Washington Post,* October 27, 2018; the story was posted at 7:42 p.m. But the official announcement of the visit seems to have come on Monday morning, October 29, from Sarah Huckabee Sanders.

Mollie Butler's comment comes from an interview with a reporter for Canada's GlobalNews television station; the clip is still available on YouTube.

My description of Trump's visit draws on interviews with Tammy Hepps, Tracy Baton, Sara Stock Mayo, Yael Silk, Tova Weinberg, and Joshua Bloom. The *Current* article, "Thousands Gather, March to Protest Synagogue Visit from President Trump," was written by Haley Frederick and ran on October 31, 2018.

9. THE SYMBOLS

I have known David Shribman for over ten years; we first met because he was a mentor to college students of mine who spent the summer working at the *Post-Gazette.* I consider him a friend, and in the acrimonious drama that marked the end of his tenure, it's fair to say that I was on his side (not that anybody asked me, and not that he ever shared more with me than was in the public record). Nevertheless, I believe I have described what happened fairly. Both Shribman and his former boss, *Post-Gazette* owner John Block, spoke with me about the newspaper's coverage of the Tree of Life shooting; pursuant to Shribman's separation agreement, both studiously avoided the topic of Shribman's firing. His *New York Times* essay about the shooting is cited above, in the notes to the Prologue.

I interviewed Danielle Kranjec and Drew Medvid in person. I met Drew at Pitt, in the company of five other Pitt students who were assembling an exhibit about the Tree of Life synagogue and the shooting: Emily Dickson, Kruthika Doreswamy, Maja Lynn, Liam Sims, and Claire Singer. They talked candidly about what it was like to be college students a couple miles away when the shooting happened.

The history of the Starbucks windows was narrated to me by Melissa Lysaght and Nicole Flannery, and Jamie Lebovitz told me about collecting and hanging the Stars of David.

10. THE HIGH SCHOOL

A book could and should be written about the big, rich, historic, diverse place that is Taylor Allderdice High School. I got to know it, a little bit, by interviewing principal James McCoy, teachers Michele Halloran, Mina Levenson, and Jonathan Parker, and students including Evan DeWitt, Giavanna Gibson, Kiara Gill, Elana Hochheiser, Sara Liang, Emily Pressman, and Isabel Smith.

11. THE HISTORY

People in Squirrel Hill will be the first to tell you that their neighborhood is special, then the first to say that they have no idea how it got to be that way. University of Pittsburgh historian Adam Shear, a transplant who grew up in Washington, D.C., then lived in New Haven, Boston, and Philadelphia, was so intrigued by Squirrel Hill's uniqueness that he organized a yearlong seminar on the question. The Squirrel Hill Project ran during the 2012–13 school year, and it featured lectures by Deborah Dash Moore, Thomas Sugrue, Barbara Burstin, and Rachel Kranson. The lectures are viewable online at jewish studies.pitt.edu, and Kranson (who also teaches at Pitt and lives in Squirrel Hill) sent me the text of her lecture "Jewish Anxieties over Suburbanization, 1945–1965," which helped shape my thinking.

Speaking of Kranson, I interviewed her for this chapter. I also interviewed Burstin, then later shared a dinner with her and local newspaper editor John Allison. I can't remember who picked up the tab, but I fear that I was not allowed to pay, a fact that I hereby disclose. Howard Rieger and his wife, Beverly Siegel, both spoke with me, and Rieger sent me dozens of pages of documents from the Renaissance Campaign, which were not easily accessible—he had to dig them up from somewhere, and I am very grateful for the effort. The most useful of these documents, and one I quote from, is "Renaissance: Building Continuity in Our Community," April 15, 1996. Conversations with architect Dan Rothschild always gave me more context, and reminded me how little I know.

My research for this chapter led me to many books, including Feldman's *The Jewish Experience in Western Pennsylvania: A History, 1755–1945*, mentioned above in the notes to the Prologue; Amy Shevitz, *Jewish Communities on the Ohio River: A History* (Lexington: University Press of Kentucky, 2007)—my quotations are from pp. 187–88; and Helen Wilson, ed., *Squirrel Hill: A Neighborhood History* (Charleston, S.C.: History Press, 2017)—not scholarly, but charming, chockablock with photographs and with names that would otherwise be lost, and to my mind indispensable.

For more on the redlining maps, the Mapping Inequality project, by the Digital Scholarship Lab at the University of Richmond, is a superb online resource—dsl.richmond.edu—and it's where you will find, among other things, several maps of the East Liberty neighborhood. The article I quote from, to describe the HOLC city surveys and redlining, is Daniel Aaronson, Daniel Hartley, and Bhashkar Mazumder, "The Effects of the 1930s HOLC 'Redlining' Maps," Federal Reserve Bank of Chicago, 2019. Also see Bruce Mitchell and Juan Franco, "HOLC 'Redlining' Maps: The Persistent Structure of Segregation and Economic Inequality" (Washington, D.C.: National Community Reinvestment Coalition, 2018), which gives a haunting analysis of the long-term effects of HOLC's map project; for further reading, its bibliography would be a great place to start. The document is online at https://ncrc.org/holc/.

For facts about the racial makeup of Pittsburgh, Cleveland, and other cities, I relied on the U.S. Census Bureau, which is online at census.gov. For the Jewish composition of Squirrel Hill, the East End, and Greater Pittsburgh today, see Matthew Boxer, Matthew A. Brookner, Janet Krasner Aronson, and Leonard Saxe, *The Greater Pittsburgh Jewish Community Study* (Brandeis University, 2017). And the earlier Jewish population studies, including *The Jewish Community of Pittsburgh: A Population Study, 1963* (a fascinating relic, truly), can be seen at jewishdatabank.org.

12. THE VISITORS

Shira Hanau interviewed Bob Ossler for her article "Christian Chaplain and Fireman Ministers to Squirrel Hill's Brokenhearted," *New York Jewish Week,* November 1, 2018. I interviewed Nimrod Eisenberg, Nina Butler, Daniel Butler, Daniel Wasserman, Daniel Yolkut, Andrea Wedner, Ron Wedner, and Rose McGee. For more on McGee, see Julie Kendrick, "A Recipe for Change," *Minnesota Good Age,* November 4, 2019, and Adam Reinherz, "Cranes and Pies Swoop in After Shabbat Services," *Pittsburgh Jewish Chronicle,* February 22, 2019.

I allowed the "high-ranking executive at a Jewish philanthropy" to remain anonymous because he was expressing a view, about well-meaning interlopers, that was widely held and that, for obvious reasons, people were reluctant to state publicly.

The New York City holy societies got good hometown press, both from the

New York Post (see Max Jaeger, "Brooklyn Group to Collect Blood of Synagogue Shooting Victims for Burial," October 28, 2018) and *The Yeshiva World,* an Orthodox publication (the news brief, "Misaskim Heading to Pittsburgh to Assist Local Chevra Kaddisha," October 28, 2018, has no byline).

The quotation about the Jewish bikers' ride to Tree of Life is from "The Pittsburgh Ride of Reflection," by Andy Réti, posted at the website of the Jewish Motorcylists Alliance (jewishmotorcyclistsalliance.com) on September 9, 2019.

13. THE MONEY

Shay Khatiri gave me multiple interviews, took my phone calls, and shared old emails; he also sent screenshots from GoFundMe, Facebook, and other platforms he has utilized as he has made his way, and his money, in America.

The *HuffPost* article "Where to Donate to Honor Each of the 26 Sandy Hook Shooting Victims," by Caroline Bologna, ran on December 14, 2017, and was later updated February 13, 2018.

On the murders in Charleston, see Jennifer Berry Hawes, *Grace Will Lead Us Home: The Charleston Church Massacre and the Hard, Inspiring Journey to Forgiveness* (New York: St. Martin's, 2019). On church corruption, see her article "SLED Opens Investigation into Emanuel AME Church over Finances, Including Donations," *Post and Courier,* October 31, 2019.

My thanks to Jeffrey Finkelstein, Adam Hertzman, Chuck Perlow, Meryl Ainsman, Susan Brownlee, Stephen Cohen, and several anonymous sources for answering my questions about the money and its distribution.

14. THE SCENE OF THE CRIME

This chapter is based on numerous interviews with Daniel Leger, Ellen Leger, Barry Werber, and Joe Charny. I would have understood if they had declined to talk with me. I was asking them difficult questions about a terrible day in their lives. I am grateful.

Among the many reports of the shooting that I read, an exceptionally useful one, in particular for Joe Charny's recollections, was Kyle Swenson, "'I Looked Up, and There Were All These Dead Bodies': Witness Describes Horror of Synagogue Massacre," *Washington Post,* October 28, 2018.

The WTAE town hall is, as of now, available online, at wtae.com/article /replay-project-community-town-hall-parkland-to-pittsburgh-stronger -together/27088062.

15. THE BUILDING

Tree of Life members who talked with me about the building included Michael Eisenberg, Laurie Zittrain Eisenberg, Irwin Harris, and Alan Hausman. Barb Feige, who during the period of my research was hired as the congregation's executive director, answered many queries. Jeffrey Myers spoke with me, as noted above. Eric Lidji, archivist at the Rauh, gave me historical context on Tree of Life (now Tree of Life*Or L'Simcha).

It was hard to know how to write about Chuck Diamond. No other name in Squirrel Hill elicits such strong, and divergent, opinions. "Rabbi Chuck" invited me to his house, where we talked for two hours; he continued to answer questions, by telephone and email, for many months. Considering that he had reason to believe that he might not come off so well, it was an act of great generosity, even courage, to keep cooperating. I hope that I have been fair to him.

For her recollections about Diamond's time at Camp Ramah, I thank Staci Bush. Daniel Schiff offered his perspective on the future of Jewish infrastructure in Squirrel Hill. For more on the botched circumcision, see Michael Walsh, "Pittsburgh Rabbi Getting Sued for Allegedly Severing Newborn's Penis," *Daily News*, December 29, 2013.

On Columbine, see Jack Healy, "Columbine High School Will Not Be Torn Down and Rebuilt," *New York Times*, July 24, 2019. On Parkland, see Scott Travis, "New Stoneman Douglas Building Will Be Ready for Classes in the Fall," *South Florida Sun-Sentinel*, January 16, 2020, and Dave Cullen, *Parkland* (New York: Harper, 2019).

16. THE SPRINGTIME

I attended the Shavuot event at Maggie Feinstein's house, the Allderdice graduation, and the Tisha B'Av services at Beth Shalom. I supplemented my own observations with interviews with Daniel Yolkut, Eric Lidji, Keshira haLev Fife, Maggie Feinstein, Evan DeWitt, Sara Stock Mayo, Jeremy Markiz, Cindy Snyder, Miri Rabinowitz, and Tammy Hepps.

I wanted to learn more about the great sums, much of it federal tax dollars, spent on "resilience" and "healing" after 10/27. By federal statute, Department of Justice money is available for communities that have suffered mass violence, and the 10.27 Healing Partnership was granted some of that money, although as of this writing it has not been paid out. The partnership has also received money, some of it a loan, from the Jewish Federation, and in-kind support from the JCC, where it is housed. So far, it has released no summary of its activities or how many people it has served. Maggie Feinstein, who when I attended the

Shavuot event at her house had already been hired as the director of the 10.27 Healing Partnership, told me that the center was collecting statistics on unique visitors and engagements, materials downloaded from its website, calls and inquiries received, and more; when I asked her for these statistics in May 2020, and again in July 2020, she told me that she could not provide them. "This is a manual tallying," she wrote on July 9, 2020, by email, "as the database that we are using is the state's and then we have other data in spreadsheets. I am pulled in many directions right now and this is not of obvious priority at this point." On November 2, 2020, in his reply to an email I had sent posing these questions again, a representative from the 10.27 Healing Partnership's public relations firm declined to answer.

In addition to asking for statistics on usage, I also asked for a copy of the government report recommending the funding of her center—its budget is $715,000 a year—which Feinstein refused to provide. I filed a Freedom of Information Act request to obtain the report, and on August 20, 2020, I received 49 pages of the 132 relevant to my request; the others, which I believe contained most of the important information I sought, the government withheld. In the pages I was sent, the amount requested from the federal government—the majority of which, it seems, would fund the center—was $3,863,606. But again, nobody at the center has responded to questions about how much of the money was allocated or how it has been used.

Jonathan Perlman discussed his depression and struggles in Toby Tabachnick, "Rabbi Jonathan Perlman Speaks on the Massacre, the Media and Moving Forward," *Pittsburgh Jewish Chronicle*, August 21, 2019.

17. THE HIGH HOLY DAYS

For the High Holy Days, I bounced between Tree of Life's services and New Light's; what I did not hear myself I heard about from others. Jeffrey Myers was gracious enough to send me the text of his sermons. Andrew Exler spoke to me and then stayed in touch with updates; his efforts to start a young people's group at Tree of Life were hampered by COVID-19, when it came. Jonathon W. Jensen, the rector of Calvary Episcopal Church, sat with me in his office and talked about his offer to host Tree of Life for the High Holy Days.

Tree of Life's vision for the future of its building was ever-evolving; as of the High Holy Days, the latest hopes were outlined in Adam Reinherz, "Tree of Life Shares Vision of Reopening," *Pittsburgh Jewish Chronicle*, October 18, 2019.

But then, on July 10, 2020, Carol Sikov Gross, by then the president of Tree of Life*Or L'Simcha, sent an email to her congregation announcing its new fundraising initiative: "Lipton Strategies has been engaged to work with us to conduct a comprehensive multi-million dollar local and national fundraising capital campaign. . . . We will be building a campaign leadership team over the summer with plans to launch the 'silent phase'—initial major donor engagements—in the fall. . . .

"Rothschild Doyno Collaborative, led by Daniel Rothschild, who many of you know from our Listening Sessions and numerous projects in the Pittsburgh Jewish community, has been retained to lead us through a three-month programming services review. . . . The outcome of the study will provide valuable information to begin the design process for the renovation."

At the time Gross sent this email, the COVID-19 economic depression had hit the Jewish community very hard. There was concern that the JCC would not be able to pay its bills, and synagogue membership was sure to decline. Many were skeptical that Tree of Life could raise millions of dollars, or that it should, at such a time as this.

18. THE ANNIVERSARY

I was at the anniversary event at Soldiers & Sailors, although for precise quotations I relied on publicly available video. I talked about the event and its aftermath with many people, including Jonathan Perlman, Amy Bardack, Stephen Cohen, Cindy Snyder, Danielle Kranjec, Daniel Leger, Howard Fienberg, Tammy Hepps, and a number of sources who did not wish to be quoted.

About the word *anniversary:* some members of the community of victims and survivors decided that using the word to describe the date October 27 was insensitive, because they believed it refers principally to happy events. I disagree. To take one counterexample among thousands, here is *The New York Times,* fifty years after Martin Luther King, Jr., was assassinated: "But on the 50th *anniversary* of his death, it is worth noting how his message and his priorities had evolved by the time he was shot on that balcony at the Lorraine Motel in Memphis in 1968." The italics are mine.

EPILOGUE

I met Robert "Zach" Zacharias three times: first in his office at Carnegie Mellon, several months later at Kelly's Bar & Lounge, in East Liberty (where I also got to meet his brother), and again the following fall, when we bumped into each other at an event at the JCC. On top of those conversations, he was also a quick and thorough respondent over email. Lynn Hyde was good enough to keep me updated on the progress of her conversion, and Dan Leger must fear that my questions will never stop. As for Eric Lidji, reading *haftarah* at New Light: he tried to keep this a secret, but one Saturday I caught him in the act. I hope he'll forgive me.

Index

Page numbers in *italics* refer to illustrations.

Illustration Credits

MARK OPPENHEIMER is the author of five books, including *Knocking on Heaven's Door: American Religion in the Age of Counterculture* and *The Newish Jewish Encyclopedia.* He was the religion columnist for *The New York Times* from 2010 to 2016 and has written for *The New York Times Magazine, GQ, Mother Jones, The Nation,* and *The Believer,* among other publications. The host of *Tablet* magazine's podcast *Unorthodox,* Oppenheimer has taught at Stanford, Wellesley, and Yale, where since 2006 he has directed the Yale Journalism Initiative. He lives with his family in New Haven, Connecticut.

A NOTE ON THE TYPE

This book was set in Minion, a typeface produced by the Adobe Corporation specifically for the Macintosh personal computer and released in 1990. Designed by Robert Slimbach, Minion combines the classic characteristics of old-style faces with the full complement of weights required for modern typesetting.

Composed by North Market Street Graphics,
Lancaster, Pennsylvania

Printed and bound by Berryville Graphics,
Berryville, Virginia

Designed by Cassandra J. Pappas